CBSE Term II
2022

Economics

Class XI

CBSE Term II 2022

Economics

Class XI

- Complete Theory Covering NCERT
- Case Based Questions
- Short/Long Answer Type Questions
- 3 Practice Papers with Explanations

Author
Pratima Jain Roy

ARIHANT PRAKASHAN (School Division Series)

CBSE Term II
2022

ARIHANT PRAKASHAN (School Division Series)

卐 **Administrative & Production Offices**

Regd. Office

'Ramchhaya' 4577/15, Agarwal Road, Darya Ganj, New Delhi -110002
Tele: 011- 47630600, 43518550

卐 **Head Office**

Kalindi, TP Nagar, Meerut (UP) - 250002, Tel: 0121-7156203, 7156204

卐 **Sales & Support Offices**

Agra, Ahmedabad, Bengaluru, Bareilly, Chennai, Delhi, Guwahati, Hyderabad, Jaipur, Jhansi, Kolkata, Lucknow, Nagpur & Pune.

卐 **ISBN :** 978-93-25796-77-5

PO No : TXT-XX-XXXXXXX-X-XX

Published by Arihant Publications (India) Ltd.

For further information about the books published by Arihant, log on to www.arihantbooks.com or e-mail at info@arihantbooks.com

Follow us on   

Contents

PART A

CHAPTER 01	Measures of Dispersion	**3-20**
CHAPTER 02	Measures of Correlation	**21-37**
CHAPTER 03	Index Numbers	**38-55**

PART B

CHAPTER 01	Producer's Behaviour	**59-80**
CHAPTER 02	Supply and Price Elasticity of Supply	**81-97**
CHAPTER 03	Forms of Market and Price Determination	**98-114**

Practice Papers (1-3) — **117-130**

Syllabus

CBSE Term II Class XI

Theory : 40 Marks	Time : 2 Hours	Marks
PART A	**Statistics for Economics**	
	Statistical Tools and Interpretation – Measures of Dispersion, Correlation, Index Number	17
	Sub Total	**17**
PART B	**Introductory Microeconomics**	
	Producer Behaviour and Supply	13
	Forms of Market and Price Determination under perfect competition with simple applications	10
	Sub Total	**23**
	Total	**40**
PART C	**Project Work (Part 2): 10 Marks**	

PART A   **STATISTICS FOR ECONOMICS**

Unit 3   **Statistical Tools and Interpretation**

Measures of Dispersion - absolute dispersion (standard deviation); relative dispersion (coefficient of variation)

Correlation – meaning and properties, scatter diagram; Measures of correlation - Karl Pearson's method (two variables ungrouped data)

Introduction to Index Numbers - meaning, types - wholesale price index, consumer price index, uses of index numbers; Inflation and index numbers.

PART B **INTRODUCTORY MICROECONOMICS**

Unit 6   **Producer Behaviour and Supply**

Meaning of Production Function – Short-Run and Long-Run Total Product, Average Product and Marginal Product.

Returns to a Factor

Cost: Short run costs - total cost, total fixed cost, total variable cost; Average cost; Average fixed cost, average variable cost and marginal cost-meaning and their relationships.

Revenue - total, average and marginal revenue - meaning and their relationship.

Supply, market supply, determinants of supply, supply schedule, supply curve and its slope, movements along and shifts in supply curve, price elasticity of supply; measurement of price elasticity of supply - percentage-change method.

Unit 7   **Forms of Market and Price Determination under Perfect Competition with simple applications.**

Perfect competition - Features; Determination of market equilibrium and effects of shifts in demand and supply.

Simple Applications of Demand and Supply: Price ceiling, price floor.

PART C **PROJECT IN ECONOMICS**

Guidelines as given in class XII curriculum

CBSE Circular

Exam Scheme Term I & II

केन्द्रीय माध्यमिक शिक्षा बोर्ड

(शिक्षा मंत्रालय, भारत सरकार के अधीन एक स्वायत संगठन)

CENTRAL BOARD OF SECONDARY EDUCATION

(An Autonomous Organisation under the Ministryof Education, Govt. of India)

CBSE/DIR (ACAD)/2021

Date: July 05, 2021
Circular No: Acad-51/2021

All the Heads of Schools affiliated to CBSE

**Subject: Special Scheme of Assessment for Board Examination Classes X
and XII for the Session 2021-22**

COVID 19 pandemic caused almost all CBSE schools to function in a virtual mode
for most part of the academic session of 2020-21. Due to the extreme risk
associated with the conduct of Board examinations during the second wave in April
2021, CBSE had to cancel both its class X and XII Board examinations of the year
2021 and results are to be declared on the basis of a credible, reliable, flexible and
valid alternative assessment policy. This, in turn, also necessitated deliberations
over alternative ways to look at the learning objectives as well as the conduct of the
Board Examinations for the academic session 2021-22 in case the situation remains
unfeasible.

CBSE has also held stake holder consultations with Government schools as well as
private independent schools from across the country especially schools from the
remote rural areas and a majority of them have requested for the rationalization of
the syllabus, similar to last year in view of reduced time permitted for organizing
online classes. The Board has also considered the concerns regarding differential
availability of electronic gadgets, connectivity and effectiveness of online teaching
and other socio-economic issues specially with respect to students from
economically weaker section and those residing in far flung areas of the country. In
a survey conducted by CBSE, it was revealed that the rationalized syllabus notified
for the session 2020-21 was effective for schools in covering the syllabus and
helped learners in achieving learning objectives in a less stressful manner.

In the above backdrop and in line with the Board's continued focus on assessing
stipulated learning outcomes by making the examinations competencies and core
concepts based, student-centric, transparent, technology-driven, and having
advance provision of alternatives for different future scenarios, the following
schemes are introduced for the Academic Session for Class X and Class XII 2021-22.

केन्द्रीय माध्यमिक शिक्षा बोर्ड
(शिक्षा मंत्रालय, भारत सरकार के अधीन एक स्वायत संगठन)
CENTRAL BOARD OF SECONDARY EDUCATION
(An Autonomous Organisation under the Ministryof Education, Govt. of India)

<u>Special Scheme for 2021-22</u>

A. Academic session to be divided into 2 Terms with approximately 50% syllabus in each term:

The syllabus for the Academic session 2021-22 will be divided into 2 terms by following a systematic approach by looking into the interconnectivity of concepts and topics by the Subject Experts and the Board will conduct examinations at the end of each term on the basis of the bifurcated syllabus. This is done to increase the probability of having a Board conducted classes X and XII examinations at the end of the academic session.

B. The syllabus for the Board examination 2021-22 will be rationalized similar to that of the last academic session to be notified in July 2021. For academic transactions, however, schools will follow the curriculum and syllabus released by the Board vide Circular no. F.1001/CBSE-Acad/Curriculum/2021 dated 31 March 2021. Schools will also use alternative academic calendar and inputs from the NCERT on transacting the curriculum.

C. Efforts will be made to make Internal Assessment/ Practical/ Project work more credible and valid as per the guidelines and Moderation Policy to be announced by the Board to ensure fair distribution of marks.

<u>Details of Curriculum Transaction</u>

- Schools will continue teaching in distance mode till the authorities permit in-person mode of teaching in schools.

- **Classes IX-X: Internal Assessment** (throughout the year-irrespective of Term I and II) would include the *3 periodic tests, student enrichment, portfolio and practical work/ speaking listening activities/ project.*

- **Classes XI-XII: Internal Assessment** (throughout the year-irrespective of Term I and II) would include end of topic or unit tests/ exploratory activities/ practicals/ projects.

- Schools would create a student profile for all assessment undertaken over the year and retain the evidences in digital format.

- CBSE will facilitate schools to upload marks of Internal Assessment on the CBSE IT platform.

- Guidelines for Internal Assessment for all subjects will also be released along with the rationalized term wise divided syllabus for the session 2021-22.The Board would also provide additional resources like sample assessments, question banks, teacher training etc. for more reliable and valid internal assessments.

केन्द्रीय माध्यमिक शिक्षा बोर्ड
(शिक्षा मंत्रालय, भारत सरकार के अधीन एक स्वायत संगठन)

CENTRAL BOARD OF SECONDARY EDUCATION
(An Autonomous Organisation under the Ministryof Education, Govt. of India)

Term I Examinations:

- At the end of the first term, the Board will organize **Term I Examination** in a flexible schedule to be conducted between November-December 2021 with a window period of 4-8 weeks for schools situated in different parts of country and abroad. Dates for conduct of examinations will be notified subsequently.

- The Question Paper will have Multiple Choice Questions (MCQ) including case-based MCQs and MCQs on assertion-reasoning type. Duration of test will be **90 minutes** and it will cover only the rationalized syllabus of **Term I only** (i.e. approx. 50% of the entire syllabus).

- Question Papers will be sent by the CBSE to schools along with marking scheme.

- The exams will be conducted under the supervision of the External Center Superintendents and Observers appointed by CBSE.

- The responses of students will be captured on OMR sheets which, after scanning may be directly uploaded at CBSE portal or alternatively may be evaluated and marks obtained will be uploaded by the school on the very same day. The final direction in this regard will be conveyed to schools by the Examination Unit of the Board.

- Marks of the **Term I** Examination will contribute to the final overall score of students.

Term II Examination/ Year-end Examination:

- At the end of the second term, the Board would organize **Term II or Year-end Examination** based on the rationalized syllabus of Term II only (i.e. approximately 50% of the entire syllabus).

- This examination would be held around **March-April 2022** at the examination centres fixed by the Board.

- The paper will be of **2 hours duration** and have questions of different formats (case-based/ situation based, open ended- short answer/ long answer type).

- In case the situation is not conducive for normal descriptive examination **a 90 minute MCQ based exam** will be conducted at the end of the Term II also.

- Marks of the Term II Examination would contribute to the final overall score.

केन्द्रीय माध्यमिक शिक्षा बोर्ड

(शिक्षा मंत्रालय, भारत सरकार के अधीन एक स्वायत संगठन)

CENTRAL BOARD OF SECONDARY EDUCATION

(An Autonomous Organisation under the Ministryof Education, Govt. of India)

Assessment / Examination as per different situations

A. In case the situation of the pandemic improves and students are able to come to schools or centres for taking the exams.

Board would conduct Term I and Term II examinations at schools/centres and the theory marks will be distributed equally between the two exams.

B. In case the situation of the pandemic forces complete closure of schools during November-December 2021, but Term II exams are held at schools or centres.

Term I MCQ based examination would be done by students online/offline from home - in this case, the weightage of this exam for the final score would be reduced, and weightage of Term II exams will be increased for declaration of final result.

C. In case the situation of the pandemic forces complete closure of schools during March-April 2022, but Term I exams are held at schools or centres.

Results would be based on the performance of students on Term I MCQ based examination and internal assessments. The weightage of marks of Term I examination conducted by the Board will be increased to provide year end results of candidates.

D. In case the situation of the pandemic forces complete closure of schools and Board conducted Term I and II exams are taken by the candidates from home in the session 2021-22.

Results would be computed on the basis of the Internal Assessment/Practical/Project Work and Theory marks of Term-I and II exams taken by the candidate from home in Class X / XII subject to the moderation or other measures to ensure validity and reliability of the assessment.

In all the above cases, data analysis of marks of students will be undertaken to ensure the integrity of internal assessments and home based exams.

Dr. Joseph Emmanuel
Director (Academics)

PART A
Statistics for Economics

Measures of Dispersion

In this Chapter...

- Introduction
- Standard Deviation

Introduction

Measures of dispersion help to determine the spread or scatteredness of values from a measure of central tendency. They help to assess the extent to which values in a distribution differ from the average of the distribution.

Types of Measures of Dispersion

On the basis of the mode of expression, measures of dispersion can be classified as

1. **Absolute Measures** They are measures of dispersion which are expressed in terms of the original units of a series as rupees, kilogram, etc. The various absolute measures of dispersion are—Range, inter-quartile range, quartile deviation, mean deviation and standard deviation.

2. **Relative Measures** They are the measures of dispersion of a series expressed as a percentage or ratio of the average. These measures do not depend on the units of measurement. Relative measures of dispersion are—Coefficient of range, coefficient of quartile deviation, coefficient of mean deviation, coefficient of standard deviation and coefficient of variation.

Note *As per latest syllabus, in this chapter we will discuss standard deviation and coefficient of variation.*

Methods of Assessing the Extent of Dispersion

The methods of assessing the extent of dispersion in a series can be classified in three categories

1. **Method Based on Spread of Values** Under this method, dispersion is computed on the basis of spread of value, i.e., by computing the differences between the values of the series. The measures of dispersion based on spread of values are—Range, inter-quartile range and quartile deviation.

2. **Method Based on Average** Under this method, dispersion is computed on the basis of difference between the values of a series and the computed average of the series. The measures of dispersion based on average are—Mean deviation and standard deviation.

3. **Graphical Method** Under this method, dispersion is computed graphically. Lorenz curve helps to assess dispersion graphically.

Standard Deviation

Standard deviation is the positive square root of the sum of square of deviations of various values from their arithmetic mean divided by the sample size.

It is an absolute measure of dispersion and is assessed on the basis of average, i.e., mean.

Standard deviation is denoted by the small Greek letter σ (read as sigma).

Coefficient of Standard Deviation

To compare the variability in two series, relative measure of standard deviation is found out. It is known as coefficient of standard deviation. Symbolically,

Coefficient of Standard Deviation $= \dfrac{\sigma}{\overline{X}}$, where

$\sigma =$ Standard Deviation, and

$\overline{X} =$ Mean

Calculation of Standard Deviation and its Coefficient

Calculation of standard deviation in different series is discussed below

In Individual Series

In individual series, standard deviation can be calculated with the help of actual mean method, direct method and short-cut or assumed mean method.

These methods are discussed ahead

1. **Actual Mean Method** In this method, deviations are taken from actual mean.

   The following steps are used to calculate standard deviation by this method

   Step 1 Obtain the sum of values and denote it by ΣX. Divide ΣX by n to find out actual mean $\overline{X}$.

   Step 2 Calculate deviation of values from actual mean and denote it as d.

   Step 3 Square up the deviation and obtain the sum of d^2 and denote it as Σd^2.

   Step 4 Obtain the standard deviation by applying the formula,

   $$\sigma = \sqrt{\dfrac{\Sigma d^2}{n}} \text{ where,}$$

   $\Sigma d^2 =$ Sum of square of deviations from mean

   $n =$ Number of items

   Step 5 Calculate coefficient of standard deviation by applying the given formula,

   Coefficient of Standard Deviation $= \dfrac{\sigma}{\overline{X}}$

Example 1. Calculate standard deviation and its coefficient from the following data through actual mean method 10, 15, 25, 20, 30, 40, 50, 10.

Ans.

Calculation of Standard Deviation and its Coefficient

Values (X)	$d\ (X-\overline{X}),\ \overline{X}=25$	d^2
10	-15	225
15	-10	100
25	0	0
20	-5	25
30	$+5$	25
40	$+15$	225
50	$+25$	625
10	-15	225
$\Sigma X = 200$		$\Sigma d^2 = 1,450$

Here, Number of observation $(n) = 8$

Mean $(\overline{X}) = \dfrac{\Sigma X}{n} = \dfrac{200}{8} = 25$

$$\sigma = \sqrt{\dfrac{\Sigma d^2}{n}}$$

$$= \sqrt{\dfrac{1,450}{8}} = \sqrt{181.25} = 13.463$$

$\therefore$ Standard Deviation $(\sigma) = 13.463$

$\therefore$ Coefficient of Standard Deviation

$$= \dfrac{\sigma}{\overline{X}} = \dfrac{13.463}{25} = 0.54$$

2. **Direct Method** In this method, standard deviation is calculated without finding out the deviations. The steps involved in the direct method are

   Step 1 Calculate the actual mean $(\overline{X})$ of the observations.

   Step 2 Square the observations and obtain the sum, i.e., ΣX^2.

   Step 3 Apply the alongside formula to calculate standard

   deviation $\sigma = \sqrt{\dfrac{\Sigma X^2}{n} - (\overline{X})^2}$

   where, $\Sigma X^2 =$ Sum of square of observations,

   $\overline{X} =$ Arithmetic mean and

   $n =$ Number of observations

   Step 4 Calculate coefficient of standard deviation by applying the given formula,

   Coefficient of Standard Deviation $= \dfrac{\sigma}{\overline{X}}$

Example 2. Calculate the standard deviation and its coefficient by direct method.

Values	5	8	7	11	14

Ans.

Calculation of Standard Deviation and its Coefficient

Values (X)	X^2
5	25
8	64
7	49
11	121
14	196
$\Sigma X = 45$	$\Sigma X^2 = 455$

Here, number of observations $(n) = 5$

Arithmetic Mean $(\overline{X}) = \dfrac{\Sigma X}{n} = \dfrac{45}{5} = 9$

Now, Standard Deviation

$$\sigma = \sqrt{\dfrac{\Sigma X^2}{n} - (\overline{X})^2} = \sqrt{\dfrac{455}{5} - (9)^2} = \sqrt{10} = 3.16$$

$\Rightarrow$ Standard Deviation $(\sigma) = 3.16$

and Coefficient of SD $= \dfrac{\sigma}{\overline{X}} = \dfrac{3.16}{9} = 0.35$

3. **Assumed Mean Method or Short-cut Method** While using this method, the deviations are taken from assumed mean. The following steps are used to calculate standard deviation

Step 1 Assume any number as mean and obtain deviation of every value from the assumed mean. These deviations are represented by d.

Step 2 Find the sum of these deviations and express it as Σd.

Step 3 Square up the deviations and express it as d^2.

Step 4 Find the sum of square of deviation as Σd^2.

Step 5 Apply the following formula to obtain the standard deviation $\sigma = \sqrt{\dfrac{\Sigma d^2}{n} - \left(\dfrac{\Sigma d}{n}\right)^2}$

where, n = Number of observations,
Σd^2 = Sum of square of deviations
Σd = Sum of deviations

Step 6 Find arithmetic mean with the help of the following formula, $\overline{X} = A + \dfrac{\Sigma d}{n}$,

where, A = Assumed Mean, and
Σd = Sum of deviations

Step 7 Find coefficient of standard deviation by applying the given formula, Coefficient of Standard

Deviation $= \dfrac{\sigma}{\overline{X}}$

Example 3. Calculate standard deviation and its coefficient from the following data through assumed mean method

Values	10	15	25	20	30	40	50	10

Ans. Let assumed mean, $(A) = 30$

Calculation of Standard Deviation and its Coefficient

Values (X)	$d\,(X - A),$ $A = 30$	d^2
10	− 20	400
15	− 15	225
25	− 5	25
20	− 10	100
30	0	0
40	10	100
50	20	400
10	− 20	400
$n = 8$	$\Sigma d = -40$	$\Sigma d^2 = 1{,}650$

Here, $\Sigma d^2 = 1{,}650$, $n = 8$, $\Sigma d = -40$

Standard Deviation $(\sigma) = \sqrt{\dfrac{\Sigma d^2}{n} - \left(\dfrac{\Sigma d}{n}\right)^2}$

$$\Rightarrow \quad \sigma = \sqrt{\dfrac{1{,}650}{8} - \left(\dfrac{-40}{8}\right)^2}$$

$$= \sqrt{206.25 - (-5)^2} = \sqrt{206.25 - 25}$$

$$= \sqrt{181.25} = 13.463$$

and Mean $(\overline{X}) = A + \dfrac{\Sigma d}{n} = 30 + \dfrac{(-40)}{8} = 30 - 5 = 25$

$\therefore$ Coefficient of $\sigma = \dfrac{\sigma}{\overline{X}} = \dfrac{13.463}{25} = 0.538$

In Discrete Series

In discrete series, standard deviation can be calculated with the help of actual mean method, direct method, short-cut or assumed mean method and step deviation method. These methods are discussed ahead

1. **Actual Mean Method** The following steps are used to calculate standard deviation by actual mean method

Step 1 Compute arithmetic mean by applying the given formula,
$$\overline{X} = \Sigma f X / \Sigma f$$

Step 2 Calculate deviations of values from actual mean and denote it as d.

Step 3 Square the deviations to find d^2 to determine fd.

Step 4 Multiply f and d^2 to obtain fd^2.

Step 5 Find the sum of fd^2 and express it as Σfd^2.

Step 6 Now, apply the given formula to compute standard deviation $\sigma = \sqrt{\dfrac{\Sigma fd^2}{\Sigma f}}$, where symbols have their meanings as defined above.

Step 7 Use the given formula to find the coeffficient of standard deviation.

$$\text{Coefficient of } \sigma = \dfrac{\sigma}{\overline{X}}$$

Example 4. Calculate standard deviation and its coefficient from the following data

Income Per Day	10	20	30	40	50	60
Number of Workers	10	20	25	20	15	10

Ans.   **Calculation of Standard Deviation and its Coefficient**

Income per day (X)	Frequency (f)	fX	$d\,(X-\overline{X}),$ $\overline{X}=34$	d^2	fd^2
10	10	100	-24	576	5,760
20	20	400	-14	196	3,920
30	25	750	-4	16	400
40	20	800	6	36	720
50	15	750	16	256	3,840
60	10	600	26	676	6,760
$\Sigma f = n = 100$		$\Sigma fX = 3,400$			$\Sigma fd^2 = 21,400$

Here, sum of frequencies, $\Sigma f = 100$

$$\therefore \quad \text{Mean}\quad (\overline{X}) = \dfrac{\Sigma fX}{\Sigma f} = \dfrac{3,400}{100} = 34$$

$$\text{Standard deviation } (\sigma) = \sqrt{\dfrac{\Sigma fd^2}{\Sigma f}} = \sqrt{\dfrac{21,400}{100}}$$

$$= \sqrt{214} = 14.63$$

$$\text{Coefficient of Standard Deviation} = \dfrac{\sigma}{\overline{X}} = \dfrac{14.63}{34} = 0.43$$

2. **Direct Method** The following steps are used to calculate standard deviation by direct method

Step 1 Compute arithmetic mean by applying the given formula, $\overline{X} = \Sigma f\,X \times /\Sigma f$

Step 2 Square the values of X to get X^2.

Step 3 Multiply X^2 with respective frequencies to get fX^2. Obtain the sum of fX^2 as $\Sigma f X^2$.

Step 4 Apply the following formula to get standard deviation, $\sigma = \sqrt{\dfrac{\Sigma f X^2}{\Sigma f} - (\overline{X})^2}$, where symbols have their usual meanings.

Step 5 Obtain the coefficient of standard deviation with the help of given formula, Coefficient of

$$\sigma = \dfrac{\sigma}{\overline{X}}$$

Example 5. Calculate standard deviation and its coefficient by the direct method.

Size	5	10	15	20
Frequency	2	1	4	3

Ans.   **Calculation of Standard Deviation and its Coefficient**

Size (X)	Frequency (f)	fX	X^2	fX^2
5	2	10	25	50
10	1	10	100	100
15	4	60	225	900
20	3	60	400	1,200
	$\Sigma f = n = 10$	$\Sigma fX = 140$		$\Sigma fX^2 = 2,250$

Here, $\Sigma fX^2 = 2,250,\ \Sigma f = 10,\ \Sigma fX = 140$

$$\text{Arithmetic Mean } (\overline{X}) = \dfrac{\Sigma fX}{\Sigma f} = \dfrac{140}{10} = 14$$

$$\text{Standard Deviation } (\sigma) = \sqrt{\dfrac{\Sigma fx^2}{\Sigma f} - (\overline{X})^2}$$

$$\Rightarrow \qquad \sigma = \sqrt{\dfrac{2,250}{10} - (14)^2}$$

$$= \sqrt{225 - 196}$$

$$= \sqrt{29} = 5.38$$

and $\text{Coefficient of } \sigma = \dfrac{\sigma}{\overline{X}} = \dfrac{5.38}{14} = 0.38$

3. **Assumed Mean Method or Short-cut Method** The following steps are used to calculate standard deviation by assumed mean method

Step 1 From the given values of X, assume a value as mean and calculate deviations from this mean denoting them as d.

Step 2 Multiply deviations with corresponding frequencies to obtain 'fd'.

Step 3 Multiply 'fd' with 'd' to obtain fd^2.

Step 4 Find Σfd and Σfd^2.

Step 5 Apply the following formula to obtain standard deviation,

$$\sigma = \sqrt{\dfrac{\Sigma fd^2}{\Sigma f} - \left(\dfrac{\Sigma fd}{\Sigma f}\right)^2}$$, where variables have the same meaning as discussed above.

Step 6 Find arithmetic mean with the help of given formula, $\overline{X} = A + \dfrac{\Sigma fd}{\Sigma f}$

Step 7 Find coefficient of standard deviation with the help of given formula,

$$\text{Coefficient of } \sigma = \dfrac{\sigma}{\overline{X}}$$

Example 6. Calculate standard deviation and its coefficient from the following data using assumed mean method

Size	5	6	7	8	9	10
Frequency	9	12	15	8	4	2

Ans. Let, assumed mean, $A = 7$

Calculation of Standard Deviation and its Coefficient

Size (X)	Frequency (f)	$d\,(X-A),$ $A=7$	fd	fd^2
5	9	-2	-18	36
6	12	-1	-12	12
7	15	0	0	0
8	8	$+1$	8	8
9	4	$+2$	8	16
10	2	$+3$	6	18
	$\Sigma f = 50$		$\Sigma fd = -8$	$\Sigma fd^2 = 90$

Standard Deviation (σ)

$$= \sqrt{\dfrac{\Sigma fd^2}{\Sigma f} - \left(\dfrac{\Sigma fd}{\Sigma f}\right)^2} = \sqrt{\dfrac{90}{50} - \left(\dfrac{-8}{50}\right)^2} = \sqrt{1.8 - 0.026}$$

$$= \sqrt{1.77} \Rightarrow \sigma = 1.33$$

Now, $\overline{X} = A + \dfrac{\Sigma fd}{\Sigma f} = 7 + \left(\dfrac{-8}{50}\right) = 7 - 0.16 = 6.84$

$\therefore$ Coefficient of $\sigma = \dfrac{\sigma}{\overline{X}} = \dfrac{1.33}{6.84} = 0.19$

4. **Step Deviation Method** This method can be used if the deviations are divisible by a common factor. The following steps are used to calculate standard deviation by step deviation method

Step 1 From the given values of X, assume a value as mean and calculate deviations from this mean denoting them as d.

Step 2 Divide the deviations by a common factor c to obtain d'.

Step 3 Multiply step deviation (d') with corresponding frequency to obtain fd'.

Step 4 Multiply fd' with d' to obtain fd'^2.

Step 5 Find $\Sigma fd'$ and $\Sigma fd'^2$.

Step 6 Apply the following formula to get standard deviation,

$$\sigma = \sqrt{\dfrac{\Sigma fd'^2}{\Sigma f} - \left(\dfrac{\Sigma fd'}{\Sigma f}\right)^2} \times c, \text{ where variables have}$$

the same meaning as discussed above.

Step 7 Find arithmetic mean by applying the given formula, $\overline{X} = A + \dfrac{\Sigma fd'}{\Sigma f} \times c$

Step 8 Find coefficient of standard deviation with the help of the given formula,

$$\text{Coefficient of } \sigma = \dfrac{\sigma}{\overline{X}}$$

Example 7. Calculate standard deviation and coefficient of standard deviation from the following data

Values	140	150	160	170	180	190	200
Frequency	3	5	8	12	7	5	2

Ans. Let assumed mean, $A = 170$ and $c = 10$

Calculation of Standard Deviation and its Coefficient

Values (X)	Frequency (f)	$d\,(X-A),$ $A=170$	$d'\,(d/c),$ $c=10$	fd'	fd'^2
140	3	-30	-3	-9	27
150	5	-20	-2	-10	20
160	8	-10	-1	-8	8
170	12	0	0	0	0
180	7	10	1	7	7
190	5	20	2	10	20
200	2	30	3	6	18
	$\Sigma f = 42$			$\Sigma fd' = -4$	$\Sigma fd'^2 = 100$

Here, $\Sigma fd' = -4$, $\Sigma fd'^2 = 100$, $\Sigma f = 42$

Standard Deviation $(\sigma) = \sqrt{\dfrac{\Sigma fd'^2}{\Sigma f} - \left(\dfrac{\Sigma fd'}{\Sigma f}\right)^2} \times c$

$\Rightarrow \qquad \sigma = \sqrt{\dfrac{100}{42} - \left(\dfrac{-4}{42}\right)^2} \times 10$

$$= \sqrt{2.38 - 0.009} \times 10$$

$$= \sqrt{2.371} \times 10 = 1.54 \times 10 = 15.4$$

Hence, Standard Deviation $(\sigma) = 15.4$

Now, Mean $(\overline{X}) = A + \dfrac{\Sigma fd'}{\Sigma f} \times c$

$$= 170 + \left(\dfrac{-4}{42}\right) \times 10 = 169.04$$

$\therefore \qquad$ Coefficient of $\sigma = \dfrac{\sigma}{\overline{X}} = \dfrac{15.4}{169.04} = 0.091$

In Continuous Series

In continuous series also, standard deviation can be calculated with the help of actual mean method, direct method, short-cut or assumed mean method and step deviation method. These methods are discussed ahead

1. **Actual Mean Method** The given steps should be followed for computing standard deviation and its coefficient by this method

   Step 1 Find the mid-values (m) of the class intervals and compute arithmetic mean by applying the given formula, $\overline{X} = \Sigma fm/\Sigma f$

   Step 2 Calculate deviations of mid-values from actual mean and denote it as d.

   Steps 3, 4, 5, 6 and 7 are the same as discussed in discrete series.

Exmaple 8. From the following data, calculate arithmetic mean, standard deviation and its coefficient

Marks	0–10	10–20	20–30	30–40	40–50
Number of Students	1	3	5	4	2

Ans.   **Calculation of Arithmetic Mean, Standard Deviation and its Coefficient**

Marks (X)	Number of Students (f)	Mid-point (m)	fm	$d\,(m-\overline{X})$, $\overline{X}=27$	fd	fd^2
0–10	1	5	5	-22	-22	484
10–20	3	15	45	-12	-36	432
20–30	5	25	125	-2	-10	20
30–40	4	35	140	8	32	256
40–50	2	45	90	18	36	648
	$\Sigma f = 15$		$\Sigma fm = 405$			$\Sigma fd^2 = 1,840$

$$\text{Mean } (\overline{X}) = \frac{\Sigma fm}{\Sigma f} = \frac{405}{15} = 27$$

$$\text{Standard Deviation } (\sigma) = \sqrt{\frac{\Sigma fd^2}{\Sigma f}} = \sqrt{\frac{1,840}{15}}$$

$$= \sqrt{122.67} = 11.076$$

$$\text{and Coefficient of } \sigma = \frac{\sigma}{\overline{X}} = \frac{11.076}{27} = 0.41$$

2. **Direct Method** The following steps are used to calculate standard deviation by direct method

   Step 1 Find the mid-values of the class intervals and compute arithmetic mean by applying the given formula, $\overline{X} = \Sigma fm/\Sigma f$

   Step 2 Square the mid-value (m) to get m^2.

   Steps 3, 4 and 5 are the same as in the case of discrete series.

Example 9. Calculate standard deviation and its coefficient by direct method.

Marks	0–10	10–20	20–30	30–40	40–50
Number of Students	4	3	6	5	2

Ans.   **Calculation of Standard Deviation and its Coefficient**

Marks (X)	Number of Students (f)	Mid-point (m)	fm	m^2	fm^2
0–10	4	5	20	25	100
10–20	3	15	45	225	675
20–30	6	25	150	625	3,750
30–40	5	35	175	1,225	6,125
40–50	2	45	90	2,025	4,050
	$\Sigma f = 20$		$\Sigma fm = 480$		$\Sigma fm^2 = 14,700$

Here, $\Sigma fm^2 = 14,700; \Sigma f = 20$

$$\Sigma fm = 480$$

$$\text{Arithmetic Mean } (\overline{X}) = \frac{\Sigma fm}{\Sigma f}$$

$$= \frac{480}{20} = 24$$

$$\text{Standard Deviation } (\sigma) = \sqrt{\frac{\Sigma fm^2}{\Sigma f} - (\overline{X})^2}$$

$$\Rightarrow \qquad \sigma = \sqrt{\frac{14,700}{20} - (24)^2}$$

$$= \sqrt{735 - 576}$$

$$= \sqrt{159} = 12.61 \text{ marks}$$

$$\text{and Coefficient of } \sigma = \frac{\sigma}{\overline{X}} = \frac{12.61}{24} = 0.525$$

3. **Assumed Mean Method or Short-cut Method** The following steps are used to calculate standard deviation by assumed mean method

   Step 1 Find the mid-values of the class intervals. From these mid-values, assume a value as mean and calculate deviations from this mean denoting them as 'd'.

   Steps 2, 3, 4, 5, 6 and 7 are the same as discussed in discrete series.

Example 10. Find out the standard deviation and its coefficient from the following frequency distribution, using assumed mean method.

Age (in years)	18–28	28–38	38–48	48–58
Number of Employees	5	8	10	7

Ans. Let assumed mean, $A = 33$

Calculation of Standard Deviation and its Coefficient

Age (in years) (X)	Number of Employees (f)	Mid-point (m)	$d(m-A)$, $A=33$	fd	fd^2
18–28	5	23	-10	-50	500
28–38	8	33	0	0	0
38–48	10	43	$+10$	$+100$	1,000
48–58	7	53	$+20$	$+140$	2,800
	$\Sigma = 30$			$\Sigma fd = 190$	$\Sigma fd^2 = 4,300$

$$\text{Standard Deviation } (\sigma) = \sqrt{\frac{\Sigma fd^2}{\Sigma f} - \left(\frac{\Sigma fd}{\Sigma f}\right)^2}$$

$$= \sqrt{\frac{4,300}{30} - \left(\frac{190}{30}\right)^2} = \sqrt{143.33 - \left(\frac{19}{3}\right)^2}$$

$$= \sqrt{143.33 - 40.11} = \sqrt{103.22} = 10.16$$

$\therefore$ Standard Deviation $= 10.16$

Now, Mean $(\overline{X}) = A + \dfrac{\Sigma fd}{\Sigma f}$

$$= 33 + \left(\frac{190}{30}\right) = 33 + 6.333 = 39.33$$

$\therefore$ Coefficient of $\sigma = \dfrac{\sigma}{\overline{X}} = \dfrac{10.16}{39.33} = 0.26$

4. **Step Deviation Method** This method can be used if the deviations are divisible by a common factor.
   The following steps are used to calculate standard deviation by this method

   Step 1 Find the mid-values of the class intervals. From these mid-values assume a value as mean and calculate deviations from this mean denoting them as d'.

   Steps 2, 3, 4, 5, 6, 7 and 8 are the same as discussed in discrete series.

Example 11. Calculate standard deviation and its coefficient from the following frequency distribution

Age (in years)	0–5	5–10	10–15	15–20
Number of Students	50	37	60	25

Ans.

Calculation of Standard Deviation and its Coefficient

Age (in years)	Number of Students (f)	Mid-point (m)	$d(m-A)$, $A = 12.5$	$d'\left(\dfrac{d}{c}\right)$, $c = 5$	fd'	fd'^2
0-5	50	2.5	-10	-2	-100	200
5-10	37	7.5	-5	-1	-37	37
10-15	60	12.5	0	0	0	0
15-20	48	17.5	5	1	48	48
	$\Sigma f = 200$				$\Sigma fd' = -89$	$\Sigma fd'^2 = 285$

$$\text{Standard Deviation } (\sigma) = \sqrt{\frac{\Sigma fd'^2}{\Sigma f} - \left(\frac{\Sigma fd'}{\Sigma f}\right)^2} \times c$$

$$= \sqrt{\frac{285}{200} - \left(\frac{-89}{200}\right)^2} \times 5$$

$$= \sqrt{1.425 - 0.198} \times 5$$

$$= \sqrt{1.227} \times 5 = 1.108 \times 5$$

$$\sigma = 5.54$$

$$\text{Mean } (\overline{X}) = A + \left(\frac{\Sigma fd'}{\Sigma f} \times C\right) = 12.5 + \left(\frac{-89}{200} \times 5\right)$$

$$= 12.5 - 2.225 \quad \therefore \quad \overline{X} = 10.275$$

$$\text{Coefficient of } \sigma = \frac{\sigma}{\overline{X}} = \frac{5.54}{10.275} = 0.54$$

Variance

Variance is another measure of dispersion which is based on standard deviation. It means the square of standard deviation.

Symbolically,

$$\text{Variance} = (\text{Standard Deviation})^2$$

$$= (\sigma^2)$$

Also $\sqrt{\text{Variance}} = \text{Standard Deviation } (\sigma)$

Coefficient of Variation

It is the percentage variation in the mean, the standard deviation being considered as the total variation in the mean. It represents the variation of a series in percentage and is computed as follows,

$$\text{Coefficient of Variation} = \frac{\text{Standard Deviation } (\sigma)}{\text{Mean} (\overline{X})} \times 100$$

Chapter Practice

Objective Questions

- ### Multiple Choice Questions

1. Standard deviation is always computed from
   (a) mean
   (b) mode
   (c) median
   (d) geometric mean

Ans. (a) mean

2. Coefficient of variation is given by
   (a) $\dfrac{\sigma}{\overline{X}}$
   (b) $\dfrac{\overline{X}}{\sigma}$
   (c) $\dfrac{\overline{X}}{\sigma} \times 100$
   (d) $\dfrac{\sigma}{\overline{X}} \times 100$

Ans. (d) $\dfrac{\sigma}{\overline{X}} \times 100$

3. Which of the following is a unit free number?
   (a) SD
   (b) Variance
   (c) MD
   (d) CV

Ans. (d) Coefficient of variation measures the variation in the given series from their average values without considering any unit.

4. The standard deviation of a data set is expressed in the
   (a) same unit as the observations in the data set
   (b) square of the unit of the observation
   (c) square root of the unit of the observation
   (d) None of the above

Ans. (a) same unit as the observations in the data set

5. Standard deviation is .... of the arithmetic average of the squares of the deviations measured from the mean.
   (a) square root
   (b) cube root
   (c) sum total
   (d) None of these

Ans. (a) square root

6. Standard deviation is .... measure of dispersion.
   (a) absolute
   (b) relative
   (c) crude
   (d) Both (a) and (b)

Ans. (a) absolute

7. Which of the following mathematical sign is used to denote standard deviation?
   (a) Ω
   (b) σ
   (c) σ^2
   (d) Σ

Ans. (c) σ^2

8. Greater the value of standard deviation, ... is the consistency of data.
   (a) lesser
   (b) greater
   (c) constant
   (d) None of these

Ans. (b) Standard deviation is a measure of consistency of the series, thus higher value of standard deviation indicates greater consistency.

9. **Statement I** Variance is the square of standard deviation for any type of statistical series.

   Statement II As the sample size increases, variance becomes equal to standard deviation.

   Alternatives
   (a) Statement I is correct and Statement II is incorrect
   (b) Statement II is correct and Statement I is incorrect
   (c) Both the statements are correct
   (d) Both the statements are incorrect

Ans. (a) Variance is the square of standard deviation and thus never becomes equal to standard deviation.

10. Which of the following statement is true about the most important disadvantage of standard deviation?
   (a) It is used in many other statistical techniques
   (b) It doesn't takes into account all the values in the data set
   (c) It is a sensitive measure of dispersion
   (d) It is difficult to calculate manually

Ans. (d) It is difficult to calculate manually

11. **Statement I** Coefficient of variation is used to check the consistency of the data.
   Statement II Standard deviation can never be calculated without arithmetic mean.

   Alternatives
   (a) Statement I is correct and Statement II is incorrect
   (b) Statement II is correct and Statement I is incorrect
   (c) Both the statements are correct
   (d) Both the statements are incorrect

Ans. (a) Calculation of standard deviation does not always required using actual mean, it can be calculated using assumed mean as well.

12. The calculated value of standard deviation can never be ....
- (a) less than one
- (b) more than one
- (c) negative
- (d) more than variance

Ans. (c) Standard deviation is calculated by squaring up the difference between the variable, thus can never be negative.

13. Which of the following is not true about the measures of dispersion?
- (a) It serve to locate the distribution
- (b) Indicates high or low uniformity of the items
- (c) Reveals how items are spread out on either side of the centre
- (d) Difference or variation among the values

Ans. (a) Dispersion is not used to locate the position of the variable rather it is used to measure the fluctuations in the given series.

14. Given below are the relative measures of dispersion except
- (a) coefficient of variation
- (b) coefficient of standard deviation
- (c) standard deviation
- (d) Both (a) and (b)

Ans. (c) Standard deviation is an absolute measure of dispersion as it is presented as a proportionate number.

15. When the actual mean is multiplied with the coefficient of variation, it becomes equal to ....
- (a) variance
- (b) coefficient of standard deviation
- (c) standard deviation
- (d) coefficient of arithmetic mean

Ans. (c) standard deviation

16. The minimum value or the lower limit of variance can be ....
- (a) −1
- (b) 0
- (c) 1
- (d) None of these

Ans. (b) The minimum value of variance is zero, which indicates no fluctuation in a given series.

17. Standard deviation remains unchanged due to change in which of the following?
- (a) Change of Origin
- (b) Change of Scale
- (c) Change of Data
- (d) All of these

Ans. (a) Standard deviation remains unchanged due to change in origin and it takes the square of the difference in the variables.

18. Choose the incorrect statement from the options given below.
- (a) Standard deviation is not based upon all the items of the series
- (b) Standard deviation is the square root of variance

- (c) Coefficient of standard deviation is a relative measure of dispersion
- (d) All of the above

Ans. (a) Standard deviation is calculated considering all the items of a given series.

19. For calculation standard deviation by step deviation method which of the following mean is used?
- (a) Actual mean
- (b) Assumed mean
- (c) Combined mean
- (d) Any of these

Ans. (b) Assumed mean

• Assertion-Reasoning MCQs

Direction (Q. Nos. 1 to 4) *There are two statements marked as Assertion (A) and Reason (R). Read the statements and choose the appropriate option from the options given below.*
- (a) Both Assertion (A) and Reason (R) are true and Reason (R) is the correct explanation of Assertion (A)
- (b) Both Assertion (A) and Reason (R) are true, but Reason (R) is not the correct explanation of Assertion (A)
- (c) Assertion (A) is false, but Reason (R) is true
- (d) Both are false

1. **Assertion** (A) Any measure of central tendency can be used to compute standard deviation.

Reason (R) Standard deviation gives best result when calculated from median.

Ans. (d) Standard deviation is only calculated using arithmetic mean.

2. **Assertion** (A) If the Variance of a series is 36, its standard deviation will be 6.

Reason (R) Variance is the square of standard deviation.

Ans. (a) Both Assertion (A) and Reason (R) are true and Reason (R) is the correct explanation of Assertion (A)

3. **Assertion** (A) Standard deviation cannot be calculated in a mid-value frequency distribution.

Reason (R) Mid-value frequency distribution need to be converted into exclusive frequency distribution to calculate standard deviation.

Ans. (d) Standard deviation is the most useful measure of dispersion which can be calculated in all types of frequency distributions.

4. **Assertion** (A) When two statistical series are compared, a series with lower coefficient of variation is considered as consistent.

Reason (R) Lower value of coefficient of variation indicates lower fluctuation in the given distribution.

Ans. (a) Both Assertion (A) and Reason (R) are true and Reason (R) is the correct explanation of Assertion (A)

• Case Based MCQs

1. Direction *Read the following case study and answer the question no. (i) to (vi) on the basis of the same.*

You're given the following information about the average salaries of people working in different fields.

	Marketing	Education	Banking	Technology
Mean Salary	4,000	4,500	6,000	8,500
Variance	10,000	25,000	90,000	40,000

(i) Based upon the above data, what will be the standard deviation of the banking sector?
   (a) 90,000   (b) 9,000
   (c) 300   (d) 30

Ans. (c) Standard deviation is the under root of variance thus, when variance in 90,000, standard deviation will be 300.

(ii) The coefficient of standard deviation of the education sector will be equal to ....
   (a) 0.03   (b) 0.3
   (c) 3.33   (d) Can't be determined

Ans. (a) Coefficient of standard deviation is calculated as the ratio of standard deviation and its arithmetic mean. Here, standard deviation will be 158.113 and mean is given as 4,500, therefore, coefficient of standard deviation will be 0.03.

(iii) **Statement I** Coefficient of variation of marketing sector as per the above data is 2.5.

     Statement II Coefficient of variation presents information in percentage form.

     Alternatives
   (a) Statement I is correct and Statement II is incorrect
   (b) Statement II is correct and Statement I is incorrect
   (c) Both the statements are correct
   (d) Both the statements are incorrect

Ans. (c) Both the statements are correct

(iv) Which of the following sectors from the above data is most consistent?
   (a) Marketing   (b) Education
   (c) Banking   (d) Technology

Ans. (d) Technology sector shows the lowest coefficient of variation thus, considered as most consistent among all other.

(v) **Assertion** (A) Marketing sector shows the least value of coefficient of variation in the given data.

    Reason (R) Lower value of coefficient of variation makes it least consistent among all the given sectors.

    Alternatives
   (a) Both Assertion (A) and Reason (R) are true and Reason (R) is the correct explanation of Assertion (A)
   (b) Both Assertion (A) and Reason (R) are true, but Reason (R) is not the correct explanation of Assertion (A)
   (c) Assertion (A) is false, but Reason (R) is true
   (d) Both are false

Ans. (d) Marketing sector doesn't have the least value of CV and lower CV indicates higher consistency.

(vi) Which of the following sectors pays highest salary on an average?
   (a) Marketing   (b) Education
   (c) Banking   (d) Technology

Ans. (d) Technology

PART 2
Subjective Questions

• Short Answer (SA) Type Questions

1. Mention the objectives of various measures of dispersion.

Ans. Objectives of measures of dispersion are
   (i) Measures of dispersion help in statistical investigation.
   (ii) They help to determine the reliability of an average.
   (iii) They help to compare the variability of two or more series.
   (iv) They serve as the basis of computation of other statistical measures such as correlation, etc.
   (v) They help to control the variation of the data from the central value.

2. What features should a good measure of dispersion possess?

Ans. Features/Properties of a good measure of dispersion are
   (i) It should be rigidly defined.
   (ii) It should be simple to understand.
   (iii) It should be easy to calculate.
   (iv) It should be based on all the observations of the series.
   (v) It should be least affected by sampling fluctuations.
   (vi) It should be capable of further algebraic treatment.
   (vii) It should not be affected by extreme values.

3. Briefly explain the concept of standard deviation using its formula to calculate the same.

Ans. The positive square root of the sum of square of deviations of various values from their mean divided by the sample size is called standard deviation. The idea of standard deviation was first given by Karl Pearson in 1893.

$$\text{Symbolically, } \sigma = \sqrt{\frac{\Sigma d^2}{n}}$$

It fulfils all the requisites of a good measure of dispersion except that it is sensitive to extreme values.

4. State some important merits of standard deviation.

Ans. Some important merits of standard deviation

    (i) It is based on all values of the series.

    (ii) It is an exact and definite measure of dispersion.

    (iii) It is least affected by fluctuations in sampling because samples are based on all values of the series.

    (iv) It is suitable for further algebraic treatment.

5. State some important demerits of standard deviation.

Ans. Some important demerits of standard deviation are

    (i) It is difficult to calculate as compared to other measures of dispersion.

    (ii) It is unduly affected by extreme values of the series as it is based on all the items.

    (iii) It cannot be used to compare two series expressed in different units.

6. What are the properties of standard deviation?

Ans. The properties of standard deviation are as follows

    (i) Standard deviation is the most popular measure of dispersion.

    (ii) It is not affected by change in origin, but is affected by change in scale.

    (iii) A distribution with lesser coefficient of variation shows greater consistency, homogeneity and uniformity, whereas a distribution with greater coefficient of variation is considered more scattered.

    (iv) For two or more groups, it is possible to measure the combined standard deviation.

7. Write the correct formula of calculating following measures of dispersion

    (i) Coefficient of Standard Deviation

    (ii) Coefficient of Variation

    (iii) Variance

Ans. Formula for computing

    (i) Coefficient of Standard Deviation $= \dfrac{\sigma}{\overline{X}}$

    (ii) Coefficient of Variation $= \dfrac{\sigma}{\overline{X}} \times 100$

    (iii) Variance $= \sigma^2$, where

        σ = Standard Deviation, and
        $\overline{X}$ = Arithmetic Mean

8. The sum of square of deviations for 10 observations taken from mean 50 is 25. Find the coefficient of variation.

Ans. Given,

    Number of observations $(n) = 10$

          Mean $(\overline{X}) = 50$

    Sum of square of deviations $(\Sigma d^2) = 25$

    We know that $\sigma = \sqrt{\dfrac{\Sigma d^2}{n}}$

    On substituting the variables, we get

$$\sigma = \sqrt{\dfrac{25}{10}} = 1.58$$

Coefficient of Variation $= \dfrac{\sigma}{\overline{X}} \times 100$

$$= \dfrac{1.58}{50} \times 100 = 3.16$$

9. Calculate the standard deviation from the given data.

$$10, 15, 20, 25, 30, 35, 40$$

Ans. **Calculation of Standard Deviation**

S.No.	X	$d\,(X-A),$ $A = 25$	d^2
1	10	-15	225
2	15	-10	100
3	20	-5	25
4	25	0	0
5	30	5	25
6	35	10	100
7	40	15	225
$n = 7$		$\Sigma d = 0$	$\Sigma d^2 = 700$

$$\sigma = \sqrt{\dfrac{\Sigma d^2}{n} - \left(\dfrac{\Sigma d}{n}\right)^2} \sqrt{\dfrac{700}{7} - \left(\dfrac{0}{7}\right)^2} = \sqrt{100}$$

$$\therefore \qquad \sigma = 10$$

10. Find out mean and standard deviation of the marks obtained by 10 students in statistics.

S.No.	1	2	3	4	5	6	7	8	9	10
Marks	43	48	65	57	31	60	37	48	78	59

Ans. Let the assumed mean be 53 i.e., $A = 53$.

Calculation of Mean and Standard Deviation

Marks (X)	$d\,(X-A), A = 53$	d^2
43	-10	100
48	-5	25
65	$+12$	144
57	$+4$	16
31	-22	484
60	$+7$	49
37	-16	256
48	-5	25
78	$+25$	625
59	$+6$	36
$n = 10$	$\Sigma d = -4$	$\Sigma d^2 = 1,760$

$$\overline{X} = A + \dfrac{\Sigma d}{n} = 53 + \dfrac{-4}{10} = 53 - 0.4 = 52.6$$

$$\sigma = \sqrt{\frac{\Sigma d^2}{n} - \left(\frac{\Sigma d}{n}\right)^2}$$

$$= \sqrt{\frac{1,760}{10} - \left(\frac{-4}{10}\right)^2}$$

$$= \sqrt{176 - 0.16} = \sqrt{175.84}$$

$$\therefore \qquad \sigma = 13.26$$

11. Calculate standard deviation and coefficient of variation from the following data with the help of direct method

S. No.	1	2	3	4	5
Marks	10	12	13	15	20

Ans. **Calculation of Standard Deviation and Coefficient of Variation**

Marks (X)	X^2
10	100
12	144
13	169
15	225
20	400
$\Sigma X = 70, n = 5$	$\Sigma X^2 = 1,038$

$$\overline{X} = \frac{\Sigma X}{n} = \frac{70}{5} = 14$$

$$\sigma = \sqrt{\frac{\Sigma X^2}{n} - \left(\frac{\Sigma X}{n}\right)^2} = \sqrt{\frac{1,038}{5} - \left(\frac{70}{5}\right)^2}$$

$$= \sqrt{207.6 - 196} = \sqrt{11.6} = 3.41$$

$$\text{Coefficient of Variation (CV)} = \frac{\sigma}{\overline{X}} \times 100 = \frac{3.4}{14} \times 100$$

$$= 24.35\%$$

12. Find the standard deviation by assumed mean method.

X	10	20	30	40	50	60
Frequency	4	6	9	8	5	10

Ans. **Calculation of Standard Deviation**

X	Frequency (f)	$d (X - A)$, $A = 30$	fd	fd^2
10	4	-20	-80	1,600
20	6	-10	-60	600
30	9	0	0	0
40	8	10	80	800
50	5	20	100	2,000
60	10	30	300	9,000
	$\Sigma f = 42$		$\Sigma fd = 340$	$\Sigma fd^2 = 14,000$

$$\sigma = \sqrt{\frac{\Sigma fd^2}{\Sigma f} - \left(\frac{\Sigma fd}{\Sigma f}\right)^2}$$

$$= \sqrt{\frac{14,000}{42} - \left(\frac{340}{42}\right)^2}$$

$$= \sqrt{333.3 - (8.09)^2}$$

$$= \sqrt{333.3 - 65.45}$$

$$= \sqrt{267.85}$$

$$\therefore \qquad \sigma = 16.37$$

13. Find the standard deviation from the given data, using step deviation method.

X	7.5	17.5	27.5	37.5	47.5
Frequency	10	8	15	6	4

Ans. **Calculation of Standard Deviation**

X	Frequency (f)	$d'\left(\dfrac{X - A}{c}\right)$, $A = 27.5, c = 10$	fd'	fd'^2
7.5	10	-2	-20	40
17.5	8	-1	-8	8
27.5	15	0	0	0
37.5	6	1	6	6
47.5	4	2	8	16
	$\Sigma f = 43$		$\Sigma fd' = -14$	$\Sigma fd'^2 = 70$

$$\sigma = \sqrt{\frac{\Sigma fd'^2}{\Sigma f} - \left(\frac{\Sigma fd'}{\Sigma f}\right)^2} \times c$$

$$= \sqrt{\frac{70}{43} - \left(\frac{-14}{43}\right)^2} \times 10$$

$$= \sqrt{1.63 - 0.106} \times 10$$

$$= \sqrt{1.524} \times 10$$

$$\therefore \qquad \sigma = 1.23 \times 10 = 12.3$$

14. If the coefficient of variation of X-series is 14.6% and that of Y-series is 36.9% and their mean are 101.2 and 101.25 respectively, find their standard deviation.

Ans. (i) For series X

$$\text{Coefficient of Variation (CV)} = \frac{\sigma}{\overline{X}} \times 100$$

$$\because \qquad CV = 14.6 \text{ and } \overline{X} = 101.2,$$

on substituting the values, we get

$$\therefore \qquad 14.6 = \frac{\sigma}{101.2} \times 100$$

$$\Rightarrow \qquad \sigma = \frac{14.6 \times 101.2}{100}$$

$$\Rightarrow \quad \sigma = \frac{1,477.52}{100} = 14.78$$

(ii) For series 'Y'

$$CV = \frac{\sigma}{\overline{X}} \times 100$$

$\because \quad CV = 36.9$ and $\overline{X} = 101.25$,

on substituting the values, we get

$$\therefore \quad 36.9 = \frac{\sigma}{101.25} \times 100$$

$$\Rightarrow \quad \sigma = \frac{36.9 \times 101.25}{100}$$

$$\Rightarrow \quad \sigma = \frac{3,736.125}{100} = 37.36$$

15. The coefficient of variations of two series are 58% and 69% and their standard deviations are 21.2 and 15.6. What are their mean?

Ans. (i) For Ist series, Coefficient of Variation (CV)

$$= \frac{\sigma}{\overline{X}} \times 100, \ CV = 58 \text{ and } \sigma = 21.2$$

On substituting the values,

we get $\quad 58 = \frac{21.2}{\overline{X}} \times 100$

$$\therefore \quad \overline{X} = \frac{21.2}{58} \times 100 = 36.55$$

(ii) For IInd series, $\ CV = \frac{\sigma}{\overline{X}} \times 100, \ CV = 69$ and $\sigma = 15.6$

On substituting the values,

we get $\quad 69 = \frac{15.6}{\overline{X}} \times 100,$

$$\therefore \quad \overline{X} = \frac{15.6}{69} \times 100 = 22.6$$

16. The sum of 10 values is 100 and the sum of their squares is 1,090. Find out the coefficient of variation. **(NCERT)**

Ans. Given that, $\Sigma X = 100, n = 10, \Sigma X^2 = 1,090$

$$\therefore \quad \overline{X} = \frac{\Sigma X}{n} = \frac{100}{10} = 10 \quad \because \Sigma X^2 = 1,090$$

$$\therefore \quad \sigma = \sqrt{\frac{\Sigma X^2}{n} - (\overline{X})^2} = \sqrt{\frac{1,090}{10} - (10)^2}$$

$$= \sqrt{9} = 3$$

Coefficient of Variation (CV) $= \frac{\sigma}{\overline{X}} \times 100$

$$= \frac{3}{10} \times 100 = 30$$

• Long Answer (LA) Type Questions

1. Find the standard deviation by the step deviation method.

Class Interval	0–10	10–20	20–30	30–40	40–50	50–60
Frequency (f)	16	12	10	15	12	8

Ans.

Calculation of Standard Deviation

Class Interval	Frequency (f)	Mid-value (m)	$d(m-A)$, $A=25$	$d'\left(\dfrac{d}{c}\right), c=10$	d'^2	fd'	fd'^2
0–10	16	5	−20	−2	4	−32	64
10–20	12	15	−10	−1	1	−12	12
20–30	10	25	0	0	0	0	0
30–40	15	35	10	1	1	15	15
40–50	12	45	20	2	4	24	48
50–60	8	55	30	3	9	24	72
	$\Sigma f = 73$					$\Sigma fd' = 19$	$\Sigma fd'^2 = 211$

$$\sigma = \sqrt{\frac{\Sigma fd'^2}{\Sigma f} - \left(\frac{\Sigma fd'}{\Sigma f}\right)^2} \times c = \sqrt{\frac{211}{73} - \left(\frac{19}{73}\right)^2} \times 10 = \sqrt{2.89 - 0.067} \times 10 = \sqrt{2.82} \times 10 = 1.68 \times 10$$

$$\therefore \quad \sigma = 16.8$$

2. Calculate the coefficient of variation for the following data.

Weight (in kg)	0–20	20–40	40–60	60–80	80–100
Number of Persons	81	40	66	49	14

Ans.

Calculation of Coefficient of Variation

Weight	Frequency (f)	Mid-value (m)	$d = m - A$ $(A = 50)$	$d' = \dfrac{d}{c}\,(c = 20)$	fd'	fd'^2
0–20	81	10	-40	-2	-162	324
20–40	40	30	-20	-1	-40	40
40–60	66	50	0	0	0	0
60–80	49	70	$+20$	$+1$	$+49$	49
80–100	14	90	$+40$	$+2$	$+28$	56
	$\Sigma f = 250$				$\Sigma fd' = -125$	$\Sigma fd'^2 = 469$

$$\overline{X} = A + \frac{\Sigma fd'}{\Sigma f} \times c = 50 + \frac{(-125)}{250} \times 20 = 50 - \frac{2{,}500}{250} = 50 - 10$$

$$\therefore \quad \overline{X} = 40$$

$$\sigma = \sqrt{\frac{\Sigma fd'^2}{\Sigma f} - \left(\frac{\Sigma fd'}{\Sigma f}\right)^2} \times c = \sqrt{\frac{469}{250} - \left(\frac{-125}{250}\right)^2} \times 20 = \sqrt{1.876 - 0.25} \times 20 = \sqrt{1.626} \times 20$$

$$\Rightarrow \quad \sigma = 1.275 \times 20 = 25.50$$

$$\therefore \quad \text{Coefficient of Variation (CV)} = \frac{\sigma}{\overline{X}} \times 100 = \frac{25.50}{40} \times 100 = 63.75\%$$

3. Calculate standard deviation and coefficient of variation from the following data.

Marks	Below 20	Below 40	Below 60	Below 80	Below 100
Number of Students	8	20	50	70	80

Ans. Since, less than distribution (marks) is given, we first convert it into an exclusive distribution (marks).

Calculation of Standard Deviation and Coefficient of Variation

Marks	Number of Students (f)	Mid-value (m)	$d = m - A$ $(A = 50)$	$d' = \dfrac{d}{c}\,(c = 20)$	fd'	fd'^2
0–20	8	10	-40	-2	-16	32
20–40	12	30	-20	-1	-12	12
40–60	30	50	0	0	0	0
60–80	20	70	$+20$	$+1$	$+20$	20
80–100	10	90	$+40$	$+2$	$+20$	40
	$\Sigma f = 80$				$\Sigma fd' = 12$	$\Sigma fd'^2 = 104$

$$\overline{X} = A + \frac{\Sigma fd'}{\Sigma f} \times c = 50 + \frac{12}{80} \times 20 = 53$$

$$\sigma = \sqrt{\frac{\Sigma fd'^2}{\Sigma f} - \left(\frac{\Sigma fd'}{\Sigma f}\right)^2} \times c = \sqrt{\frac{104}{80} - \left(\frac{12}{80}\right)^2} \times 20 = \sqrt{1.3 - 0.0225} \times 20 = \sqrt{1.2775} \times 20 = 1.130 \times 20 = 22.60$$

$$\text{Coefficient of Variation (CV)} = \frac{\sigma}{\overline{X}} \times 100 = \frac{22.60}{53} \times 100 = 42.64\%$$

4. Calculate the coefficient of variation of the given continuous series.

More than	0	10	20	30	40	50	60	70
Cumulative Frequency	100	90	75	50	20	10	5	0

Ans. Since, 'more than' distribution is given, we first convert it into exclusive distribution.

Calculation of Coefficient of Variation

Class Interval	Frequency (f)	Mid-value (m)	$d = m - A$ $(A = 35)$	$d' = \dfrac{d}{c}(c=10)$	fd'	fd'^2
0–10	10	5	−30	−3	−30	90
10–20	15	15	−20	−2	−30	60
20–30	25	25	−10	−1	−25	25
30–40	30	35	0	0	0	0
40–50	10	45	10	1	10	10
50–60	5	55	20	2	10	20
60–70	5	65	30	3	15	45
70–80	0	75	40	4	0	0
	$\Sigma f = 100$				$\Sigma fd' = -50$	$\Sigma fd'^2 = 250$

$$\overline{X} = A + \frac{\Sigma fd'}{\Sigma f} \times c = 35 + \frac{-50}{100} \times 10 = 35 - \frac{500}{100} = 35 - 5$$

$$\therefore \qquad \overline{X} = 30$$

$$\sigma = \sqrt{\frac{\Sigma fd'^2}{\Sigma f} - \left(\frac{\Sigma fd'}{\Sigma f}\right)^2} \times c = \sqrt{\frac{250}{100} - \left(\frac{50}{100}\right)^2} \times 10 = \sqrt{2.5 - 0.25} \times 10 = \sqrt{2.25} \times 10 = 1.5 \times 10 = 15$$

$$\text{Coefficient of Variaton (CV)} = \frac{\sigma}{\overline{X}} \times 100 = \frac{15}{30} \times 100$$

$$\therefore \qquad CV = 50\%.$$

5. Calculate the standard deviation from the following series

Class	0–10	10–20	20–30	30–40	40–50	50–60	60–70
Frequency	2	4	6	8	6	4	2

Ans.
Calculation of Coefficient of Variation

Class Interval (X)	Frequency (f)	Mid-value (m)	fm	m^2	fm^2
0–10	2	5	10	25	50
10–20	4	15	60	225	900
20–30	6	25	150	625	3,750
30–40	8	35	280	1,225	9,800
40–50	6	45	270	2,025	12,150
50–60	4	55	220	3,025	12,100
60–70	2	65	130	4,225	8,450
	$\Sigma f = 32$		$\Sigma fm = 1,120$		$\Sigma fm^2 = 47,200$

$$\text{Mean, } \overline{X} = \frac{\Sigma fm}{\Sigma f} = \frac{1,120}{32} = 35$$

$$\text{Standard Deviation, } (\sigma) = \sqrt{\frac{\Sigma fm^2}{\Sigma f} - (\overline{X})^2} \;\Rightarrow\; (\sigma) = \sqrt{\frac{47,200}{32} - (35)^2} \;\Rightarrow\; (\sigma) = \sqrt{1,475 - 1,225}$$

or, $(\sigma) = \sqrt{250} = 15.81$

Hence, standard deviation of the above series is 15.81.

6. A batsman is to be selected for a cricket team. The choice is between X and Y on the basis of their five previous scores which are

X	25	85	40	80	120
Y	50	70	65	45	80

Which batsman should be selected if we want,

(i) a higher scorer, or

(ii) a more reliable batsman in the team?　**(NCERT)**

Ans. **Batsman X**

Calculation of Mean and Coefficient of Variation

X	$d(X - \overline{X}), \overline{X} = 70$	d^2
25	-45	2,025
85	$+15$	225
40	-30	900
80	10	100
120	50	2,500
$\Sigma X = 350$		$\Sigma d^2 = 5,750$

$$\overline{X} = \frac{\Sigma X}{n} = \frac{350}{5} = 70 \Rightarrow \sigma = \sqrt{\frac{\Sigma d^2}{n}} = \sqrt{\frac{5,750}{5}} = 33.91$$

$$CV = \frac{\sigma}{\overline{X}} \times 100 = \frac{33.91}{70} \times 100 = 48.44$$

Batsman Y

Calculation of Mean and Coefficient of Variation

Y	$d(Y - \overline{Y}), \overline{Y} = 62$	d^2
50	-12	144
70	8	64
65	3	9
45	-17	289
80	18	324
$\Sigma Y = 310$		$\Sigma d^2 = 830$

$$\overline{Y} = \frac{\Sigma Y}{n} = \frac{310}{5} = 62$$

$$\sigma = \sqrt{\frac{\Sigma d^2}{n}} = \sqrt{\frac{830}{5}} = 12.88$$

$$CV = \frac{\sigma}{\overline{Y}} \times 100 = \frac{12.88}{62} \times 100 = 20.78$$

(i) Average of Batsman X is higher than that of Batsman Y, so he should be selected if we want a high scorer.

(ii) Batsman Y is more reliable than Batsman X. This is because the coefficient of variation of Batsman Y is less than that of Batsman X. So, on the basis of reliability, Batsman Y should be selected.

7. To check the quality of two brands of light bulbs, their life in burning hours was estimated as under for 100 bulbs of each brand.

Life (in hrs)	Number of Bulbs (Brand A)	Number of Bulbs (Brand B)
0–50	15	2
50–100	20	8
100–150	18	60
150–200	25	25
200–250	22	5
Total	100	100

(i) Which brand gives higher life?　　(ii) Which brand is more dependable?　　**(NCERT)**

Ans. **For Brand A**

Calculation of Mean and Coefficient of Variation

Life (in hrs)	Number of Bulbs (f)	Mid-value (m)	$d(m - A), A = 125$	$d'\left(\dfrac{d}{c}\right), c = 50$	d'^2	fd'	fd'^2
0–50	15	25	-100	-2	4	-30	60
50–100	20	75	-50	-1	1	-20	20
100–150	18	125	0	0	0	0	0
150–200	25	175	50	1	1	25	25
200–250	22	225	100	2	4	44	88
	$n = 100$					$\Sigma fd' = 19$	$\Sigma fd'^2 = 193$

$$\overline{X} = A + \frac{\Sigma fd'}{\Sigma f} \times c = 125 + \frac{19}{100} \times 50 = 134.5$$

$$\sigma = \sqrt{\frac{\Sigma fd'^2}{n} - \left(\frac{\Sigma fd'}{n}\right)^2} \times c = \sqrt{\frac{193}{100} - \left(\frac{19}{100}\right)^2} \times 50$$

$$= \sqrt{1.93 - 0.0361} \times 50 = \sqrt{1.8939} \times 50 = 1.376 \times 50$$

$$\therefore \qquad \sigma = 68.8$$

$$\text{Coefficient of Variation (CV)} = \frac{\sigma}{\overline{X}} \times 100 = \frac{68.8}{134.5} \times 100 = 51.15$$

For Brand B

Calculation of Mean and Coefficient of Variation

Life (in hrs)	Number of Bulbs (f)	Mid-value (m)	$d(m-A)$, $A = 125$	$d'\left(\frac{d}{c}\right), c = 50$	d'^2	fd'	fd'^2
0–50	2	25	-100	-2	4	-4	8
50–100	8	75	-50	-1	1	-8	8
100–150	60	125	0	0	0	0	0
150–200	25	175	50	1	1	25	25
200–250	5	225	100	2	4	10	20
	$n = 100$					$\Sigma fd' = 23$	$\Sigma fd'^2 = 61$

$$\overline{X} = A + \frac{\Sigma fd'}{N} \times c = 125 + \frac{23}{100} \times 50 = 125 + 11.5 = 136.5$$

$$\sigma = \sqrt{\frac{\Sigma fd'^2}{n} - \left(\frac{\Sigma fd'}{n}\right)^2} \times c = \sqrt{\frac{61}{100} - \left(\frac{23}{100}\right)^2} \times 50 = \sqrt{0.61 - 0.0529} \times 50 = \sqrt{0.5571} \times 50 = 0.75 \times 50$$

$$\therefore \qquad \sigma = 37.5$$

$$\text{Coefficient of Variation (CV)} = \frac{\sigma}{\overline{X}} \times 100 = \frac{37.5}{136.5} \times 100 = 27.47$$

(i) The average life of bulb of Brand B is comparatively higher than that of Brand A, therefore Brand B gives higher life.

(ii) The bulbs of Brand B are more dependable as CV of Brand B is less than CV of Brand A.

Chapter Test

Multiple Choice Questions

.... is an absolute measure of dispersion.
(a) Range (b) Mean deviation (c) Standard deviation (d) All of these

When dispersion of the series is expressed in terms of some relative value, it is called
(a) Relative measure (b) Absolute measure (c) Range (d) None of these

.... of dispersion expresses the variability of data in terms of the original unit.
(a) Relative measure (b) Absolute measure (c) Standard deviation (d) None of these

If the standard deviation of a data is 0.12, find the variance.
(a) 0.144 (b) 0.0144 (c) 1.44 (d) 0.00144

For calculation of coefficient of variation, which of the following is/are required?
(a) Standard deviation (b) Mean (c) Both (a) and (b) (d) None of these

Short Answer (SA) Type Questions

What are the types of measures of dispersion?

Calculate standard deviation and its coefficient from the following data through assumed mean method.

Values	10	15	25	20	30	40	50	10

Calculate the standard deviation by direct method. Values are 5, 8, 7, 9, 6.

Calculate standard deviation using assumed mean method

Size	4	5	6	7	8
Frequency	9	12	17	8	4

Which measure of dispersion is the best and why? State four reasons.

Long Answer (LA) Type Questions

Calculate standard deviation from the following data using step-deviation method.

Items	10-20	20-30	30-40	40-50	50-60	60-70	70-80
Frequency	4	8	8	16	12	6	4

Compute the following parts.

(i) Mean and standard deviations of two distributions of 100 and 150 items are 50 and 5 and 40 and 6 respectively. Find the combined standard deviation.

(ii) Write two merits and two demerits of standard deviation.

Answers

For Detailed Solutions
Scan the code

Measures of Correlation

In this Chapter...

- Meaning of Correlation
- Methods of Computing Correlation

Meaning of Correlation

Correlation studies and measures the direction and intensity of relationship between two variables, in which change in the value of one variable, is associated with change in the value of the other variable.

For example, as the summer heat rises, hill stations are crowded with more and more visitors. Ice-cream sales also increase. Thus, the rise in temperature is correlated to increase in the number of visitors to hill stations and sale of ice-creams.

Correlation and Causation

Correlation only points out the changes that occur in a given variable when some other variable changes.

However, it does not reveal anything about the cause and effect relationship. So, if two variables are correlated, it does not mean that change in one is the cause of changes in the other.

For any two correlated events, say A and B, the following relationships are possible

- A causes B, which is also referred to as **direct causation**. For example, fall in prices of mobiles have led to a rise in it's demand.

- B causes A, which is also referred to as **reverse causation**. For example, as the demand for mobile phone rises, it's prices also rise.

- A and B are consequences of a common cause but do not cause each other.
  For example, during winter sale of woollen clothes and electric heaters both increase due to fall in the temperature. So, even though sale of woollen clothes and heaters exhibit correlation, but they are not related to each other.

- A causes B and B causes A, which is also referred to as **cyclic causation**.
  For example, as national income rises, the level of aggregate demand goes up and as the level of aggregate demand rises, the national income rises.

- A causes C which causes B. It is also referred to as **indirect causation**.
  For example, the glamour and money associated with cricket attract many youngsters towards it and the other sports suffer.

- There is no connection between A and B, which is also referred to as **chance or spurious correlation**.
  For example, correlation between number of ice-creams eaten and marks scored in an examination.

Types of Correlation

On the basis of change in direction, correlation can be classified as

1. **Positive Correlation** When two related variables move together in the same direction, it is said to be positive correlation.

   For example, increase in price and increase in supply of a commodity, sale of ice-creams and high day temperature, etc.

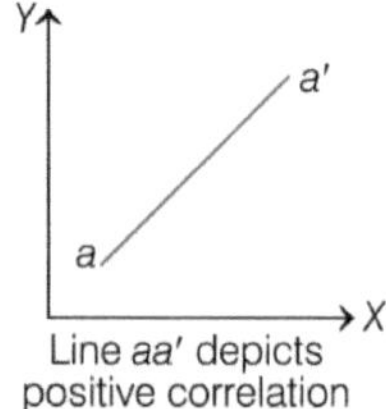

Line *aa'* depicts positive correlation

2. **Negative Correlation** When two variables move in the opposite direction, it is said to be negative correlation.

   For example, growing popularity of TV has resulted in loss of revenue for the film industry, sale of woollen garments fall with a rise in temperature.

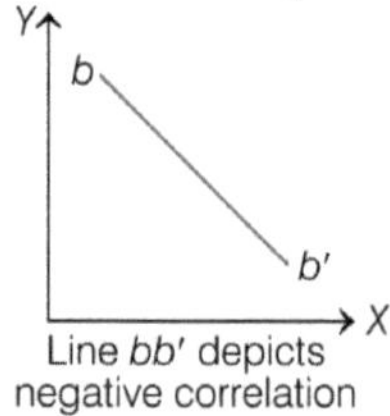

Line *bb'* depicts negative correlation

Methods of Computing Correlation

The different methods of computing correlation are enumerated below

- Scatter Diagrams
- Karl Pearson's Coefficient of Correlation or Covariance
- Spearman's Rank Correlation
- Concurrent Deviation

As per syllabus, first two methods are discussed.

Scatter Diagrams

It is a technique for visually examining the form of relationship between two variables, without calculating any numerical value. To construct a scatter diagram, independent variable is taken on X-axis and dependent variable is taken on Y-axis. The cluster of points plotted is referred to as a scatter diagram.

In a scatter diagram, the degree of closeness of scatter points and their overall direction enables us to examine the relationship between the variables.

Scatter Diagrams Depicting the Various Degrees of Correlation

1. **Positive Correlation** Points are scatterred around an upward rising line indicating the movement of the variables in the same direction,

i.e. when X rises, Y also rises and vice-versa.

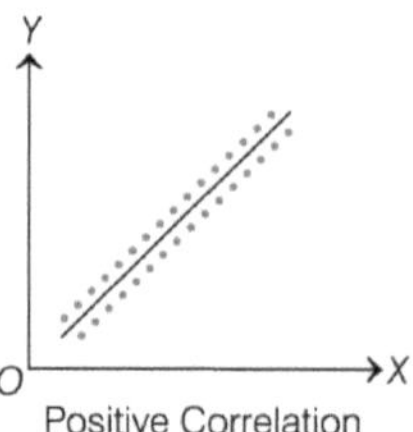

Positive Correlation

2. **Negative Correlation** Points are scatterred around a downward sloping line indicating that variables are moving in opposite directions, i.e. when X rises, Y falls and vice-versa.

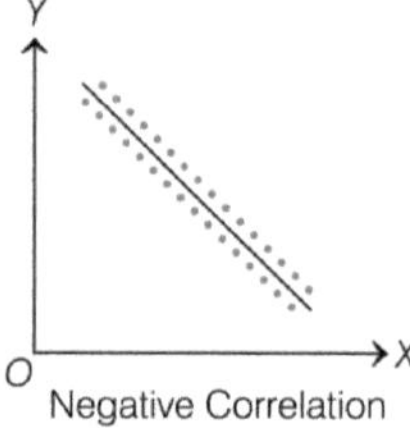

Negative Correlation

3. **No Correlation** There is no upward or downward movement in the points plotted, so variables show no correlation.

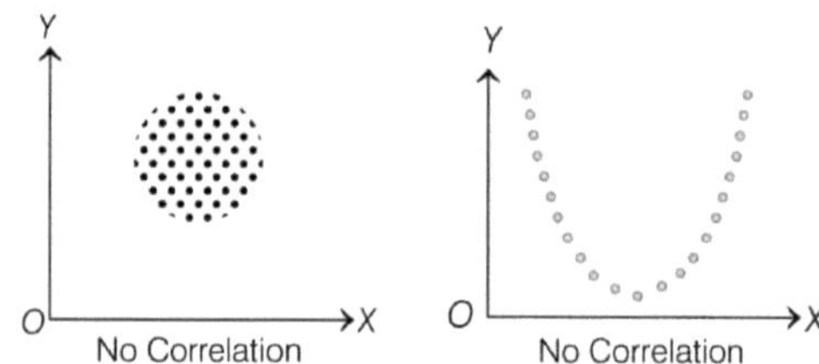

No Correlation   No Correlation

4. **Perfect Positive Correlation** Points are not scattered around the line rather, they are on the same upward slopping line, showing perfect positive correlation.

Perfect Positive Correlation

5. **Perfect Negative Correlation** Points are not scattered around the line rather, they are on the same downward sloping line, showing perfect negative correlation.

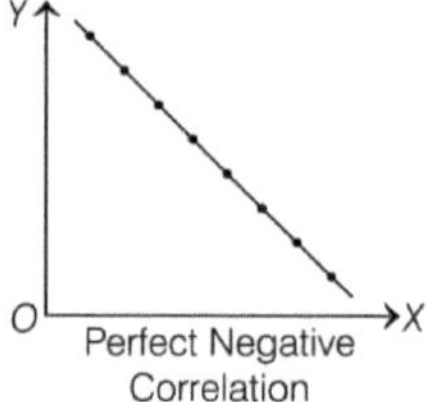

Perfect Negative Correlation

Points to be Remembered while Interpreting a Scatter Diagram

The scatter diagram can be interpreted in the following ways

- If all the points lie on a line, the correlation is perfect and said to be unity, i.e. one.
- If the scatter points are widely dispersed around the line, the correlation is low.
- Correlation is said to be linear if the scatter points lie near a line or on a line.
- If the points move from left to right upwards, the correlation is said to be positive, whereas the movement of points from left to right downwards, indicates negative correlation.
- Points falling close to each other in a straight line indicate high degree of correlation.
- If plotted points show no trend at all, then it shows absence of correlation or no correlation between the two variables.

Example 1. Following are the heights and weights of 10 students of class XI

Height (in inches)	**Weight** (in kgs)
X	**Y**
62	50
72	65
68	63
58	50
65	54
70	60
66	61
63	55
60	54
70	65

Draw a scatter diagram and indicate whether the correlation is positive or negative.

Ans. The scatter diagram of the given data is shown below

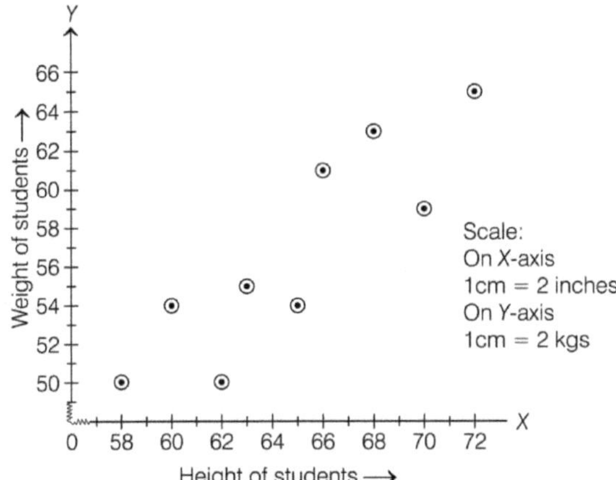

Since the points are dense i.e. close to each other, we may expect a high degree of correlation between the series of heights and weights.

Further, since the points reveal an upward trend starting from left bottom and going up towards the right top, the correlation is positive. Hence, we may expect a fairly high degree of positive correlation between height and weight of the of class XI.

Karl Pearson's Coefficient of Correlation

The scatter diagram method indicates the direction of correlation but does not give an exact value of magnitude. A mathematical method of measuring the magnitude of linear relationship between two statistical series was given by British statistician **Karl Pearson**.

"The correlation coefficient between two variables denotes as $'r_{xy}'$ is the ratio of the covariance between X and Y to the product of standard deviations of X and Y." Symbolically,

Correlation Coefficient $(r) = \dfrac{Cov(x, y)}{\sigma_x \times \sigma_y}$, where

$Cov(x, y) = $ Covariance between X and Y and is computed as, $\dfrac{\Sigma xy}{n}$,

where $\Sigma x = \Sigma(X - \overline{X})$ and $\Sigma y = \Sigma(Y - \overline{Y})$,

$\sigma_x = $ Standard Deviation of X, $\sigma_y = $ Standard Deviation of Y

Methods of Calculating Karl Pearson's Coefficient of Correlation

There are three methods to calculate coefficient of correlation by Karl Pearson's method. The steps for computation of correlation coefficient by each of the method are discussed below

1. Direct Method

Following steps are involved in the calculation of coefficient of correlation by direct method

Step 1 At first compute the values of $\overline{X}$ and $\overline{Y}$.

Step 2 Then, take deviations of observations in X series from $\overline{X}$ and denote it as x and in Y series from $\overline{Y}$ and denote it as y.

Step 3 Square the deviations and add the results to obtain Σx^2 and Σy^2.

Step 4 Multiply the corresponding deviations of the X and Y series to obtain x y and add the products to obtain $\Sigma x y$.

Step 5 Find the standard deviation of X and Y series, with the help of the following formulae,

$$\sigma_x = \sqrt{\dfrac{\Sigma x^2}{n}}, \qquad \sigma_y = \sqrt{\dfrac{\Sigma y^2}{n}}$$

Step 6 In the end, apply the following formula to calculate the value of correlation

$$r = \dfrac{\Sigma x\, y}{n \cdot \sigma_x \cdot \sigma_y},$$ where symbols have the same meaning as discussed. Alternately, the following formula can also be applied, $r = \dfrac{\Sigma x\, y}{\sqrt{\Sigma x^2 \times \Sigma y^2}}$

Example 2. Compute Karl Pearson's coefficient of correlation from the following data by direct method.

X	10	12	11	13	12	14	9	12	14	13
Y	7	9	12	9	13	8	10	12	7	13

Ans.

Calculation of Coefficient of Correlation

X	$x\,(X-\overline{X})\,\overline{X}=12$	Square of Deviation (x^2)	Y	$y\,(Y-\overline{Y})\,\overline{Y}=10$	Square of Deviation (y^2)	xy
10	−2	4	7	−3	9	6
12	0	0	9	−1	1	0
11	−1	1	12	2	4	−2
13	1	1	9	−1	1	−1
12	0	0	13	3	9	0
14	2	4	8	−2	4	−4
9	−3	9	10	0	0	0
12	0	0	12	2	4	0
14	2	4	7	−3	9	−6
13	1	1	13	3	9	3
$\Sigma X=120$	$\Sigma x=0$	$\Sigma x^2=24$	$\Sigma Y=100$	$\Sigma y=0$	$\Sigma y^2=50$	$\Sigma xy=-4$

Here, $n=10$

Mean of X series $(\overline{X})=\dfrac{\Sigma X}{n}=\dfrac{120}{10}=12$;   Mean of Y series $(\overline{Y})=\dfrac{\Sigma Y}{n}=\dfrac{100}{10}=10$

Standard deviation of X series, $(\sigma_x)=\sqrt{\dfrac{\Sigma x^2}{n}}=\sqrt{\dfrac{24}{10}}=\sqrt{2.4}=1.55$

Standard deviation of Y series, $(\sigma_y)=\sqrt{\dfrac{\Sigma y^2}{n}}=\sqrt{\dfrac{50}{10}}=\sqrt{5}=2.24$

$\because$ Karl Pearson's coefficient of correlation, $r=\dfrac{\Sigma xy}{n\cdot\sigma_x\cdot\sigma_y}$ $\therefore$ $r=\dfrac{-4}{10\times1.55\times2.24}=\dfrac{-4}{34.72}=-0.115$

There is low degree of negative correlation between X and Y.

2. Short-cut Method

The short-cut method of calculating correlation is used where the calculated values of means are in fraction. This method makes use of the assumed mean as the basis for calculation. Here deviations are taken from assumed mean.

Calculation of coefficient of correlation by short-cut method involves the following steps

Step 1 Take any convenient whole numbers as the assumed means of X and Y series.

Step 2 Take the deviations of X series from the assumed mean, so as to get dx and obtain their total i.e., Σdx.

Step 3 Take the deviations of Y series from the assumed mean so as to get dy and obtain their total i.e., Σdy.

Step 4 Square dx and obtain their total i.e. Σd^2x.

Step 5 Square dy and obtain their total i.e. Σd^2y.

Step 6 Multiply the corresponding deviations of x and y series and add these products to get $\Sigma dx\,dy$.

Step 7 Substitute the above values in the given formula to get the value of coefficient of correlation (r).

$$r=\dfrac{\Sigma dx\;dy-\dfrac{\Sigma dx\times\Sigma dy}{n}}{\sqrt{\Sigma dx^2-\dfrac{(\Sigma dx)^2}{n}}\times\sqrt{\Sigma dy^2-\dfrac{(\Sigma dy)^2}{n}}} \quad Or \quad \dfrac{\Sigma dx\,dy\cdot n-(\Sigma dx)(\Sigma dy)}{\sqrt{\Sigma dx^2\cdot n-(\Sigma dx)^2}\times\sqrt{\Sigma dy^2\cdot n-(\Sigma dy)^2}}$$

where symbols have the same meaning as discussed.

Example 3. Calculate Karl Pearson's coefficient of correlation between the following two series by short-cut method.

X	24	27	28	28	29	30	32	33	35	35	40
Y	18	20	22	25	22	28	28	30	27	30	22

Ans.

Calculation of Coefficient of Correlation

X	$dx(X-A), A=32$	dx^2	Y	$dy(Y-A), A=25$	dy^2	$dx\,dy$
24	-8	64	18	-7	49	56
27	-5	25	20	-5	25	25
28	-4	16	22	-3	9	12
28	-4	16	25	0	0	0
29	-3	9	22	-3	9	9
30	-2	4	28	3	9	-6
32	0	0	28	3	9	0
33	1	1	30	5	25	5
35	3	9	27	2	4	6
35	3	9	30	5	25	15
40	8	64	22	-3	9	-24
$n=11$	$\Sigma dx=-11$	$\Sigma dx^2=217$		$\Sigma dy=-3$	$\Sigma dy^2=173$	$\Sigma dx\,dy=98$

$$r = \frac{n\,\Sigma dxdy - (\Sigma dx)(\Sigma dy)}{\sqrt{\Sigma dx^2 \cdot n - (\Sigma dx)^2} \times \sqrt{\Sigma dy^2 \cdot n - (\Sigma dy)^2}} = \frac{98 \times 11 - (-11)(-3)}{\sqrt{217 \times 11 - (-11)^2} \times \sqrt{173 \times 11 - (-3)^2}}$$

$$= \frac{1,078 - 33}{\sqrt{2,387 - 121} \times \sqrt{1,903 - 9}} = \frac{1,045}{\sqrt{2,266} \times \sqrt{1,894}} = \frac{1,045}{47.6 \times 43.52} = 0.505 \ \text{(approx)}$$

It shows medium degree of positive correlation between X and Y series.

3. **Step Deviation Method** The step deviation method of calculating correlation is used when the values of the variables are large and are divisible by a common factor.

Calculation of coefficient of correlation by step deviation method involves the following steps

Step 1 Take any convenient whole numbers as the assumed means of X and Y series.

Step 2 Take the deviations of X series from the assumed mean, so as to get dx and obtain their total, i.e. $\Sigma\,dx$.

Step 3 Take the deviations of Y series from the assumed mean so as to get dy and obtain their total, i.e. $\Sigma\,dy$.

Step 4 Now, divide dx and dy by some common factor as $dx' = \dfrac{dx}{c_1}$ and $dy' = \dfrac{dy}{c_2}$, here c_1 is common factor for series X and c_2 is common factor for series Y. dx' and dy' are step deviations.

Step 5 $\Sigma dx'$ and $\Sigma dy'$ are found by adding the step deviations.

Step 6 Step deviations of the two series are multiplied as $dx' \times dy'$ and products are added to obtain $\Sigma dx'dy'$.

Step 7 Squares of the step deviations dx'^2 and dy'^2 are added upto, find out $\Sigma dx'^2$ and $\Sigma dy'^2$.

Step 8 Finally, coefficient of correlation is calculated using the following formula

$$r = \frac{\Sigma dx'dy' - \dfrac{\Sigma dx' \times \Sigma dy'}{n}}{\sqrt{\left[\Sigma dx'^2 - \dfrac{\Sigma dx'^2}{n}\right]} \times \sqrt{\left[\Sigma dy'^2 - \dfrac{\Sigma dy'^2}{n}\right]}}$$

where symbols have the same meaning as discussed.

Example 4. Calculate coefficient of correlation between the price and quantity demanded.

Price (in ₹)	5	10	15	20	25
Demand (in kg)	40	35	30	25	20

Ans.

Calculation of Coefficient of Correlation

X	$dx\,(X-A),$ $A=15$	$dx'\left(\dfrac{dx}{c_1}\right),$ $c_1=5$	dx'^2	Y	$dy\,(Y-A),$ $A=30$	$dy'\left(\dfrac{dy}{c_2}\right),$ $c_2=5$	dy'^2	$dx'\,dy'$
5	−10	−2	4	40	10	2	4	−4
10	−5	−1	1	35	5	1	1	−1
15	0	0	0	30	0	0	0	0
20	5	1	1	25	−5	−1	1	−1
25	10	2	4	20	−10	−2	4	−4
$n=5$		$\Sigma dx'=0$	$\Sigma dx'^2=10$			$\Sigma dy'=0$	$\Sigma dy'^2=10$	$\Sigma dx'dy'=-10$

$$\text{Coefficient of Correlation }(r)=\frac{\Sigma dx'\,dy'-\dfrac{\Sigma dx'\times\Sigma dy'}{n}}{\sqrt{\left[\Sigma dx'^2-\dfrac{(\Sigma dx')^2}{n}\right]}\times\sqrt{\left[\Sigma dy'^2-\dfrac{(\Sigma dy')^2}{n}\right]}}=\frac{-10-\dfrac{0}{5}}{\sqrt{10-\dfrac{0}{5}}\times\sqrt{10-\dfrac{0}{5}}}$$

$$=\frac{-10}{\sqrt{10}\times\sqrt{10}}=\frac{-10}{10}=-1$$

$$\therefore \qquad r=-1$$

This is a situation of perfectly negative correlation between price and quantity demanded.

Computation of Correlation Coefficient without Finding Deviations

If the values of dependent and independent variables are small, then Karl Pearson's Correlation Coefficient can also be computed with the help of given formula,

$$r=\frac{\Sigma XY}{\sqrt{\Sigma X^2\times\Sigma Y^2}},\text{ where,}$$

ΣXY = Sum of products of values of series X and series Y. ΣX^2 = Sum of squares of values of series X.

ΣY^2 = Sum of squares of values of series Y.

Properties of Correlation Coefficient

- Correlation coefficient (r) has no unit. It is a pure number. It means units of measurement are not part of r.
- A negative value of r indicates an inverse relation. A change in one variable is associated with change in the other variable in the opposite direction.
- If r is positive the two variables move in the same direction.
- If $r = 0$, the two variables are uncorrelated or they are not linearly correlated.
- If $r = 1$ or $r = -1$, the correlation is perfect. The relation between them is exact.
- A high value of r indicates strong linear relationship. Its value is said to be high when it is close to $+1$ or -1.
- A low value of r indicates a weak linear relation. Its value is said to be low when it is close to zero.
- The value of the correlation coefficient lies between minus one and plus one,
  i.e. $-1\le r\le 1$
- The value of r is unaffected by the change of origin and change of scale.

Chapter Practice

Objective Questions

- **Multiple Choice Questions**

1. Which of the following techniques deals with the association between two or more variables?
(a) Index number   (b) Correlation
(c) Dispersion   (d) None of these
Ans. (b) Correlation

2. When two variables move together in the same direction, it is said to be
(a) no correlation   (b) negative correlation
(c) positive correlation   (d) zero correlation
Ans. (c) positive correlation

3. Correlation is an analysis of ...... between two or more variables.
(a) relationship   (b) covariation
(c) determination   (d) calculation
Ans. (b) covariation

4. If all the points lie on the same downward sloping line, the correlation is said to be
(a) perfect correlation
(b) perfect positive correlation
(c) perfect negative correlation
(d) negative correlation
Ans. (c) Downward sloping line indicates inverse relationship between variable X and Y and as they lie in a straight line, it indicates perfect negative correlation.

5. Scatter diagram can be used to indicate which of the following degrees of correlation?
(a) Perfect positive correlation
(b) Perfect negative correlation
(c) No correlation   (d) All of the above
Ans. (d) All of the above

6. A modified version of Karl Pearson's formula is
(a) $r = \dfrac{\Sigma xy}{\Sigma x^2 \cdot \Sigma y^2}$ (b) $r = \dfrac{\Sigma xy}{\sqrt{\Sigma x^2 \times \Sigma y^2}}$

(c) $r = \dfrac{\Sigma xy}{n\,\Sigma X^2 \cdot \Sigma Y^2}$ (d) $r = \dfrac{\Sigma xy}{n\,\delta_x \cdot \delta_y}$

Ans. (b) $r = \dfrac{\Sigma xy}{\sqrt{\Sigma x^2 \times \Sigma y^2}}$

7. Karl Pearson's coefficient of correlation indicates the ...... and also the degree of relationship between the two variables.
(a) direction   (b) relation
(c) interpretation   (d) None of these
Ans. (a) Karl Pearson's method is the most useful method of correlation, which can be used to indicate direction as well as magnitude of change.

8. The coefficient of correlation is independent of
(a) change of scale only
(b) change of origin only
(c) both change of scale and origin
(d) None of the above
Ans. (c) Coefficient of correlation remains unaffected due to change in either scale or origin.

9. When the mean of series is a decimal number, then which method should be used for computing Karl Pearson's coefficient of correlation?
(a) Direct Method   (b) Short-cut Method
(c) Step Deviation Method   (d) None of these
Ans. (b) Under short-cut method of computing correlation, assumed mean is used in place of actual mean. Thus, it can be used when actual mean comes in decimal points.

10. Which of the following pair is correctly matched?

Column I (Method)		Column II (Formula)
A. Direct Method	(i)	$r = \dfrac{\Sigma dxdy \cdot n - (\Sigma dx)(\Sigma dy)}{\sqrt{\Sigma dx^2 \cdot n - (\Sigma dx)^2} \times (\sqrt{\Sigma dy^2 \cdot n - (\Sigma dy)^2}}$
B. Short-cut Method	(ii)	$r = \dfrac{\Sigma xy}{n \cdot \sigma_x \cdot \sigma_y}$
C. Step Deviation Method	(iii)	$r = \dfrac{\Sigma dx'dy' \cdot n - (\Sigma dx')(\Sigma dy')}{\sqrt{\Sigma dx'^2 \cdot n - (\Sigma dx')^2} \times \sqrt{\Sigma dy'^2 \cdot n - (\Sigma dy')^2}}$

Codes
(a) A–(i)   (b) B–(ii)
(c) C–(iii)   (d) None of these
Ans. (c) C–(iii)

11. The minimum limit of correlation under Karl Pearson's method is

   (a) −1   (b) 0

   (c) 1   (d) None of these

Ans. (a) Minimum limit of correlation is −1 as coefficient of correlation ranges from −1 to 1.

12. **Statement I** Correlation is a multivariate analysis.

Statement II Partial correlation considers all other variables to be constant.

Alternatives

   (a) Statement I is correct and Statement II is incorrect

   (b) Statement II is correct and Statement I is incorrect

   (c) Both the statements are correct

   (d) Both the statements are incorrect

Ans. (c) Both the statements are correct

13. **Statement I** Non-linear correlation is also called curvy linear correlation.

Statement II Numerical measure of correlation is called coefficient of determination.

Alternatives

   (a) Statement I is correct and Statement II is incorrect

   (b) Statement II is correct and Statement I is incorrect

   (c) Both the statements are correct

   (d) Both the statements are incorrect

Ans. (a) Statement I is correct and Statement II is incorrect

14. If the dots in a scatter diagram fall on a narrow band, it indicates a ....degree of correlation.

   (a) zero   (b) high

   (c) low   (d) None of these

Ans. (c) low

15. Coefficient of correlation lies between

   (a) 0 and +1   (b) 0 and −1

   (c) −1 and +1   (d) − 3 and +3

Ans. (c) −1 and +1

• Assertion–Reasoning MCQs

Direction (*Q. Nos. 1 to 4*) *There are two statements marked as Assertion (A) and Reason (R). Read the statements and choose the appropriate option from the options given below.*

   (a) Both Assertion (A) and Reason (R) are true and Reason (R) is the correct explanation of Assertion (A)

   (b) Both Assertion (A) and Reason (R) are true, but Reason (R) is not the correct explanation of Assertion (A)

   (c) Assertion (A) is false, but Reason (R) is true

   (d) Both Assertion (A) and Reason (R) are false

1. **Assertion** (A) Sale of ice-cream increases during summer, shows positive correlation.

Reason (R) When two variables move in same direction, it shows positive correlation.

Ans. (b) Sale of ice cream and season indicates cause and effect relationship and this relation as per question is positive.

2. **Assertion** (A) Correlation analysis is a means for examining inter relationships systematically.

Reason (R) Causation explain the cause and effect relationship between variables.

Ans. (b) Correlation is a measure of interrelation between two variables and does not indicate the cause and effect relationship.

3. **Assertion** (A) Karl Pearson's method is non-mathematical in nature.

Reason (R) Degree of correlation helps in identifying the nature of correlation between variables.

Ans. (c) Karl Pearson's method is purely a mathematical method which is used to measure the magnitude of change in the two or more variables.

4. **Assertion** (A) Broadly, there only two types of correlation i.e., positive and negative.

Reason (R) The correlation is said to be positive when the variables move together in the same direction, the correlation is negative when they move in opposite directions.

Ans. (b) There are only two types of correlation i.e., positive and negative correlation, rest of the degrees are the sub-types of positive and negative correlation only.

• Case Based MCQs

1. **Direction** *Read the following case study and answer the question no. (i) to (vi) on the basis of the same.*

Coefficient of correlation is an important statistical tool which is used to measure the relationship between two variables. This is not only useful in the field of statistics but also used in other disciplines like Economics, Geography, Psychology.

In the present time due to the outbreak of Covid-19 corona virus, demand has gradually come down in almost all areas. As per the latest estimates, demand for car has decreased after the nationwide lockdown is lifted in phased manner.

   (i) What will be the coefficient of correlation between demand for car and varied level of income due to nationwide lockdown?

     (a) Positive correlation   (b) Negative correlation

     (c) Perfect positive correlation   (d) No correlation

Ans. (a) Due to lockdown, income level declined which further led to fall in demand for cars and thus, indicates positive correlation between the two.

(ii) If one variable change exactly in the reverse direction of the other variable, ... should be the degree of correlation.

(a) positive correlation

(b) negative correlation

(c) perfect positive correlation

(d) perfect negative correlation

Ans. (d) perfect negative correlation

(iii) Which of the following tools can be used to know the pattern of demand during lockdown?

(a) Correlation

(b) Causation

(c) Both (a) and (b)

(d) Neither (a) nor (b)

Ans. (b) Causation

(iv) Which method of calculating correlation uses actual mean?

(a) Karl Pearson's coefficient of correlation

(b) Scatter diagram method

(c) Spearman's rank correlation method

(d) Both (a) and (c)

Ans. (a) Karl Pearson's coefficient of correlation

(v) In perfect positive correlation, the value of 'r' is ....

(a) -1 (b) 0

(c) 1 (d) infinity

Ans. (c) 1

(vi) The correlation between using mask and being injected by the virus will be

(a) positive   (b) negative

(c) Not correlated   (d) Either (a) or (b)

Ans. (b) Wearing mask reduces the chance of being infected by the virus, thus shows an inverse relationship between the two.

PART 2
Subjective Questions

• Short Answer (SA) Type Questions

1. What do you understand by 'spurious' or 'non-sense' correlation?

Ans. If there is no evident or sensible connection between two variables, then the correlation between these variables is said to be spurious, non-sense or chance correlation. For example, correlation between rainfall recorded and production of steel.

These two variables are not connected by any way. So, the correlation between these variables is said to be spurious.

2. Consider the examples given below

(i) As price falls, demand for product 'A' increases.

(ii) Effect of adequate irrigation facilities, fertilisers and pesticides on per hectare productivity of wheat.

On the basis of above examples explain the main difference between simple correlation and multiple correlation.

Ans. The first example involves only two variables, viz. price and demand. Therefore, it relates to simple correlation.

The second example involves more than two variables, i.e., how the productivity of wheat is affected by use of irrigation facilities, fertilisers and pesticides. Therefore, it relates to multiple correlation.

The main difference between simple correlation and multiple correlation is

Simple Correlation	Multiple Correlation
When the relationship between only two variables is studied, it is called simple correlation.	When the relationship among three or more than three variables is studied simultaneously, it is called multiple correlation.

3. Why is 'r' preferred to covariance as a measure of association? **(NCERT)**

Ans. Both, correlation coefficient and covariance measure the degree of linear relationship between two variables but correlation coefficient is generally preferred to covariance.

It is due to the following reasons

(i) The correlation coefficient (r) has no unit.

(ii) The correlation coefficient is independent of origin as well as scale.

4. Can r lie outside the -1 and 1 range depending on the type of data? **(NCERT)**

Ans. No, the value of the correlation coefficient lies between minus one and plus one i.e., $-1 \le r \le 1$. If the value of r is outside this range in any type of data, it indicates error in calculation as in between two or more variables, there can be either a perfect or an imperfect relationship. A perfect relationship is indicated by -1 or 1 and imperfect relationships are indicated by a value between -1 and 1, excluding 0.

5. List some variables where accurate measurement is difficult. **(NCERT)**

Ans. Accurate measurement is difficult in case of

(i) Qualitative variables such as beauty, intelligence, honesty, etc.

(ii) It is also difficult to measure subjective variables such as poverty, development, etc, which are interpreted differently by different people.

(iii) Where the cause and effect relationship is not known.

6. Interpret the values of r as 1, −1 and 0.   **(NCERT)**

Ans. (i) If $r = 0$, the two variables are uncorrelated. There is no linear relation between them. However, other types of relation may be there and hence the variables may not be independent.

(ii) If $r = 1$, the correlation is perfectly positive. The relation between them is exact in the sense that if one increases,

the other also increases in the same proportion and if one decreases, the other also decreases in the same proportion.

(iii) If $r = -1$, the correlation is perfectly negative. The relation between them is exact in the sense that if one increases, the other decreases in the same proportion and if one decreases, the other increases in the same proportion.

7. Draw a scatter diagram and indicate the nature of correlation.

X	10	20	30	40	50	60	70	80
Y	5	10	15	20	25	30	35	40

Ans. Now, we plot the points on a graph paper which is shown below

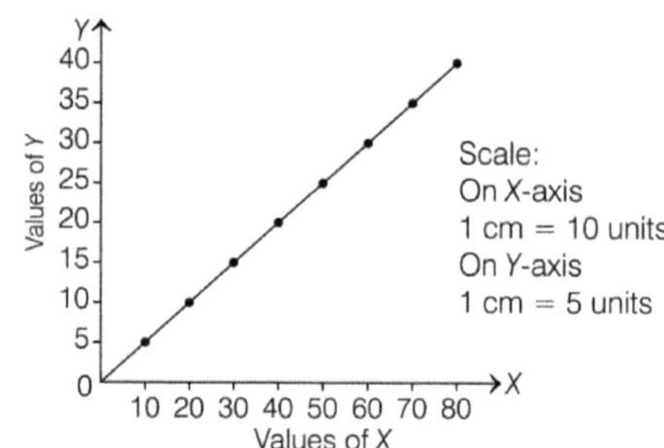

The diagram indicates that there is perfect positive correlation between the values of the two variables X and Y.

8. Draw a scatter diagram and interpret whether the correlation is positive or negative.

X	4	5	6	7	8	9	10	11	12	13	14	15
Y	78	72	66	60	54	48	42	36	30	24	18	12

Ans. The pair of points are (4, 78), (5, 72), (6, 66), (7, 60), (8, 54), (9, 48), (10, 42), (11, 36), (12, 30), (13, 24), (14, 18) and (15, 12).

Now we plot the points on a graph paper, which is shown below

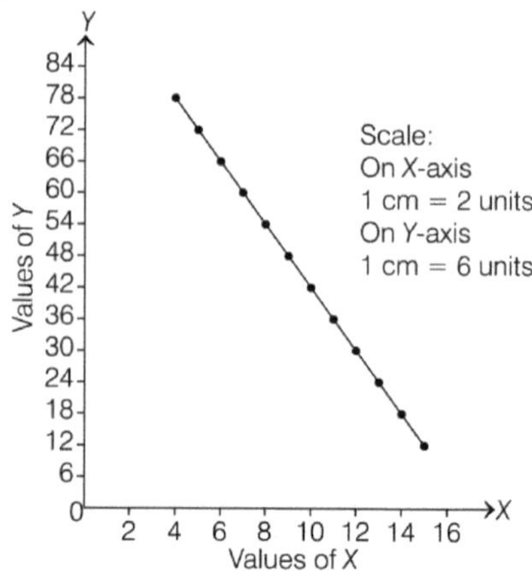

The diagram indicates that there is perfect negative correlation between the values of the two variables X and Y.

9. Calculate Karl Pearson's coefficient of correlation between X and Y from the following data
$$n = 8, \overline{X} = 11, \overline{Y} = 10, \Sigma x^2 = 184, \Sigma y^2 = 148, \Sigma xy = 164$$

Ans. Given that, $n = 8, \overline{X} = 11, \overline{Y} = 10, \Sigma x^2 = 184, \Sigma y^2 = 148$ and $\Sigma xy = 164$. Applying the formula,
$$r = \frac{\Sigma xy}{\sqrt{\Sigma x^2 \times \Sigma y^2}} = \frac{164}{\sqrt{184 \times 148}}$$
$$= \frac{164}{\sqrt{27,232}}$$
$$= \frac{164}{164.02} = 0.99$$

10. The following results are obtained regarding two series. Compute coefficient of correlation, when sum of products of deviations of X and Y series from their respective mean is 122.

	X Series	Y Series
Number of Items	15	15
Arithmetic Mean	25	18
Standard Deviation	3.01	3.03

Ans. We are given that, $n = 15, \overline{X} = 25, \sigma_x = 3.01,$
$$\overline{Y} = 18, \sigma_y = 3.03$$
and
$$\Sigma xy = 122$$
$$r = \frac{\Sigma xy}{n \cdot \sigma_x \cdot \sigma_y} = \frac{122}{15 \times 3.01 \times 3.03} = \frac{122}{136.80} = 0.89$$

11. Give the advantages of Karl Pearson's coefficient of correlation.

Ans. The advantages of Karl Pearson's coefficient of correlation are

(i) Karl Pearson's coefficient of correlation indicates the relationship as positive or negative and thus direction of the relationship can be ascertained.

(ii) This measure gives summarised and precise quantitative figure of correlation which can be interpreted easily and can provide meaningful results.

(iii) This coefficient of correlation indicates the direction and also the degree of relationship between the two variables. It shows whether the relationship is high, moderate or low.

12. Give the disadvantages of Karl Pearson's coefficient of correlation.

Ans. The disadvantages of Karl Pearson's coefficient of correlation are

(i) The value of coefficient is affected by extreme items.

(ii) The calculation process consumes a lot of time.

(iii) Correlation coefficient needs very careful interpretation, otherwise it may be misinterpreted.

13. From the following data, calculate Karl Pearson's coefficient of correlation.

X	6	2	10	4	8
Y	9	11	?	8	7

Arithmetic mean of X and Y series are 6 and 8, respectively.

Ans. Let the missing value be a

$$\overline{Y} = \frac{\Sigma Y}{n} = \frac{9 + 11 + a + 8 + 7}{5} = \frac{35 + a}{5}$$

$$\Rightarrow \qquad 8 = \frac{35 + a}{5} \quad \Rightarrow \quad 40 = 35 + a \quad \Rightarrow \quad a = 5$$

Thus, the completed series is

X	6	2	10	4	8
Y	9	11	5	8	7

Now, we find coefficient of correlation.

Calculation of Coefficient of Correlation

X	$x\,(X - \overline{X})$	x^2	Y	$y\,(Y - \overline{Y})$	y^2	xy
6	0	0	9	1	1	0
2	−4	16	11	3	9	−12
10	4	16	5	−3	9	−12
4	−2	4	8	0	0	0
8	2	4	7	−1	1	−2
$\Sigma X = 30$		$\Sigma x^2 = 40$	$\Sigma Y = 40$		$\Sigma y^2 = 20$	$\Sigma xy = -26$

Here, $\quad n = 5, \Sigma X = 30, \Sigma x^2 = 40, \Sigma Y = 40, \Sigma y^2 = 20$ and $\Sigma xy = -26$

$$\therefore \qquad r = \frac{\Sigma xy}{\sqrt{\Sigma x^2 \times \Sigma y^2}}$$

$$= \frac{-26}{\sqrt{40 \times 20}} = \frac{-26}{\sqrt{800}} = \frac{-26}{28.28} = -0.9193$$

It indicates that there is high degree of negative correlation between X and Y.

14. Calculate the correlation coefficient between X and Y and comment on the relationship. **(NCERT)**

X	−3	−2	−1	1	2	3
Y	9	4	1	1	4	9

Ans.

Calculation of Coefficient of Correlation

X	X^2	Y	Y^2	XY
−3	9	9	81	−27
−2	4	4	16	−8
−1	1	1	1	−1
1	1	1	1	1
2	4	4	16	8
3	9	9	81	27
$\Sigma X = 0$	$\Sigma X^2 = 28$	$\Sigma Y = 28$	$\Sigma y^2 = 196$	$\Sigma xy = 0$

Here, $n = 6,\ \Sigma XY = 0,\ \Sigma X^2 = 28$ and $\Sigma Y^2 = 196$

$$\therefore \quad r = \frac{\Sigma XY}{\sqrt{\Sigma X^2 \times \Sigma Y^2}} = \frac{0}{\sqrt{28 \times 196}} = 0$$

$r = 0$ shows that there is absence of correlation between the variables X and Y but we observe that it remains a non-linear correlation between the two variables as $y = x^2$. So, in this question, the correlation coefficients fails to indicate the correct relationship between these two variables.

15. Calculate the correlation coefficient between X and Y and comment on their relationship. **(NCERT)**

X	1	3	4	5	7	8
Y	2	6	8	10	14	16

Ans.

Calculation of Coefficient of Correlation

X	Y	XY	X^2	Y^2
1	2	2	1	4
3	6	18	9	36
4	8	32	16	64
5	10	50	25	100
7	14	98	49	196
8	16	128	64	256
$\Sigma X = 28$	$\Sigma Y = 56$	$\Sigma XY = 328$	$\Sigma X^2 = 164$	$\Sigma Y^2 = 656$

Here, $n = 6, \Sigma XY = 328,\ \Sigma X^2 = 164$ and $\Sigma Y^2 = 656$

$$\therefore \quad r = \frac{\Sigma XY}{\sqrt{\Sigma X^2 \times \Sigma Y^2}}$$

$$= \frac{328}{\sqrt{164 \times 656}} = \frac{328}{328} = 1$$

As the correlation coefficient between the two variables is $+ 1$, so the two variables are perfectly positively correlated.

16. Compute Karl Pearson's coefficient of correlation by direct method and interpret the result.

Marks in Mathematics	15	18	21	24	27
Marks in Accountancy	25	25	27	31	32

Ans. Let X and Y denote marks in mathematics and accountancy, respectively.

Calculation of Coefficient of Correlation

X	$x\,(X-\overline{X}),$ $\overline{X}=21$	x^2	Y	$y\,(Y-\overline{Y})$ $\overline{Y}=28$	y^2	xy
15	−6	36	25	−3	9	18
18	−3	9	25	−3	9	9
21	0	0	27	−1	1	0
24	3	9	31	3	9	9
27	6	36	32	4	16	24
$\Sigma X=105$		$\Sigma x^2=90$	$\Sigma Y=140$		$\Sigma y^2=44$	$\Sigma xy=60$

Here, $\Sigma X=105$, $\Sigma Y=140$, $\Sigma xy=60$, $\Sigma x^2=90$ and $\Sigma y^2=44$

$$\overline{X}=\frac{\Sigma X}{n}=\frac{105}{5}=21;\ \ \overline{Y}=\frac{\Sigma Y}{n}=\frac{140}{5}=28;\ \ r=\frac{\Sigma xy}{\sqrt{\Sigma x^2\times\Sigma y^2}}=\frac{60}{\sqrt{90\times44}}=\frac{60}{\sqrt{3,960}}=\frac{60}{62.928}=0.95$$

It indicates that there is high degree of positive correlation between marks in mathematics and accountancy.

• Long Answers (LA) Type Questions

1. Calculate the correlation coefficient between the height of fathers in inches (X) and their sons (Y).   **(NCERT)**

X	65	66	57	67	68	69	70	72
Y	67	56	65	68	72	72	69	71

Ans.

Calculation of Coefficient of Correlation

X	$x(X-\overline{X})\ \overline{X}=66.75$	x^2	Y	$y\,(Y-\overline{Y})\ \overline{Y}=67.5$	y^2	xy
65	− 1.75	3.0625	67	− 0.5	0.25	0.875
66	− 0.75	0.5625	56	− 11.5	132.25	8.625
57	− 9.75	95.0625	65	− 2.5	6.25	24.375
67	0.25	0.0625	68	0.5	0.25	0.125
68	1.25	1.5625	72	4.5	20.25	5.625
69	2.25	5.0625	72	4.5	20.25	10.125
70	3.25	10.5625	69	1.5	2.25	4.875
72	5.25	27.5625	71	3.5	12.25	18.375
$\Sigma X=534$		$\Sigma x^2=1,435$	$\Sigma Y=540$		$\Sigma y^2=194$	$\Sigma xy=73$

Here, $n=8$, $\Sigma X=534$, $\Sigma x^2=1435$, $\Sigma Y=540$, $\Sigma y^2=194$ and $\Sigma xy=73$

Now, $\overline{X}=\dfrac{\Sigma X}{n}=\dfrac{534}{8}=66.75$, and $\overline{Y}=\dfrac{\Sigma Y}{n}=\dfrac{540}{8}=67.5$

$$r=\frac{\Sigma xy}{\sqrt{\Sigma x^2\times\Sigma y^2}}=\frac{73}{\sqrt{143.5\times194}}=\frac{73}{\sqrt{27,839}}=\frac{73}{166.85}=0.438$$

It indicates that there is low degree of positive correlation between heights of fathers and sons.

2. Calculate coefficient of correlation between age group and rate of mortality from the following data.

Age Group	0–20	20–40	40–60	60–80	80–100
Rate of Mortality	350	280	540	760	900

Ans. Since, class interval are given for age, so mid value should be used for the calculation of r.

Calculation of Coefficient of Correlation

Age Group	Mid-value (X)	$dx(X-A),$ $A=50$	$dx'\left(\dfrac{dx}{c_1}\right),$ $c_1=20$	dx'^2	Rate of Mortality (Y)	$dy(Y-A),$ $A=540$	$dy'\left(\dfrac{dx}{c_2}\right),$ $c_2=10$	dy'^2	$dx'dy'$
0–20	10	-40	-2	4	350	-190	-19	361	38
20–40	30	-20	-1	1	280	-260	-26	676	26
40–60	50	0	0	0	540	0	0	0	0
60–80	70	20	1	1	760	220	$+22$	484	22
80–100	90	40	2	4	900	360	$+36$	1,296	72
			$\Sigma dx'=0$	$\Sigma dx'^2=10$			$\Sigma dy'=13$	$\Sigma dy'^2=2,817$	$\Sigma dx'dy'=158$

Here, $n=5, \Sigma dx'=0, \Sigma dx'^2=10, \Sigma dy'=13, \Sigma dy'^2=2,817$ and $\Sigma dx'\,dy'=158$

Now,
$$r=\frac{\Sigma dx'dy'-\dfrac{\Sigma dx'\times \Sigma dy'}{n}}{\sqrt{\Sigma dx'^2-\dfrac{(\Sigma dx')^2}{n}}\times \sqrt{\Sigma dy'^2-\dfrac{(\Sigma dy')^2}{n}}}=\frac{158-\dfrac{0\times 13}{5}}{\sqrt{10-\dfrac{(0)^2}{5}}\times \sqrt{2,817-\dfrac{(13)^2}{5}}}=\frac{158}{\sqrt{10-0}\times \sqrt{2,817-\dfrac{169}{5}}}$$

$$=\frac{158}{\sqrt{10}\times \sqrt{2,817-33.8}}=\frac{158}{\sqrt{10}\times \sqrt{2,783.2}}=\frac{158}{3.16\times 52.8}=\frac{158}{166.8}=+\,0.95$$

There is high degree of positive correlation between age group and rate of mortality.

3. From the following data, calculate coefficient of correlation between age and playing habits.

Age Group	20–30	30–40	40–50	50–60	60–70
Number of Students	25	60	40	20	20
Number of Regular Players	10	30	12	2	1

Ans. First, we shall find the percentage of regular players in the following way

Calculation of Percentage of Regular Players

Number of Students	Number of Regular Players	Percentage of Regular Players
25	10	$\dfrac{10}{25}\times 100=40$
60	30	$\dfrac{30}{60}\times 100=50$
40	12	$\dfrac{12}{40}\times 100=30$
20	2	$\dfrac{2}{20}\times 100=10$
20	1	$\dfrac{1}{20}\times 100=5$

Denoting mid-value of age as X and percentage of regular players as Y.

Calculation of Coefficient of Correlation

Age Group	Mid-value (X)	dx $(X-A)$, $A=45$	$dx'\left(\dfrac{dx}{c_1}\right)$, $c_1=10$	dx'^2	Percentage of Regular Players (Y)	dy $(Y-A)$, $A=30$	$dy'\left(\dfrac{dy}{c_2}\right)$, $c_2=5$	dy'^2	$dx'dy'$
20–30	25	−20	−2	4	40	10	2	4	−4
30–40	35	−10	−1	1	50	20	4	16	−4
40–50	45	0	0	0	30	0	0	0	0
50–60	55	10	1	1	10	−20	−4	16	−4
60–70	65	20	2	4	5	−25	−5	25	−10
			$\Sigma dx'=0$	$\Sigma dx'^2=10$			$\Sigma dy'=-3$	$\Sigma dy'^2=61$	$\Sigma dx'dy'=-22$

Here, $n=5, \Sigma dx'=0, \Sigma dx'^2=10, \Sigma dy'=-3, \Sigma dy'^2=61$

and $\Sigma dx'dy'=-22$

$$\therefore \quad r = \frac{\Sigma dx'dy' - \dfrac{\Sigma dx' \times \Sigma dy'}{n}}{\sqrt{\Sigma dx'^2 - \dfrac{(\Sigma dx')^2}{n}} \times \sqrt{\Sigma dy'^2 - \dfrac{(\Sigma dy')^2}{n}}} = \frac{-22 - \dfrac{0 \times -3}{5}}{\sqrt{10 - \dfrac{(0)^2}{5}} \times \sqrt{61 - \dfrac{(-3)^2}{5}}}$$

$$= \frac{-22}{\sqrt{10} \times \sqrt{61-1.8}} = \frac{-22}{\sqrt{10} \times \sqrt{59.2}} = \frac{-22}{3.16 \times 7.69} = \frac{-22}{24.3} = -0.90$$

It indicates that there is a high degree of negative correlation between age and playing habits. It shows that as age increases, the tendency to play decreases.

4. From the data given below, calculate Karl Pearson's coefficient of correlation between density of population and death rate by step deviation method.

Region	Area (in sq km)	Population	Death
A	200	40,000	480
B	150	75,000	1,200
C	120	72,000	1,080
D	80	20,000	280

Ans. First of all, we shall compute density of population i.e., population per sq km and death rate per 1,000.

$$\text{Density of Population} = \frac{\text{Population}}{\text{Area}}, \quad \text{Death Rate} = \frac{\text{Number of Deaths}}{\text{Population}} \times 1,000$$

Calculation of Coefficient of Correlation

Region	Density (X)	$dx\,(X-A)$, $A=500$	$dx'\left(\dfrac{dx}{c_1}\right)$, $c_1=50$	dx'^2	Death Rate (Y)	$dy\,(Y-A)$, $A=16$	$dy'\left(\dfrac{dy}{c_2}\right)$, $c_2=1$	dy'^2	$dx'dy'$
A	200	−300	−6	36	12	−4	−4	16	24
B	500	0	0	0	16	0	0	0	0
C	600	100	2	4	15	−1	−1	1	−2
D	250	−250	−5	25	14	−2	−2	4	10
			$\Sigma dx'=-9$	$\Sigma dx'^2=65$			$\Sigma dy'=-7$	$\Sigma dy'^2=21$	$\Sigma dx'dy'=32$

Here, $dx' = -9$, $\Sigma dx'^2 = 65$, $\Sigma dy' = -7$, $\Sigma dy'^2 = 21$ and $\Sigma dx'dy' = 32$

$$\therefore \quad r = \dfrac{\Sigma dx'\, dy' - \dfrac{\Sigma dx' \times \Sigma dy'}{n}}{\sqrt{\Sigma dx'^2 - \dfrac{(\Sigma dx')^2}{n}} \times \sqrt{\Sigma dy'^2 - \dfrac{(\Sigma dy')^2}{n}}}$$

$$= \dfrac{32 - \dfrac{(-9 \times -7)}{4}}{\sqrt{65 - \dfrac{(-9)^2}{4}} \times \sqrt{21 - \dfrac{(-7)^2}{4}}} = \dfrac{32 - 15.75}{\sqrt{65 - 20.25} \times \sqrt{21 - 12.25}}$$

$$= \dfrac{16.25}{\sqrt{44.75} \times \sqrt{8.75}} = \dfrac{16.25}{6.69 \times 2.96} = \dfrac{16.25}{19.80} = 0.82$$

There is high degree of positive correlation between density of population and death rate.

5. Calculate coefficient of correlation between the price and quantity supplied (using short-cut method)

Price (₹)	4	6	7	12	20
Supply (kg)	6	12	18	20	24

Ans.

Calculation of Coefficient of Correlation

Price (X)	Deviation $(dx = X - A)$ $A = 12$	Square of Deviation (dx^2)	Supply (Y)	Deviation $(dy = Y - A)$ $A = 18$	Square of Deviation (dy^2)	Multiple of deviations $(dxdy)$
4	−8	64	8	−10	100	80
6	−6	36	12	−6	36	36
7	−5	25	18	0	0	0
12	0	0	20	2	4	0
20	8	64	24	6	36	48
$N = 5$	$\Sigma dx = -11$	$\Sigma dx^2 = 189$	$N = 5$	$\Sigma dx = -8$	$\Sigma dy^2 = 176$	$\Sigma dxdy = 164$

$$r = \dfrac{\Sigma dxdy - \dfrac{(\Sigma dx) \times (\Sigma dy)}{N}}{\sqrt{\Sigma dx^2 - \dfrac{(\Sigma dx)^2}{N}} \times \sqrt{\Sigma dy^2 - \dfrac{(\Sigma dy)^2}{N}}}$$

$$= \dfrac{164 - \dfrac{(-11) \times (-8)}{5}}{\sqrt{189 - \dfrac{121}{5}} \times \sqrt{176 - \dfrac{64}{5}}}$$

$$= \dfrac{164 - \dfrac{88}{5}}{\sqrt{189 - 24.2} \times \sqrt{176 - 12.8}}$$

$$= \dfrac{164 - 17.6}{\sqrt{164.8} \times \sqrt{163.2}}$$

$$= \dfrac{146.4}{12.84 \times 12.77} = \dfrac{146.4}{163.97} = 0.89$$

Chapter Test

Multiple Choice Questions

1. Which of the following represents cyclic causation?

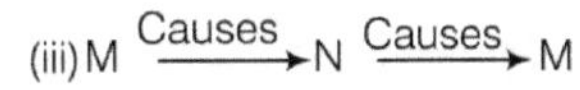

(i) L Causes $\Big\langle$ M / N   (ii) M $\xrightarrow{\text{Causes}}$ L $\xrightarrow{\text{Causes}}$ N   (iii) M $\xrightarrow{\text{Causes}}$ N $\xrightarrow{\text{Causes}}$ M

Alternatives

(a) Only (i) (b) Only (ii) (c) Only (iii) (d) None of these

2. The curve cc' depicts
(a) linear positive correlation
(b) non-linear positive correlation
(c) linear negative positive correlation
(d) non-linear negative correlation

3. The value of correlation coefficient of two variables 'alpha' and 'beta' has been computed as 0.39. What does this value convey?
(a) High degree of positive correlation
(b) Moderate degree of positive correlation
(c) Low degree of positive correlation
(d) Very low degree of positive correlation

4. The techniques which provide the decision maker a systematic and powerful means of analysis to explore policies for achieving predetermined goals are called.......... .
(a) Correlation techniques
(b) Mathematical techniques
(c) Quantitative techniques
(d) None of these

Short Answers (SA) Type Questions

1. "Correlation is preferred to covariance as a measure of association." Explain.

2. Calculate the coefficient of correlation from the following data $\Sigma xy = 4{,}880$, $\sigma_x = 28.70$, $\sigma_y = 18.02$, $n = 10$

3. Compute coefficient of correlation from the following data

	X Series	Y Series
Mean	15	28
Sum of Squares of Deviation from Mean	144	225

Sum of products of deviation of X and Y series from their respective mean is 20. Number of pairs of observations is 10.

4. Does correlation imply causation?

5. What are the properties of Karl Pearson's coefficient of correlation?

Long Answers (LA) Type Questions

1. Calculate coefficient of correlation between the X and Y variables.

X	43	48	56	64	67	70
Y	128	120	138	143	141	152

2. From the following data, calculate coefficient of correlation between age and playing habits.

Age Group	20-30	30-40	40-50	50-60	60-70
Number of Students	25	60	40	20	20
Number of Regular Players	10	30	12	2	1

Answers

Multiple Choice Questions

1. (c)   2. (d)   3. (c)   4. (c)

For Detailed Solutions

Scan the code

CHAPTER 03

Index Numbers

In this Chapter

- Concept of Index Number
- Consumer Price Index (CPI)
- Wholesale Price Index (WPI)

Concept of Index Number

Index numbers are used to measure changes in the variables such as price and quantity of goods and services across two time periods.

It is the ratio of a measure taken for one time period called as **current period** to the same measure taken for another time period, commonly known as **base period.** It is a unit free measure. The measures or variables under consideration may be

- The price of a particular commodity like wheat, gold, steel, etc or a group of commodities like consumer goods, cereals, etc.
- Volume of trade, factory production, industrial and agriculture production, exports or imports, prices of stocks or shares, sales or profits of a firm and so on.
- The national income of a country, wage structure of workers in various sectors, bank deposits, cost of living of persons of a particular community, class or profession, etc.

Mathematically, Index Number for Period N

$$= \left(\frac{\text{Value of variable under consideration in Period } N}{\text{Value of variable under consideration in Base Period}} \right) \times 100$$

Advantages/Uses of Index Number

1. **A Barometer of Economic Progress** With the help of index numbers, a comparison in the value of money in different years can be made easily. If the value of money rises, then it signifies that the country has progressed and vice-versa.

2. **Importance for the Government** The change in the value of money has a direct effect on the public, so government adopts suitable fiscal and monetary policy according to the results of index number.

3. **Throws Light on Economic Condition** Index numbers are very helpful in comparing the economic condition of a particular group of people in two different periods.

4. **Fixation of Wages or Policy-making** The money wages can be revised according to the proportionate change in the cost of living. The cost of living index number guides the government and the executives for the fixation and revision of wages.

5. **Importance for the Producer** Price index number helps the producer to decide whether he should expand the production or he should reduce the production. If price level is rising, it means profit margin is high and production can be increased.

6. **Measure to Remove Inequality of Income** Index number of wholesale price also indicates about the regional disparity.

   So, different measures can be taken for the proper distribution of wealth and ensuring that inequalities of income are checked.

Types of Index Number

Index number can be broadly classified into the following two categories

1. **Price Index Numbers** These index numbers measure the general changes in the prices. They can be further categorised as

(i) **Wholesale Price Index** The wholesale price index measures the changes in the wholesale prices.

(ii) **Retail/Consumer Price Index** This price index measures the changes in retail prices.

2. **Quantity Index Numbers** These index numbers measure the changes in the quantity of goods produced in the periods under review.

Methods of Constructing Index Number

Following are the main methods of constructing an index number

I. Simple Index Number

In simple index number, all items under consideration are given equal weightage, i.e., all goods and services are to be given equal importance. There are two methods of constructing simple index number

1. Simple Aggregative Method

In this method, the sum total of prices of base and current years are considered while computing the index number. Following steps should be followed while computing index number by this method

Step 1 Find the sum of prices of all the goods and services under consideration for the current year and denote it as Σp_1.

Step 2 Find the sum of prices of all the goods and services under consideration for the base year and denote it as Σp_0.

Step 3 Apply the given formula to compute the price index number, $P_{01} = \dfrac{\Sigma p_1}{\Sigma p_0} \times 100$, where symbols have their usual meaning.

Example 1. With the help of the following data, calculate index number for 2020 taking 2015 as base year

Commodity	Price in 2015 (in ₹)	Price in 2020 (in ₹)
A	100	145
B	90	130
C	145	200
D	180	275
E	85	150

Ans. **Calculation of Index Number by Simple Aggregative Method**

Commodity	Price in 2015 (p_0)	Price in 2020 (p_1)
A	100	145
B	90	130
C	145	200
D	180	275
E	85	150
	$\Sigma p_0 = 600$	$\Sigma p_1 = 900$

$$P_{01} = \frac{\Sigma p_1}{\Sigma p_0} \times 100 = \frac{900}{600} \times 100 = 150$$

It means that there is a net increase of 50% in the price of commodities in 2020 as compared to the price of 2015.

2. Simple Average of Price Relative Method

In this method, the average of price relatives is considered while computing the index number. Following steps should be followed while computing index number by this method

Step 1 Compute the price relatives of the given items with the help of the following formula,

$$\text{Price Relative}\,(I) = \frac{p_1}{p_0} \times 100$$

Step 2 Find the sum of the price relatives so computed and express it as ΣI.

Step 3 Apply the given formula to find index number as an average of price relatives, $P_{01} = \dfrac{\Sigma I}{n}$, where

ΣI = Sum of price relatives and n = Number of items

Example 2. Construct index number by simple average of price relative method for 2021 taking the price of 2016 as base from the data given below

Commodity	Price (in ₹)	
	2016	**2021**
A	30	45
B	40	50
C	60	72
D	80	88
E	10	13

Ans. **Construction of Index Number using Simple Average of Price Relative Method**

Commodity	Price (in ₹)		Price Relative = $\left(\dfrac{p_1}{p_0} \times 100\right)$
	2016 (p_0)	**2021 (p_1)**	
A	30	45	$\dfrac{45}{30} \times 100 = 150$
B	40	50	$\dfrac{50}{40} \times 100 = 125$
C	60	72	$\dfrac{72}{60} \times 100 = 120$
D	80	88	$\dfrac{88}{80} \times 100 = 110$
E	10	13	$\dfrac{13}{10} \times 100 = 130$
$n = 5$			$\Sigma I = 635$

$$P_{01} = \frac{\Sigma I}{n} = \frac{635}{5} = 127$$

II. Weighted Index Number

They are the index number in which different items of the series are accorded different weightage, depending upon their relative importance. There are two methods of constructing weighted index number

1. Weighted Average of Price Relative Method

According to this method, weighted index number is simply the weighted arithmetic mean of price relatives. The steps to be followed while computing this index number are given below

Step 1 Compute the price relatives of the given items with the help of the following formula,

$$\text{Price Relative } (I) = \frac{p_1}{p_0} \times 100$$

Step 2 Multiply the price relative so computed with the given weights to find IW.

Step 3 Find the sum of IW to obtain ΣIW.

Step 4 Find the sum of the weights to obtain ΣW.

Step 5 Apply the given formula to compute index number by this method $P_{01} = \dfrac{\Sigma IW}{\Sigma W}$, where symbols have the same meaning as defined above.

Example 3. From the following data, construct a weighted index number for 2020 with 2010 as base year.

Commodity	Weight	Price (in ₹)	
		2010	2020
Wheat	15	10	15
Rice	10	8	16
Pulses	5	5	10
Milk	4	2	4
Oil	6	4	6
Sugar	7	3	6
Salt	3	1	2

Ans. **Construction of Weighted Index Number**

Commodity	Weight (W)	Price (in ₹) 2010 (p_0)	Price (in ₹) 2020 (p_1)	Price Relative (I) ($p_1/p_0 \times 100$)	IW
Wheat	15	10	15	150	2,250
Rice	10	8	16	200	2,000
Pulses	5	5	10	200	1,000
Milk	4	2	4	200	800
Oil	6	4	6	150	900
Sugar	7	3	6	200	1,400
Salt	3	1	2	200	600
					$\Sigma IW = 8,950$

$$\text{Weighted Index Number} = \frac{\Sigma IW}{\Sigma W}$$

$$= \frac{8,950}{50} = 179$$

2. Weighted Aggregative Method

Under this method, weights are assigned to various items and the weighted aggregate of the prices are obtained. There are many methods to construct weighted aggregative index number.

However, considering the scope of syllabus of class XI, we will discuss the following methods of constructing weighted aggregated index number

(i) **Laspeyre's Method** In this method, the quantity consumed in base year (q_0) is taken as weight. Following steps are to be remembered

Step 1 Multiply the current year price of various commodities with base year quantity and add the products to obtain $\Sigma p_1 q_0$.

Step 2 Multiply base year price of various commodities with base year quantity and add the products to obtain $\Sigma p_0 q_0$.

Step 3 Following formula is used to calculate Laspeyre's index number

$$P_{01} = \frac{\Sigma p_1 q_0}{\Sigma p_0 q_0} \times 100$$

(ii) **Paasche's Method** In this method, the quantity consumed in current year (q_1) is taken as weight. Following steps are to be remembered

Step 1 Multiply current year price of various commodities with current year quantities and add the products to obtain $\Sigma p_1 q_1$.

Step 2 Multiply the base year price of various commodities with the current year quantities and add the products to obtain $\Sigma p_0 q_1$.

Step 3 Following formula is used to calculate Paasche's index number $P_{01} = \dfrac{\Sigma p_1 q_1}{\Sigma p_0 q_1} \times 100$

(iii) **Fisher's Method** This method was introduced by Professor Irving Fisher. This method combines the techniques of Laspeyre's method and Paasche's method. Fisher used both base year as well as current year quantities (q_0, q_1) as weight. The given steps should be followed to compute Fisher's index number

Step 1 Multiply base year quantity with prices of base year and current year and add the products to obtain $\Sigma p_1 q_0$ and $\Sigma p_0 q_0$.

Step 2 Multiply current year quantity with prices of base year and current year and add the products to obtain $\Sigma p_1 q_1$ and $\Sigma p_0 q_1$.

Step 3 Apply the given formula to compute Fisher's index number $P_{01} = \sqrt{\dfrac{\Sigma p_1 q_0}{\Sigma p_0 q_0} \times \dfrac{\Sigma p_1 q_1}{\Sigma p_0 q_1}} \times 100$

Example 4. Construct index number of price from the data given below by applying

    (i) Laspeyre's Method   (ii) Paasche's Method
    (iii) Fisher's Method

Commodity	Base Year		Current Year	
	Price (in ₹)	Quantity	Price (in ₹)	Quantity
A	2	40	3	20
B	1.5	30	2.5	40
C	1	50	1.5	30
D	2.5	20	2	80

Ans.   **Construction of Price Index Number**

Commodity	Base Year		Current Year		$p_1 q_0$	$p_0 q_0$	$p_1 q_1$	$p_0 q_1$
	Price (p_0)	Quantity (q_0)	Price (p_1)	Quantity (q_1)				
A	2	40	3	20	120	80	60	40
B	1.5	30	2.5	40	75	45	100	60
C	1	50	1.5	30	75	50	45	30
D	2.5	20	2	80	40	50	160	200

$$\Sigma p_1 q_0 \quad \Sigma p_0 q_0 \quad \Sigma p_1 q_1 \quad \Sigma p_0 q_1$$
$$= 310 \quad = 225 \quad = 365 \quad = 330$$

    (i) **Laspeyre's Method**

$$P_{01} = \frac{\Sigma p_1 q_0}{\Sigma p_0 q_0} \times 100$$

$$= \frac{310}{225} \times 100 = 137.8$$

    (ii) **Paasche's Method**

$$P_{01} = \frac{\Sigma p_1 q_1}{\Sigma p_0 q_1} \times 100 = \frac{365}{330} \times 100 = 110.6$$

    (iii) **Fisher's Method**

$$P_{01} = \sqrt{\frac{\Sigma p_1 q_0}{\Sigma p_0 q_0} \times \frac{\Sigma p_1 q_1}{\Sigma p_0 q_1}} \times 100$$

$$= \sqrt{\frac{310}{225} \times \frac{365}{330}} \times 100$$

$$= \sqrt{1.378 \times 1.106} \times 100$$

$$= 1.23 \times 100 = 123$$

Consumer Price Index (CPI)

Consumer Price Index (CPI) measures the changes over time in the general price level of goods and services that households acquire for the purpose of consumption. CPI is considered to be an indicator of inflation in a country.

The Consumer Price Index number is also known as cost of living index number, retail price index number, price of living index number.

Different CPI for Different Consumers

The consumption patterns of consumers belonging to different strata of society are different.

So, there are different CPI based on the consumption patterns of different consumers. These are

- Consumer Price Index for Industrial Workers (CPI-IW) (constructed with 2001 as base year)
- Consumer Price Index for Agricultural Labour (CPI-AL) and Consumer Price Index for Rural Labour (CPI-RL) (constructed with 1986-87 as base year)
- Consumer Price Index for Rural, Urban and Combined Sectors (constructed with 2011-12 as base year)

Methods of Construction of Consumer Price Index Number

There are following two methods

1. Aggregative Expenditure Method

This method is the same as Laspeyre's method of constructing weighted index.

The following formula is applied for calculating index number by aggregative expenditure method

$$\text{CPI} = \frac{\Sigma p_1 q_0}{\Sigma p_0 q_0} \times 100$$

Here, $\Sigma p_1 q_0 =$ Aggregate expenditure in current year
             $\Sigma p_0 q_0 =$ Aggregate expenditure in base year.

Example 5. Find the consumer price index or cost of living index number for the current year from the following data by aggregative expenditure method.

Commodity	Base Year		Current Year	
	Price	Quantity	Price	Quantity
A	2	12	4	5
B	5	12	6	10
C	4	20	5	15
D	3	10	3	10

Ans. **Construction of Consumer Price Index Number**

Commodity	Base Year		Current Year		$p_1 q_0$	$p_0 q_0$
	Price (p_0)	Quantity (q_0)	Price (p_1)	Quantity (q_1)		
A	2	12	4	5	48	24
B	5	12	6	10	72	60
C	4	20	5	15	100	80
D	3	10	3	10	30	30
					$\Sigma p_1 q_0$ = 250	$\Sigma p_0 q_0$ = 194

$$\text{CPI} = \frac{\Sigma p_1 q_0}{\Sigma p_0 q_0} \times 100 = \frac{250}{194} \times 100 = 128.87$$

2. Family Budget Method

In this method, the family budgets of a large number of people, for whom the index is meant, are carefully studied. Then, the aggregate expenditure of an average family on various commodities is estimated.

These values constitute the weights. CPI is computed in the same manner as weighted average of price relative method. The following formula is applied to compute CPI by family budget method $\text{CPI} = \dfrac{\Sigma IW}{\Sigma W}$

where, ΣIW = Sum of products of price relative with weights ΣW = Sum of weights

Example 6. Construct the consumer price index number for 2021 on the basis of the following data using family budget method.

Items	Price in 2010 (₹)	Price in 2021 (₹)	Weight
Food	200	280	30
Rent	100	200	20
Clothing	150	120	20
Fuel and lighting	50	100	10
Miscellaneous	100	200	20

Ans. **Construction of Consumer Price Index Number for 2021**
[Base year 2010 = 100 (Family Budget Method)]

Items	Weight (W)	Price in 2010 (p_0)	Price in 2021 (p_1)	$I = \dfrac{p_1}{p_0} \times 100$	IW
Food	30	200	280	140	4,200
Rent	20	100	200	200	4,000
Clothing	20	150	120	80	1,600
Fuel and lighting	10	50	100	200	2,000
Miscellaneous	20	100	200	200	4,000
	$\Sigma W = 100$				ΣIW = 15,800

Consumer Price Index Number for 2011

$$= \frac{\Sigma IW}{\Sigma W}$$

$$= \frac{15,800}{100}$$

$$= 158$$

Weights Assigned to Different Categories of Consumption Goods

As we have discussed that while computing CPI by family budget items, different weights are assigned to various consumption goods.

The government agencies while computing CPI refer to the standard weights which are tabulate below

The Group of Items in CPI for Industrial Workers and Their Weightage

Major Group	Weight in %
Food	45.86
Pan, supari, tobacco, etc	2.38
Fuel & light	6.84
Housing	10.07
Clothing, bedding & footwear	6.53
Misc. group	28.32
General	100.00

Source *Economic Survey, Government of India.*

Wholesale Price Index (WPI)

The Wholesale Price Index measures the changes in the general price level of the country. This price index is calculated mainly on the basis of those commodities which are traded on wholesale rates such as oil, sugar, wheat, rice, etc.

This price index totally ignores the service sector. There is only one composite Wholesale Price Index for the whole country and it is computed on a weekly basis.

The methods for computation of Wholesale Price Index are the same as discussed in Consumer Price Index.

Groups for the Construction of Wholesale Price Index

The current series of wholesale price index has a base year of 2011-12. Also, in India for the construction of wholesale price index, goods are mainly classified into the following three main groups

1. **Primary Articles** This group is further divided into three sub-groups, viz. food articles, non-food articles and minerals. Primary articles have a weightage of 22.62%.

2. **Fuel and Power** In this category, items like coal, petroleum products, electricity, etc are included with a total weightage of 13.15%.

3. **Manufactured Products** This group is further divided into many sub-groups such as food products, beverages, textiles, metal products, etc. This group has a weightage of 64.23%.

The above information can be tabulated as below

The Categories in WPI and Their Weightage

Category	Weight in %
Primary Articles	22.62%
Fuel and Power	13.15%
Manufactured Products	64.23%

Source *Ministry of Statistics and Programme Implementation, 2016-17*

Other Important Index Numbers

These index numbers are also important

1. **Sensex** Sensex is the short form for Bombay Stock Exchange (BSE) Sensitive Index with 1978-79 as base.

   It is the benchmark index for the Indian stock market. It consists of 30 stocks which represent a large, well-established companies of the economy.

   If the sensex rises, it indicates that market is doing well and investors expect better earnings from companies. It also indicates a growing confidence of investors in the basic health of the economy.

   Movement in sensex should be interpreted in the following way

   - If sensex goes up, it means that the prices of the stocks of most of the companies under BSE sensex have gone up.
   - If sensex goes down, it means that prices of stocks of most of the companies under BSE sensex have gone down.

2. **Human Development Index** It is another index number used to judge the level of development of different countries.

   This index is prepared by United Nation (UN) for its member countries using threee components

   - Per capita income (measured in $PPP).
   - Gross enrollment ratio and years of schooling.
   - Life expectancy at birth.

   Based upon the index, counties are given value out of 1 and ranked accordingly.

Issues in Construction of Index Number

There are many problems faced while constructing index number. Some of the problems are as follows

1. **Determination and Definition of the Purpose** Before constructing an index number, one must define the objective. It is necessary that the purpose and scope of the desired index number must be determined and clearly defined in specified terms.

2. **Selection of Sources of Data** Data can be taken either from primary sources or from secondary sources. The source of data for the construction of index number should be carefully selected depending on the extent of coverage desired, accuracy, nature and objective of constructing the index number, etc.

3. **Selection of Base Year** Base year should be too far in the past. It must be a representative year and a year in which there were no elections, war or natural calamities.

4. **Selection of Items/Commodities** Items used for the construction of index number must be representative. The number of commodities should be neither too large nor too small. Items selected should be relevant and standardised i.e., easy to be described, recognised and understood. e.g., rice, milk, ghee, cloth, etc.

5. **Selection of the Price** In the construction of price index, the problem is whether to adopt retail price or wholesale price, controlled or open market price.

6. **Selection of Weighing Methods** We should accord suitable weightage to different items. The method of providing weightage depends upon the purpose of index number. Weighing may be according to the value or quantity.

7. **Selection of the Formula** Index number can be constructed with the help of many formulae such as Laspeyre's method, Paasche's method, Dorbish and Bowley's method, Fisher's method, etc. One has to decide about the method to be used while constructing the index number.

Index Number in Economics

There are many uses of index number in economics. These are

- Consumer Price Index (CPI) are helpful in wage negotiation, formulation of income policy, price policy, rent control, taxation and general economic policy formulation.

- The Wholesale Price Index (WPI) is used to estimate the effect of changes in prices on aggregate such as, national income, capital formation, etc.

- CPI are used in calculating the purchasing power of money and real wage.

- Index of industrial production gives us a quantitative figure about the change in production in the industrial sector.
- Agricultural production index provides us a ready reckoner of the performance of agricultural sector.
- Sensex is a useful guide for investors in the stock market. If the sensex is rising, investors are optimistic of the future performance of the economy.
- The WPI is widely used to measure the rate of inflation as discussed below.
  Inflation is a general and continuing increase in prices. If inflation becomes sufficiently large, money may lose its traditional function as a medium of exchange and as a unit of account. Its primary impact lies in lowering the value of money.

Inflation and Index Number

Inflation is described as a situation characterised by a sustained increase in the general price level. A small rise in price or an irregular price rise cannot be called inflation. Wholesale Price Index (WPI) is the most commonly accepted measure of inflation, due to following attributes

- The Wholesale Price Index (WPI) is the most widely used price index as an indicator of the rate of inflation in the economy.
- It is only general index capturing price movements in a comprehensive way and indicates movement in price of commodities in all trade and transactions.
- WPI is available on a weekly basis with the shortest possible time lag of 2 weeks.

Chapter Practice

Objective Questions

• Multiple Choice Questions

1. An index number which accounts for the relative importance of the items is known as **(NCERT)**
(a) Weighted index
(b) Simple aggregative index
(c) Simple average of relatives
(d) None of the above

Ans. (a) Weighted index

2. In most of the weighted index numbers the weight pertains to **(NCERT)**
(a) base year
(b) current year
(c) both base and current year
(d) None of these

Ans. (a) base year

3. The impact of change in the price of a commodity with little weight in the index will be **(NCERT)**
(a) small
(b) large
(c) uncertain
(d) None of these

Ans. (a) small

4. The item having the highest weight in consumer price index for industrial workers is **(NCERT)**
(a) food
(b) housing
(c) clothing
(d) None of these

Ans. (a) food

5. In general, inflation is calculated by using **(NCERT)**
(a) Wholesale Price Index
(b) Consumer Price Index
(c) Producer's Price Index
(d) None of these

Ans. (a) Wholesale Price Index

6. Which of the following devices is used for measuring differences in the magnitude of a group of related variables?
(a) Arithmetic mean
(b) Index number
(c) Correlation
(d) Mode

Ans. (b) Index number

7. Index numbers are very helpful in comparing the economic conditions of a particular group of people for ......different periods.
(a) three
(b) two
(c) four
(d) None of these

Ans. (b) two

8. **Statement I** Construction of index numbers only needs choosing commodity basket.

Statement II Index numbers have universal acceptance.

Alternatives
(a) Statement I is correct and Statement II is incorrect
(b) Statement II is correct and Statement I is incorrect
(c) Both the statements are correct
(d) Both the statements are incorrect

Ans. (b) Statement II is correct and Statement I is incorrect

9. **Statement I** An appropriate method for working out consumer price index is family budget method.

Statement II Index numbers are devices for measuring differences in the magnitude of a group of related variables.

Alternatives
(a) Statement I is correct and Statement II is incorrect
(b) Statement II is correct and Statement I is incorrect
(c) Both the statements are correct
(d) Both the statements are incorrect

Ans. (c) Both the statements are correct

10. The ...... value of index number is a pure number.
(a) average
(b) commodity
(c) price relative
(d) All of these

Ans. (c) price relative

11. Which of the following index numbers is based on the assumption that all the commodities are of equal importance?
(a) Weighted index number
(b) Simple index number
(c) Both (a) and (b)
(d) None of these

Ans. (b) Simple index number

12. Choose the correct pair.

Column I	Column II
A. Economic Barometers	(i) Only weighted Index Numbers
B. Purchasing Power of Money	(ii) Inverse of CPI
C. Base year of Index Numbers	(iii) 1990

Codes
(a) A–(i)   (b) B–(ii)
(c) C–(iii)   (d) None of these

Ans. (b) B–(ii)

13. In Laspeyre's index number, the weight pertains to
(a) base year quantities   (b) current year
(c) Both (a) and (b)   (d) None of these

Ans. (a) base year quantities

14. If Laspeyre's index is 110 and Paasche's index is 108, fisher's index will be
(a) 100   (b) 108
(c) 109   (d) None of these

Ans. (c) Fisher's index $= \sqrt{110 \times 108} = 108.99$ or 109

15. Factor Reversal Test is expressed in terms of

(a) $\dfrac{\Sigma P_1 Q_1}{\Sigma P_0 Q_0}$

(b) $\dfrac{\Sigma P_1 Q_0}{\Sigma P_0 Q_0} \times \dfrac{\Sigma P_1 Q_1}{\Sigma P_0 Q_1}$

(c) $\dfrac{\Sigma P_1 Q_1}{\Sigma Q_0 P_1}$

(d) $\dfrac{\Sigma Q_1 P_0}{\Sigma Q_0 P_0} \times \dfrac{\Sigma P_1 Q_1}{\Sigma Q_0 P_1}$

Ans. (d) $\dfrac{\Sigma Q_1 P_0}{\Sigma Q_0 P_0} \times \dfrac{\Sigma P_1 Q_1}{\Sigma Q_0 P_1}$

• Assertion-Reasoning MCQs

Direction *(Q. Nos. 1 to 5) There are two statements marked as Assertion (A) and Reason (R). Read the statements and choose the appropriate option from the options given below*
(a) Both Assertion (A) and Reason (R) are true and Reason (R) is the correct explanation of Assertion (A)
(b) Both Assertion (A) and Reason (R) are true, but Reason (R) is not the correct explanation of Assertion (A)
(c) Assertion (A) is true, but Reason (R) is false
(d) Assertion (A) is false, but Reason (R) is true

1. Assertion (A) A better way to estimate GDP accurately is to deflate input and output prices through separate indices.

Reason (R) When output prices move relatively faster than the input prices, the single deflation method overestimates GDP.

Ans. (a) Both Assertion (A) and Reason (R) are true and Reason (R) is the correct explanation of Assertion (A)

2. Assertion (A) Index number serves as the barometer for measuring the value of money in an economy.

Reason (R) Index numbers have universal acceptance thus can be applied in any case.

Ans. (b) Index number is an important statistical tool that serves as the barometer for comparison of different variables.

3. Assertion (A) Wholesale price index is used to measure the changes in the prices of goods that impacts individual.

Reason (R) Positive value of index number indicates rise in general price levels.

Ans. (d) Consumer's price index is used to measure the changes in the retail prices of the commodities.

4. Assertion (A) Value index is based upon both price and quantity.

Reason (R) Value is calculated by the product of price and quantity.

Ans. (b) Value refers to the product of price and quantity thus comprised of both base and current year's price and quantities.

5. Assertion (A) Fisher's method of index number is considered as ideal weighted method of index numbers.

Reason (R) Fisher's method passes all statistical tests of time and factor reversal.

Ans. (a) Both Assertion (A) and Reason (R) are true and Reason (R) is the correct explanation of Assertion (A)

• Case Based MCQs

1. Direction *Read the following case study graph and answer the question no. (i) to (vi) on the basis of the same.*

(i) Which year is considered as the base year for constructing Sensex in India?
 (a) 1978-79   (b) 2000-01   (c) 2004-05   (d) 2011-12

Ans. (a) 1978-79

(ii) As per the given graph, rising Sensex indicates
....
 (a) growth of economy
 (b) growth of investors profit
 (c) inflow of foreign currency
 (d) All of the above

Ans. (b) As the graph is showing an upward trend, it indicates growth of profit for the investors.

(iii) Index number is always expressed in terms of ....
 (a) percentage   (b) proportionate
 (c) Both (a) and (b)   (d) None of these

Ans. (a) percentage

(iv) .... type of average is used to calculate the value of index number.
 (a) Simple   (b) Weighted
 (c) Proportionate   (d) Both (a) and (b)

Ans. (b) Weighted

(v) The given graph shows 0.64% increase, what does it indicate?
 (a) Rise in number of stocks (b) Rise in stock prices
 (c) Fall in stock price   (d) None of these

Ans. (b) Rise in stock prices

(vi) Which year shows a decrease in stock price as per the given graph?
 (a) 2017   (b) 2018   (c) 2019   (d) 2020

Ans. (d) 2020

2. Direction *Read the following case study and answer the question no. (i) to (vi) on the basis of the same.*

We frequently see index numbers, such as the Consumer Price Index (CPI), in our daily life. Economists often use the index numbers to compare values measured at different points in time. Using an index can make quick comparisons easy. The index numbers have become a widely accepted statistical device for measuring business activity changes. A typical use of the index number technique in business is to summarize complex situations with a single performance index so that a dashboard (or report) would have enough space to show all KPIs. An index number is used to measure changes in the magnitude of a variable or group of variables regarding time, geographical location, or other characteristics such as profession.

IT professionals who need to analyse economic and business activities, but have limited experience in statistics, want to learn how to construct and interpret performance indexes. Index numbers are also not free from criticism as its base year and commodity selection requires a lot of attention and expert attention.

(i) Choose the correct statement from given below
 (a) Index numbers are cent percent accurate
 (b) There is null possibility of biasness in case of index numbers
 (c) Index number is based upon all the items given in the data
 (d) All of the above

Ans. (c) Index number is based upon all the items given in the data

(ii) Index numbers can be used in which of the following fields?
 (a) Geographical areas
 (b) Change in magnitude of a variable
 (c) Change in time periods
 (d) All of the above

Ans. (d) All of the above

(iii) Which of the following problems comes in the construction of index numbers?
 (a) Selection of base year   (b) Selection of commodities
 (c) Selection of quantities   (d) All of these

Ans. (d) All of these

(iv) **Assertion** (A) Selection of incorrect base leads to mis-leading conclusion.

 Reason (R) A year with high fluctuations in prices should not be considered as base year.

 Alternatives
 (a) Both Assertion (A) and Reason (R) are true and Reason (R) is the correct explanation of Assertion (A).
 (b) Both Assertion (A) and Reason (R) are true, but Reason (R) is not the correct explanation of Assertion (A)
 (c) Assertion (A) is true, but Reason (R) is false
 (d) Both are false

Ans. (a) Both Assertion (A) and Reason (R) are true and Reason (R) is the correct explanation of Assertion (A).

(v) Application of index numbers which is based on data related to different time period is known as ....
 (a) Time series data   (b) Temporal data
 (c) Inter-temporal data   (d) All of these

Ans. (d) All of these

(vi) Economists often use the index numbers to .... values measured at different points in time.
 (a) measure   (b) change   (c) compare   (d) All of these

Ans. (a) measure

PART 2
Subjective Questions

• Short Answer (SA) Type Questions

1. Why do we need an index number?   **(NCERT)**

Ans. Index numbers are needed because of the various advantages which pertain to the use of index numbers. These advantages

  (i) **Barometer of Economic Progress** Index numbers are a barometer for measuring the value of money and assessing the level of economic progress.

  (ii) **Importance for the Government** The government adopts suitable monetary and fiscal policies according to the changes in index numbers.

  (iii) **Throws Light on Economic Condition** Index numbers are very helpful in comparing the economic condition of a particular group of people across two time periods.

  (iv) **Fixation of Wages of Policy-making** Index numbers such as CPI and WPI help the government and executives for the fixation and revision of wages.

2. Is the change in any price reflected in a price index number?   **(NCERT)**

Ans. No, the change in any price is not reflected in a price index number. Price index numbers measure and permit comparison of the prices of certain goods included in the basket being used to compare prices in the base period with prices in the current period. Moreover, an equal rise in the price of an item with large weight and that of an item with low weight will have different implications for the overall change in the price index.

3. What are the desirable properties of the base period?   **(NCERT)**

Ans. Base period should have the following properties

  (i) The base year should be a normal year in which extraordinary events such as earthquake, flood, war, elections, etc should not have occurred.

  (ii) The period should not be too far in the past as comparison cannot be done with such a base year because policies, economic and social conditions change with time.

  (iii) Base period should be updated periodically.

  Thus, we can conclude that while selecting base period, certain factors should be considered.

4. What is the difference between a price index and a quantity index?   **(NCERT)**

Ans. The differences between a price index and a quantity index are as follows

  (i) Price index numbers measure and allow for comparison of the prices of certain goods while quantity index numbers measure the changes in the physical volume of production, construction or employment.

  (ii) Price index numbers are more widely used as compared to quantity index numbers.

  (iii) Quantity index does not indicate the real change in the purchasing power of money while price index does.

5. The Consumer Price Index for June, 2005 was 125. The food index was 120 and that of other items was 135. What is the percentage of the total weight given to food?   **(NCERT)**

Ans. Let X denote the percentage of total weight given to food and $100 - X$ denote the percentage of total weight given to other items.

$$\text{CPI} = \frac{120(X) + 135\,(100 - X)}{100}, \quad 125 = \frac{120X \times 13{,}500 - 135\,X}{100}$$

$$\Rightarrow \quad 12{,}500 = 120X + 13{,}500 - 135\,X$$

$$\Rightarrow \quad 1{,}000 = 15\,X \Rightarrow X = \frac{1{,}000}{15} = 66.67\%$$

Thus, the percentage of the total weight given to food $= 66.67\%$

6. If the salary of a person in the base year is ₹ 4,000 per annum and the current year salary is ₹ 6,000, by how much should his salary rise to maintain the same standard of living, if the CPI is 400?   **(NCERT)**

Ans. Base year salary = ₹ 4,000, Base year index = 100 (assumption), Current year index = 400
Salary required in the current year to maintain the same standard of living of base year

$$= \text{Base Year Salary} \times \frac{\text{CPI of Current Year}}{\text{CPI of Base Year}}$$

$$= 4{,}000 \times \frac{400}{100} = ₹\,16{,}000$$

Current year salary = ₹ 6,000
The increase in current salary required
$$= 16{,}000 - 6{,}000 = ₹\,10{,}000$$

7. Which method is considered 'ideal' for constructing index number and why?

Ans. Fisher's method is considered ideal for constructing index number because

  (i) It satisfies factor reversal test.

  (ii) It satisfies time reversal test.

  (iii) It is based on different weights.

8. Give the limitations of simple aggregative method of computing index number.

Ans. Although computation of index number is quite simple while using this method, yet it is not ordinarily used because of the following limitations

  (i) All items are given equal weightage.

  (ii) This measure of index number is influenced by the items which are highly priced.

  (iii) This method is affected with the change in the unit of measurement.

For example, index number computed when price of wheat is expressed in per kg, will be different from the index number computed when the price of wheat is expressed in per quintal.

9. Mr Ashok was getting ₹ 400 in the base year and ₹ 800 in the current year. If Consumer Price Index is ₹ 350, then what extra amount is required for maintaining the earlier standard of living?

Ans. For former standard of living, Ashok should get

$$= \frac{\text{Salary in Base Year} \times \text{CPI}}{100} = \frac{400 \times 350}{100} = 1,400$$

∴ Amount required for maintaining the same standard of living $= 1,400 - 800 = ₹ 600$

10. The monthly per capita expenditure incurred by workers of an industrial centre during 1980 and 2005 on the following items are given below.

The weights of these items are 75, 10, 5, 6 and 4, respectively. Prepare a weighted index number for cost of living for 2005 with 1980 as base. **(NCERT)**

Item	Price in 1980	Price in 2005
Food	100	200
Clothing	20	25
Fuel and lighting	15	20
House rent	30	40
Miscellaneous	35	65

Ans. **Construction of Consumer Price Index**

Item	W	Price in 1980 (₹) (p_0)	Price in 2005 (₹) (p_1)	$I\left(\dfrac{p_1}{p_0} \times 100\right)$	I W
Food	75	100	200	200	15,000
Clothing	10	20	25	125	1,250
Fuel and lighting	5	15	20	133.33	666.65
House rent	6	30	40	133.33	799.98
Miscellaneous	4	35	65	185.71	742.84
	$\Sigma W = 100$				$\Sigma I W = 18,459.47$

$$\text{CPI} = \frac{\Sigma IW}{\Sigma W} = \frac{18,459.47}{100} = 184.59 = 185 \text{ (approx)}$$

11. Explain briefly the process of data collection for Consumer Price Index (CPI).

Ans. Primary data is collected every month to compute rural and urban CPI in the following ways

(i) For CPI (Rural), two villages are selected from each district. Presently data is collected from 1,181 villages. Number of items for price data collection is identified through the market survey and it is around 225.

Price data is collected from selected shops in the villages every month by the Department of Posts.

(ii) For CPI (Urban), data is collected from all cities, having a population of more than 9 lakhs. Presently, total number of selected cities is 310. Number of items for price data collection is identified through the market survey and it is around 250. Each selected market is visited every month for price data collection from shops and outlets.

(iii) 4.75 lakh price data records collected from rural and urban areas are uploaded per month to the web portal of National Informatics Centre, which is the formal data collection arm of NSSO (National Sample Survey Organisation).

12. An enquiry into the budgets of the middle class families in a certain city gave the following information.

Expenses on Items	Food 35%	Fuel 10%	Clothing 20%	Rent 15%	Miscellan-eous 20%
Price in 2004 (₹)	1,500	250	750	300	400
Price in 1995 (₹)	1,400	200	500	200	250

What is the cost of living index number of 2004 as compared with 1995?

Ans. **Construction of Consumer Price Index**

Item	W (%)	Price in 1995 (₹) (p_0)	Price in 2004 (₹) (p_1)	$I\left(\dfrac{p_1}{p_0} \times 100\right)$	I W
Food	35	1,400	1,500	107.14	3,750 (approx)
Fuel	10	200	250	125.00	1,250
Clothing	20	500	750	150.00	3,000
Rent	15	200	300	150.00	2,250
Miscella-neous	20	250	400	160.00	3,200
	$\Sigma W = 100$				$\Sigma IW = 13,450$

$$\text{CPI} = \frac{\Sigma IW}{\Sigma W}$$

$$= \frac{13,450}{100} = 134.5$$

This result indicates that the CPI in the year 2004 has increased by 34.5% as compared to the year 1995.

13. Construct index number of 2015 from the given data by the simple aggregative method and the simple average of relative method.

Commodity	A	B	C	D	E	F
Price in 2015 (₹)	10	18	16	14	12	17
Price in 2010 (₹)	8	15	12	10	8	12.5

Ans.   **Construction of Index Number**

Commodity	Price in 2010 ($\overline{\rule{0.6em}{0pt}}$) ($p_0$)	Price in 2015 ($\overline{\rule{0.6em}{0pt}}$) ($p_1$)	$I\left(\dfrac{p_1}{p_0} \times 100\right)$
A	8	10	125
B	15	18	120
C	12	16	133.3
D	10	14	140
E	8	12	150
F	12.5	17	136
$n = 6$	$\Sigma p_0 = 65.5$	$\Sigma p_1 = 87$	$\Sigma I = 804.3$

(i) Simple Aggregative Method

$$P_{01} = \frac{\Sigma p_1}{\Sigma p_0} \times 100 = \frac{87}{65.5} \times 100 = 132.8$$

(ii) Simple Average of Relative Method

$$P_{01} = \frac{\Sigma I}{n} = \frac{804.3}{6} = 134.05$$

14. Construct the index number by simple average of price relative method and by simple aggregative method.

Commodity	A	B	C	D	E
Price in 2014 ($\overline{\rule{0.6em}{0pt}}$)	16	40	35	5.25	2
Price in 2015 ($\overline{\rule{0.6em}{0pt}}$)	20	60	50	6.25	1.5

Ans.   **Construction of Index Number**

Commodity	Price in 2014 ($\overline{\rule{0.6em}{0pt}}$) ($p_0$)	Price in 2015 ($\overline{\rule{0.6em}{0pt}}$) ($p_1$)	$I\left(\dfrac{p_1}{p_0} \times 100\right)$
A	16	20	125
B	40	60	150
C	35	50	142.9
D	5.25	6.25	119.05
E	2	1.50	75
$n = 5$	$\Sigma p_0 = 98.25$	$\Sigma p_1 = 137.75$	$\Sigma I = 611.95$

(i) Simple Average of Price Relative Method

$$P_{01} = \frac{\Sigma I}{n} = \frac{611.95}{5} = 122.39$$

(ii) Simple Aggregative Method

$$P_{01} = \frac{\Sigma p_1}{\Sigma p_0} \times 100 = \frac{137.75}{98.25} \times 100$$
$$= 140.20$$

15. Using the simple aggregative method, calculate the index number for the given data.

	A	B	C	D
p_1	15	22	20	27
p_0	10	20	18	25

Ans.   **Construction of Index Number**

Commodity	p_0 (Base Year)	p_1 (Current Year)
A	10	15
B	20	22
C	18	20
D	25	27
	$\Sigma p_0 = 73$	$\Sigma p_1 = 84$

$$P_{01} = \frac{\Sigma p_1}{\Sigma p_0} \times 100 \Rightarrow P_{01} = \frac{84}{73} \times 100 = 115.07$$

16. Calculate the weighted average of price relative index for 2016 on the basis of 2012 from the following data

Commodity	W	p_0	p_1
		2012	2016
A	10	15	20
B	8	10	12
C	6	5	8
D	6	10	13
E	4	4	5

Ans.   **Construction of Weighted Index Number**

Commodity	W	Price in 2012 ($\overline{\rule{0.6em}{0pt}}$) ($p_0$)	Price in 2016 ($\overline{\rule{0.6em}{0pt}}$) ($p_1$)	$I\left(\dfrac{p_1}{p_0} \times 100\right)$	IW
A	10	15	20	133.33	1,333
B	8	10	12	120.00	960
C	6	5	8	160.00	960
D	6	10	13	130.00	780
E	4	4	5	125.00	500
	$\Sigma W = 34$				$\Sigma IW = 4,533$

$$P_{01} = \frac{\Sigma IW}{\Sigma W} = \frac{4,533}{34} = 133.3$$

• Long Answer (LA) Type Questions

1. Explain briefly the various characteristics or features of index numbers.

Ans. The characteristics of index numbers are as follows

(i) **Specialised Averages** Index numbers are specialised averages as they are helpful in computing combined averages of goods and services expressed in different units. Unlike the measures of central tendency, which can compute averages of variables expressed in one unit only, index numbers can measure the averages of variables with diverse units.

(ii) **Measure the Relative Changes** Index numbers measure the relative change in the value of the variable under study. Because of this, index numbers are expressed in terms of percentage which are independent of the units of measurement.

(iii) **Measure the Net Changes** Index numbers measure net changes in a variable or group of variables. They describe net change in a single number. This facilitates the comparisons of two or more index numbers.

(iv) **Measure the Change not Capable of Direct Measurement** Index numbers are meant to study the changes in the effects of such factors which cannot be measured directly. For example, changes in business activity in a country are not capable of direct measurement but it is possible to study relative changes in business activity with the help of index number.

2. Discuss in brief, the methods of constructing weighted index numbers.

Ans. Weighted index numbers are the index number in which different items of the series are accorded different weightage, depending upon their relative importance.

There are two methods of constructing weighted index numbers

(i) **Weighted Average of Price Relative Method** According to this method, weighted index number is simply the weighted arithmetic mean of price relative. In this method, weighted sum of the price relative is divided by the sum total of the weights.

Thus, $$P_{01} = \frac{\Sigma IW}{\Sigma W}$$

(ii) **Weighted Aggregative Method** Under this method, weights are assigned to various items and instead of finding the simple aggregate of price, the weighted aggregate of the price are obtained. The different methods to compute weighted aggregative index numbers are

Laspeyre's Method This method uses the base year quantities as weights.
The following formula is used to calculate index number

$$P_{01} = \frac{\Sigma p_1 q_0}{\Sigma p_0 q_0} \times 100$$

Paasche's Method This method uses the current year quantities as weights The following formula is used to calculate index number

$$P_{01} = \frac{\Sigma p_1 q_1}{\Sigma p_0 q_1} \times 100$$

Fisher's Method This method combines the techniques of Laspeyre's method and Paasche's method and uses both base year as well as current year quantities (q_0, q_1) as weight. The formula to construct index number is

$$P_{01} = \sqrt{\frac{\Sigma p_1 q_0}{\Sigma p_0 q_0} \times \frac{\Sigma p_1 q_1}{\Sigma p_0 q_1}} \times 100$$

3. Construct index number of price for the year price of 2016 from the following data by

   (i) Laspeyre's Method   (ii) Paasche's Method   (iii) Fisher's Method

Commodity	2008		2016	
	Price	Quantity	Price	Quantity
A	10	30	12	35
B	9	10	11	15
C	8	15	10	20
D	6	20	7	25

Ans.

Construction of Price Index Number

Commodity	2008 (Base Year)		2016 (Current Year)		$p_0 q_0$	$p_0 q_1$	$p_1 q_0$	$p_1 q_1$
	p_0	q_0	p_1	q_1				
A	10	30	12	35	300	350	360	420
B	9	10	11	15	90	135	110	165
C	8	15	10	20	120	160	150	200
D	6	20	7	25	120	150	140	175
					$\Sigma p_0 q_0 = 630$	$\Sigma p_0 q_1 = 795$	$\Sigma p_1 q_0 = 760$	$\Sigma p_1 q_1 = 960$

(i) **Laspeyre's Method** $P_{01} = \dfrac{\Sigma p_1 q_0}{\Sigma p_0 q_0} \times 100 = \dfrac{760}{630} \times 100 = 120.63$

(ii) **Paasche's Method** $P_{01} = \dfrac{\Sigma p_1 q_1}{\Sigma p_0 q_1} \times 100 = \dfrac{960}{795} \times 100 = 120.75$

(iii) **Fisher's Method** $P_{01} = \sqrt{\dfrac{\Sigma p_1 q_0}{\Sigma p_0 q_0} \times \dfrac{\Sigma p_1 q_1}{\Sigma p_0 q_1}} \times 100 = \sqrt{\dfrac{760}{630} \times \dfrac{960}{795}} \times 100 = \sqrt{1.206 \times 1.207} \times 100 = \sqrt{1.455} \times 100$

$$= 1.2065 \times 100 = 120.65$$

4. Construct the following indices by taking 2014 as the base year

(i) Simple Aggregative Price Index   (ii) Index of Average of Price Relative

Item	A	B	C	D	E
Price in 2014 (₹)	6	2	4	10	8
Price in 2015 (₹)	10	2	6	12	12
Price in 2016 (₹)	15	3	8	14	16

Ans.

Construction of Price Index Number

Item	Price in 2014 (₹) (p_0)	Price in 2015 (₹) (p_1)	Price in 2016 (₹) (p_2)	$I_1 \left(\dfrac{p_1}{p_0} \times 100\right)$	$I_2 \left(\dfrac{p_2}{p_0} \times 100\right)$
A	6	10	15	166.67	250
B	2	2	3	100.00	150
C	4	6	8	150.00	200
D	10	12	14	120.00	140
E	8	12	16	150.00	200
$n = 5$	$\Sigma p_0 = 30$	$\Sigma p_1 = 42$	$\Sigma p_2 = 56$	$\Sigma I_1 = 686.67$	$\Sigma I_2 = 940$

(i) **Simple Aggregative Price Index** $P_{01} = \dfrac{\Sigma p_1}{\Sigma p_0} \times 100 = \dfrac{42}{30} \times 100 = 140$ (for 2015),

$$P_{02} = \dfrac{\Sigma p_2}{\Sigma p_0} \times 100 = \dfrac{56}{30} \times 100 = 186.67 \text{ (for 2016)}$$

(ii) **Index of Average of Price Relative** $P_{01} = \dfrac{\Sigma I_1}{n} = \dfrac{686.67}{5} = 137.34$ (for 2015),

$$P_{02} = \dfrac{\Sigma I_2}{n} = \dfrac{940}{5} = 188 \text{ (for 2016)}$$

5. The price quotation of different commodities for 2014 and 2015 are given below. Calculate the index number for 2015 with 2014 as base year by using

(i) Simple Average of Price Relative   (ii) Weighted Average of Price Relative

Commodity	Unit	Weight	Price (₹)	
			2014	2015
A	kg	5	2.00	4.50
B	quintal	7	2.50	3.20
C	dozen	6	3.00	3.50
D	kg	2	1.00	1.80

Ans.

Construction of Weighted Index Number

Commodity	Weight (W)	p_0	Price in 2015 (p_1)	$I\left(\dfrac{p_1}{p_0} \times 100\right)$	IW
A	5	2.00	4.50	$\dfrac{4.50}{2.0} \times 100 = 225$	1,125
B	7	2.50	3.20	$\dfrac{3.20}{2.50} \times 100 = 128$	896
C	6	3.00	3.50	$\dfrac{3.50}{3.00} \times 100 = 116.67$	700.02
D	2	1.00	1.80	$\dfrac{1.80}{1.00} \times 100 = 180$	360
$n = 4$	$\Sigma W = 20$			$\Sigma I = 649.67$	$\Sigma IW = 3,081.02$

(i) **Simple Average of Price Relative Method** $\quad P_{01} = \dfrac{\Sigma I}{n} = \dfrac{649.67}{4} = 162.42$

(ii) **Weighted Average of Price Relative Method** $\quad P_{01} = \dfrac{\Sigma IW}{\Sigma W} = \dfrac{3,081.02}{20} = 154.051$

6. Calculate the cost of living index number using family budget method.

Commodity	Wheat	Rice	Pulses	Ghee	Sugar	Oil	Fuel	Clothes
Units Consumed in Base Year	200	50	56	20	40	50	60	40
Price in ₹ (Base Year)	1.0	3.0	4.0	20.0	2.5	10.0	2.0	15.0
Price in ₹ (Current Year)	1.2	3.5	5.0	30.0	5.0	15.5	2.5	18.0

Ans.

Construction of Cost of Living Index Number

Commodity	Unit Consumed in Base Year (q_0)	Price in Base Year (₹) (p_0)	Price in Current Year (₹) (p_1)	$I\left(\dfrac{p_1}{p_0} \times 100\right)$	$W(p_0 q_0)$	IW
Wheat	200	1.0	1.2	120.00	200	24,000
Rice	50	3.0	3.5	116.67	150	17,500.5
Pulses	56	4.0	5.0	125.00	224	28,000
Ghee	20	20.0	30.0	150.00	400	60,000
Sugar	40	2.5	5.0	200.00	100	20,000
Oil	50	10.0	15.5	155.00	500	77,500
Fuel	60	2.0	2.5	125.00	120	15,000
Clothes	40	15.0	18.0	120.00	600	72,000
					$\Sigma W = 2,294$	$\Sigma IW = 3,14,000.5$

$$\text{CPI} = \frac{\Sigma IW}{\Sigma W} = \frac{3,14,000.5}{2,294} = 136.88$$

This result indicates that CPI in the current year has increased by 36.88% as compared to the base period.

7. The price paid and quantities purchased by a household in base and current years are given below. Calculate the additional dearness allowance to be given to the household so as to fully compensate it for the price rise, using both the Laspeyre's and Paasche's index number.

Commodity	Base Year		Current Year	
	Price (₹)	Quantity	Price (₹)	Quantity
A	30	10	40	8
B	12	20	15	18

Ans.

Construction of Price Index Number

Commodity	Base Year		Current Year		$p_0 q_0$	$p_0 q_1$	$p_1 q_0$	$p_1 q_1$
	p_0	q_0	p_1	q_1				
A	30	10	40	8	300	240	400	320
B	12	20	15	18	240	216	300	270
					$\Sigma p_0 q_0 = 540$	$\Sigma p_0 q_1 = 456$	$\Sigma p_1 q_0 = 700$	$\Sigma p_1 q_1 = 590$

Laspeyre's Index Number $\dfrac{\Sigma p_1 q_0}{\Sigma p_0 q_0} \times 100 = \dfrac{700}{540} \times 100 = 129.63$

Paasche's Index Number $\dfrac{\Sigma p_1 q_1}{\Sigma p_0 q_1} \times 100 = \dfrac{590}{456} \times 100 = 129.39$

Additional dearness allowance to be paid as per Laspeyre's Index Number = 29.63%

Additional dearness allowance to be paid as per Paasche's Index Number = 29.39%

Chapter Test

Multiple Choice Questions

1. Fisher's index number is the
   (a) arithmetic mean of index numbers of Laspeyre and Passche.   (b) harmonic mean of index number of Laspeyre and Paasche.
   (c) geometric mean of index numbers of Laspeyre and Passche.   (d) None of the above

2. Which of the following measures changes in retail price of the commodities?
   (a) Wholesale Price Index   (b) Weighted Index   (c) Consumer Price Index   (d) None of these

3. Cost of living index numbers are also used to find real wage by the process of
   (a) base shifting   (b) splicing of index number   (c) deflating of index number   (d) None of the above

4. .... is the benchmark index for the Indian stock market.
   (a) Price index   (b) Agricultural index   (c) Sensex   (d) None of these

5. Consumer Price Index number for the year 1957 was 313 with 1940 as the base year, the average monthly wages in 1957 of the workers in a factory was ₹ 160. Their real wage is
   (a) 48.40   (b) 51.12   (c) 40.30   (d) None of these

Short Answer (SA) Type Questions

1. Why is it essential to have different CPI for different categories of consumers?

2. Write any three uses of index number especially in economics.

3. What methods are used for constructing Consumer Price Index number?

4. "Index numbers measures the changes in the variables under study." Name some of the variables in which the changes are studied.

5. Calculate weighted price relatives index

Commodity	Weight in%	Base Year Price in (₹)	Current Year (₹)	Price Relative
A	40	2	4	200
B	30	5	6	120
C	20	4	5	125
D	10	2	3	150

Long Answer (LA) Type Questions

1. Calculate weighted aggregative price index from the following data using Fisher's method.

Commodity	Base Year		Current Year	
	Price (₹)	Quantity	Price (₹)	Quantity
A	2	10	4	5
B	5	12	6	10
C	4	20	5	15
D	2	15	3	10

2. Given the following data

Item	Base Year		Current Year	
	Price (₹)	Quantity	Price (₹)	Quantity
A	1	10	2	5
B	1	5	X	2

Find X, if the ratio between Laspeyre's and Paasche's index number is 28 : 27.

Answers

Multiple Choice Questions

   1. (c)   **2.** (c)   **3.** (c)   **4.** (c)   **5.** (b)

For Detailed Solutions
Scan the code

PART B

Introductory Microeconomics

CHAPTER 01

Producer's Behaviour

In this Chapter

- Production
- Concept of Cost
- Concept of Revenue

Production

A producer or a firm requires different inputs like labour, machines, land, raw materials, etc. By combining these inputs in different proportions, firms produce output. This is called the process of production. Thus, production is a process of the transformation of input into output.

Factors of Production

The inputs that a firm uses in the production process are called factors of production. It includes

1. **Factor Inputs** These factors include factors of production such as land, labour, capital and entrepreneurs. The prices of these factors are rent, wage, interest and profit respectively.

    The above factor inputs are further classified as

    (i) **Fixed Inputs** These are the inputs which do not change with the change in output, e.g. land and machine.

    (ii) **Variable Inputs** These are the inputs which change with the change in the level of output, e.g. casual labour.

2. **Non-factor Inputs** These factors include raw material and fuels.

Concept of Time Period in Production

Time period is categorised as under

1. **Market Period or Very Short Period** It is the period of time during which production factors cannot be changed at all.

2. **Short Period** It is a time period in which the producer can change only the variable factors, while the fixed factors remain constant.

3. **Long Period** It is a time period when the producer has enough time to change all the factors. In fact, all factors are variable in long-run.

Production Function

Production function is a functional relationship between inputs used and output produced by the firm. It expresses the maximum quantity of output that can be produced with any given quantities of inputs. Production function considers only the efficient use of inputs that helps in getting the maximum possible output.

A production function is defined for a given technology. If the technology improves, the level of output obtainable for different input combinations also increases.

It is expressed in terms of the following equation

$$Qx = f(L, K)$$

Here, Q_X = Production of commodity X

L = Labour, K = Capital

Here, it is assumed that only two factors of production are used for production, i.e. labour and capital.

Types of Production Function

It can be of two types which are as follows

1. **Short-run Production Function** It refers to the situation when production is increased by increasing variable input only, keeping fixed factor constant. This function is also called as **variable proportion type production function**.

Mathematically, it is expressed as

$$Q_x = f(L, \overline{K})$$

Here, Q_x = Output of commodity X,

　　L = Labour (variable factor)

　　f = Functional relation

　　$\overline{K}$ = Capital (Fixed factor)

2. **Long-run Production Function** It refers to the situation in which all the factor inputs are increased to increase the output in same proportion. In long-run, all factors variable, thus it is expressed as

$$Q_x = f(L, K)$$

Here, Q_x = Output of commodity X,

　　L = Labour, f = Functional relation

　　K = Capital

Concept of Product

There are mainly three concepts of product viz, Total Product (TP), Average Product (AP) and Marginal Product (MP).

1. **Total Product** (TP) It is the sum total of output produced by all the units of labour along with other factors of production. It is also referred to as **Total Physical Product** of the variable input.

   It is calculated as

   $$TP = \Sigma MP$$

   Or　　$= TP_1 + TP_2 + \ldots + TP_n$

   Or　　$= AP \times L$

   The shape of TP curve is steep from the origin, then begins to get flatten and eventually drops-off.

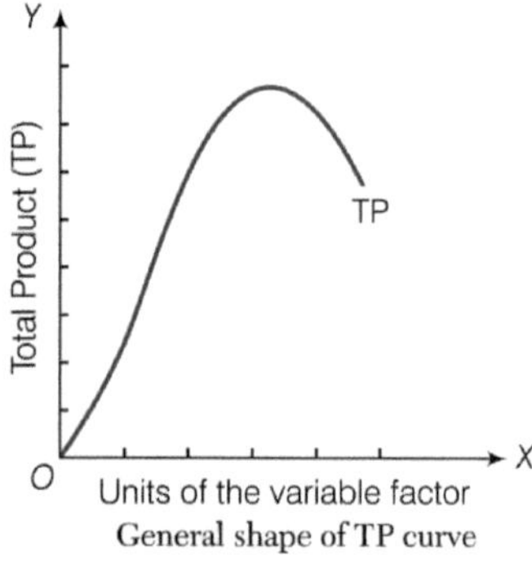
General shape of TP curve

2. **Average Product** (AP) It is per unit production of the variable factor. It is obtained by dividing the total product by the number of units of variable inputs. It is also referred to as **Average Physical Product**. The Average Product curve is hump shaped or inverted 'U' shaped. It is calculated as

$$AP = TP / L$$

As Labour (L) is taken as variable factor.

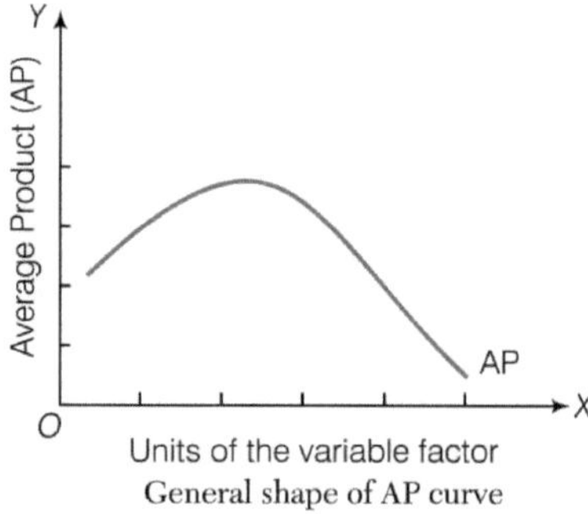
General shape of AP curve

3. **Marginal Product** (MP) It is the change in total production as a result of a unit change in the input of a variable factor. Marginal product is an addition made to the total product by employing an additional unit of variable input, keeping the other inputs unchanged. It is also referred to as **Marginal Physical Product**. It is calculated as　$MP = TP_n - TP_{n-1}$

Or　　　　　　$$MP = \frac{\Delta TP}{\Delta L}$$

The Marginal Product curve is generally inverted 'U' shape.

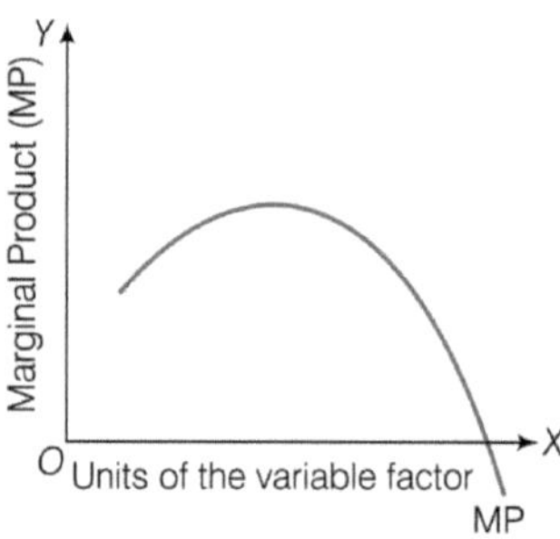
General shape of MP curve

Example 1. Calculate TP and MP when AP and L is given.

Units of Labour (L)	Average Product (AP)
1	50
2	60
3	70
4	80

Ans.

L	AP	TP = AP × L	$MP_{nth} = TP_n - TP_{n-1}$
1	50	50	50
2	60	120	70
3	70	210	90
4	80	320	110

Example 2. Calculate Total Product and Marginal Product of a firm, if its Average Product is as under

Labour	1	2	3	4	5	6
Average Product	10	12	14	12	10	8

Ans.

Units of Labour (L)	Average Product (AP)	Total Product (AP ×L)	Marginal Product ($TP_n - TP_{n-1}$)
1	10	10	—
2	12	24	14
3	14	42	18
4	12	48	6
5	10	50	2
6	8	48	−2

Returns to a Factor: Law of Variable Proportion

This law relates to short-run, in which to increase the production, only variable factor can be increased. It states that as more and more units of a variable factor are employed with fixed factors, total product increases at an increasing rate in the beginning, then increases at a diminishing rate, reaches its maximum and finally starts falling.

Assumptions of Law

Assumptions followed in the law of variable proportion are

- Technique of production does not change.
- All units of variable factor are equally efficient.
- Factors of production are not perfect substitute of each other.
- There must be some inputs whose quantity is kept fixed. Because of this, the ratio between the fixed factor and variable factor changes.

Explanation of the Law

This law may be explained with the help of following schedule and diagram (based on hypothetical data)

Units of Land	Units of Labour	Total Product	Marginal Product	Stage
1	1	2	2	
1	2	5	3	I = Increasing returns
1	3	9	4	
1	4	12	3	
1	5	14	2	II = Diminishing returns
1	6	15	1	
1	7	15	0	III = Negative returns
1	8	14	−1	

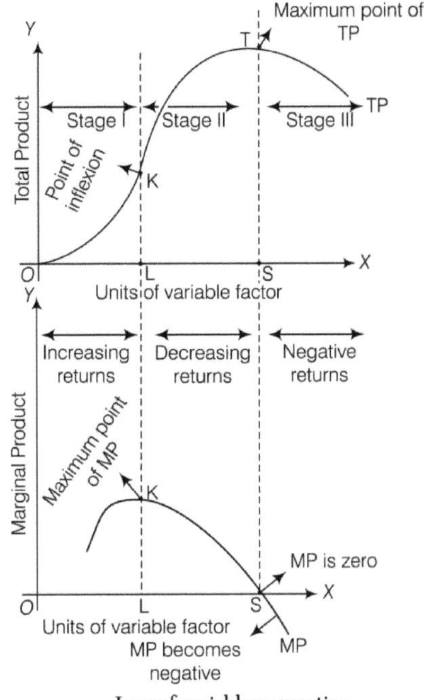

Law of variable proportion

Following observations can be made from the above table and curve

- MP rises till 3rd unit of labour are employed. In this stage, TP increases at an increasing rate. This stage is called stage of **increasing returns to factors**.
- With the use of 4th unit of labour, MP starts decreasing but remains positive and TP increases only at decreasing rate. This stage is called stage of **diminishing returns to factors**.
- At 7th unit of variable factor, when decreasing MP reduces to zero, TP is maximum and constant.
- At 8th unit of variable factor, when MP is negative, TP starts declining. This stage is called stage of **negative returns to factor**.

Stages of Law of Variable Proportion

Generally, there are three stages of law of variable proportion

1. **Stage of Increasing Returns to Factor** In the diagram, it is between O to K on the TP curve. In this zone, MP is increasing and because of this TP is increasing at an increasing rate.

   In this stage, increasing returns to a variable factor is obtained because greater use of the variable factors makes it possible to utilise the fixed indivisible factors fully and to introduce a greater degree of division of labour.

Increasing returns to a factor occur because of the following factors

- Fuller utilisation of the fixed factor.
- Increased efficiency of the variable factor.
- Better coordination between the factors.

2. **Stage of Diminishing Returns to Factor** In the diagram, it is between K to T on TP curve. In this zone, MP is decreasing but remains positive and because of this TP is increasing at a decreasing rate.

In this stage, diminishing returns to a factor is obtained because in this stage, the proportion between the variable factor such as labour has less fixed factors to work upon.

K is the **point of inflexion** where TP stops increasing at an increasing rate and instead, starts increasing at a decreasing rate.

Diminishing returns to a factor occur because of the following factors

- Fixity of the factor.
- Imperfect factor substitutability.
- Poor coordination between the factors.

3. **Stage of Negative Returns to Factor** In the diagram, it is beyond point T on TP curve. In this zone, TP starts declining because MP becomes negative.

In this stage, the variable factors become too much relative to fixed factors, disturbing the production process due to which there is a fall in total product.

Negative returns to a factor occur because of the following factors

- Limitation of fixed factor.
- Decrease in efficiency of variable factor.
- Poor coordination between the fixed factor and the variable factor.

Postponement of the Law

Postponement of law of variable proportions is possible under the two conditions given below

- When there is improvement in technology used in the process of production, so that greater output is achieved with the same inputs.
- When some substitute of the fixed factor is discovered, so that the constraint of fixity of the factor is removed.

Law of Diminishing Marginal Product

(Law of Variable Proportion in Terms of Marginal Product)

This law states that with the increase in a variable factor, keeping all other factors constant, the marginal product of the variable factor diminishes after a certain level of production and eventually becomes negative.

This law was given by classical economists and related to agriculture.

This law may be explained with the help of an imaginary schedule and diagram

Land (acre)	Labour (Units)	Total Product (Quantity)	Marginal Product (Quantity)	
5	1	50	50	
5	2	110	60	
5	3	180	70	
5	4	260	80	
5	5	340	80	
5	6	410	70	
5	7	470	60	
5	8	520	50	Law of Diminishing Marginal Product
5	9	550	30	
5	10	560	10	
5	11	560	0	
5	12	550	−10	
5	13	530	−20	

Marginal Product curve

Note *Law of diminishing marginal product operates in the second stage of law of variable proportion.*

In the above diagram, after point 'a' on MP curve, marginal product diminishes continuously, showing the law of diminishing marginal product, i.e., with the employment of 6th labour, diminishing returns operates.

Relationship between TP, AP and MP Curves

The relationship between product curves can be understood with the help of following graph

From the given curves in graph below, following observations are made on the relationship between TP and MP

- When TP increases at an increasing rate, MP also increases.
- When TP increases at a diminishing rate, MP declines, but remains positive.
- When TP reaches its maximum, MP becomes zero.
- When TP begins to decline, MP becomes negative.

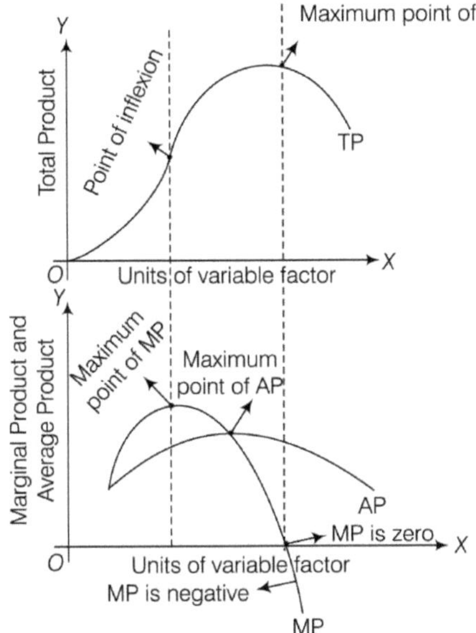

From the given curves, following observations are made on the relationship between AP and MP

- AP increases so long as MP > AP.
- AP decreases when MP < AP.
- AP is at its maximum when AP = MP.
- MP may be zero or negative, but AP continues to be positive.
- AP increases, even when MP falls but MP should lie above AP.

Example 3. Identify different phases of the law of variable proportion from the following schedule. Give reasons.

Variable Inputs (Units)	Total Product (TP) (Units)	Marginal Product (MP) (Units)
1	4	4
2	9	5
3	13	4
4	15	2
5	15	0
6	12	−3

Ans.

Variable Inputs (Units)	TP (Units)	MP (Units)	Stages of Law of Variable Proportion	
1	4	4 ⎤		TP is increasing at an increasing rate and MP is also increasing.
2	9	5 ⎦	Stage I	
3	13	4 ⎤		TP is increasing at a diminishing rate and MP starts declining.
4	15	2 ⎦	Stage II	
5	15	0 ⎤		MP becomes negative and TP falls.
6	12	−3 ⎦	Stage III	

Concept of Cost

Cost refers to the monetary and non-monetary expenditure incurred by a producer on the factor as well as non-factor inputs for producing a given amount of output of a commodity.

Cost of production incurred by producer can also be classified as

1. **Implicit Cost** This is the cost of self-owned and self-employed resources. e.g. rent of producer's own land, interest on producer's own capital.

   This cost is also referred to as non-accounting cost. This is called implicit because producers do not make payments to others for this kind of cost. It is measured in terms of opportunity cost.

2. **Explicit Cost** This cost includes those cash payments, which firms make to outsiders for hiring their services and goods. e.g. wages, payment for raw material, rent, interest, etc.

3. **Opportunity Cost** It refers to the cost of the second best alternative cost forgone. It is considered essential as it provides basis of concept of cost.

Cost Function

A cost function shows the functional relationship between output and cost of production.

Cost function is given as $C = f(Q)$

Here, C = Cost, Q = Units of output
f = Functional relationship

Cost function of a firm depends on two factors

- Quantum of goods produced.
- Prices of factors of production.
- Government taxation policy.

Short-run Costs

Short-run costs are the costs during which some factors are in fixed supply like plant and machinery. These are divided into Fixed Cost, Variable Cost, Total Cost, Marginal Cost, Average Cost, Average Fixed Cost and Average Variable Cost.

1. **Fixed Cost** (FC) or **Total Fixed Cost** (TFC) Fixed cost is the sum total of expenditure incurred by the producer on the purchase or hiring of fixed factors of production. These are also called **supplementary costs** or **overhead costs** or **indirect costs**. e.g. rent of the factory, insurance premium, salaries of the permanent employees, etc.

   These costs cannot be avoided, also they do not vary with the level of output. Fixed costs are not zero at zero level of output.

Units of Output	Fixed Cost (₹)
0	10
1	10
2	10
3	10

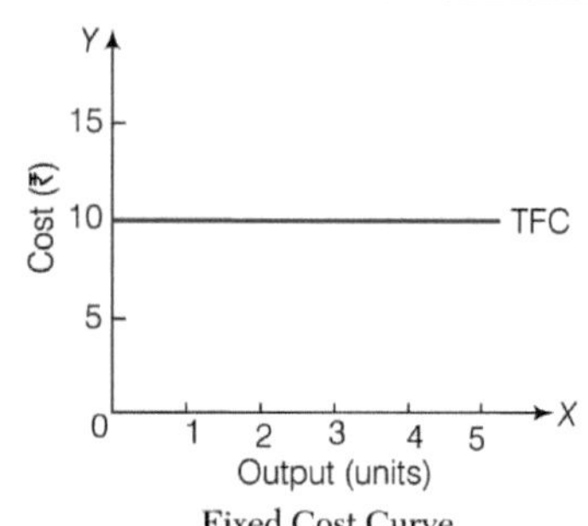
Fixed Cost Curve

   Total fixed cost curve is a straight line parallel to X-axis, indicating that total fixed cost is constant at all levels of output.

2. **Variable Cost** (VC) or **Total Variable Cost** (TVC) This is the cost incurred on hiring variable factors of production. Variable cost varies directly with the quantity of output produced. These are also called **prime costs, special costs** or **direct costs**. e.g. wages of labour, cost of raw materials, fuel, electricity, etc.

   Variable cost is defined as the expenditure incurred by a producer on the use of variable factors of production. It is zero at zero level of output.

Units of Output	Variable Cost (₹)
0	0
1	10
2	18
3	24
4	28
5	32

Total variable cost curve initially increases at decreasing rate and finally increases at an increasing rate. It is positively sloped as shown in graph below

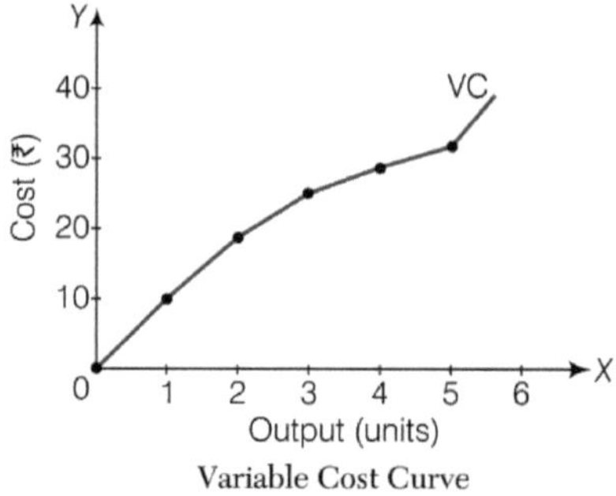
Variable Cost Curve

3. **Total Cost** (TC) Total Cost is defined as the aggregate of all costs of production at a given level of output. TC is derived by the sum total of TFC and TVC,

   i.e. $$TC = TFC + TVC.$$

Output (Units)	Fixed Cost (₹)	Variable Cost (₹)	Total Cost (₹)
0	10	0	10
1	10	10	20
2	10	18	28
3	10	24	34
4	10	28	38
5	10	32	42

Total cost curve is parallel to total variable cost curve. It shows the difference between TC and TVC, i.e. TFC, which is constant at all levels.

Because of this, the difference between TC and VC curves is the same at all levels.

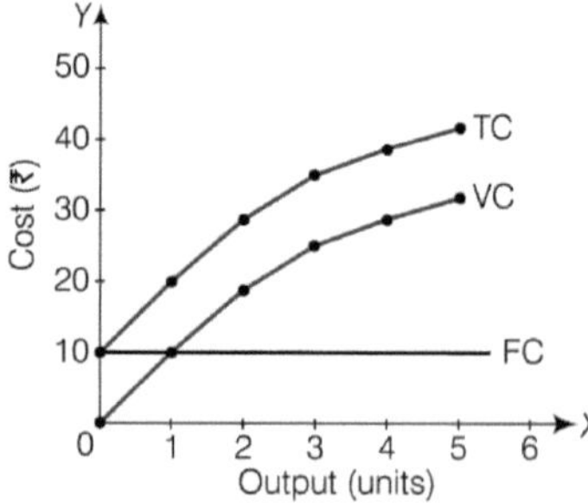

4. **Average Cost** (AC) It is the cost per unit of output produced. It is also called **unit cost of production.**

   It is obtained by dividing the Total Cost by the total number of units produced.

   $$\text{Average Cost (AC)} = \frac{\text{Total Cost (TC)}}{\text{Number of Units Produced (Q)}}$$

Output (Units)	Total Cost (₹)	Average Cost (₹)
0	10	—
1	20	20
2	28	14
3	34	11.33
4	38	9.5
5	42	8.4

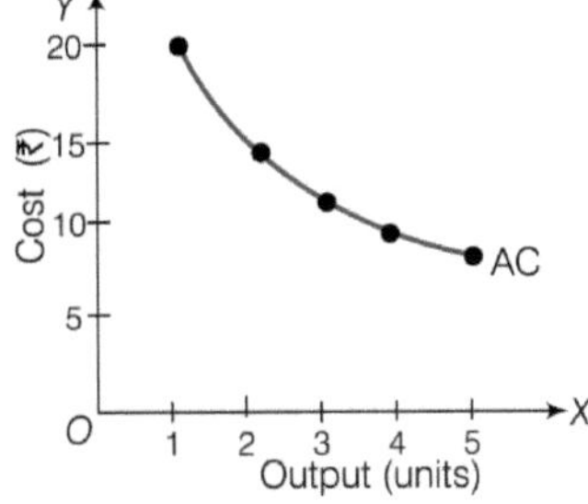

The AC curve derived from TC curve is 'U' shaped. It shows that as output increases, the value of AC falls continuously till it reaches a minimum point and then starts to rise. It comprises of

(i) **Average Fixed Cost** (AFC) It is defined as the fixed cost of producing per unit of the commodity. It is obtained by dividing TFC by the level of output.

$$AFC = \frac{TFC}{\text{Number of Units Produced (Q)}} \ Or \ \frac{TFC}{Q}$$

AFC falls continuously with the rise in the level of output however, it never becomes zero, as TFC always remains positive. The AFC curve derived from TFC curve is a rectangular hyperbola, as the area under the curve at each point is exactly the same.

(ii) **Average Variable Cost** (AVC) It is defined as the variable cost of producing per unit of the commodity.

It is obtained by dividing TVC by the level of output.

$$AVC = \frac{TVC}{\text{Number of Units Produced (Q)}} \ Or \ \frac{TVC}{Q}$$

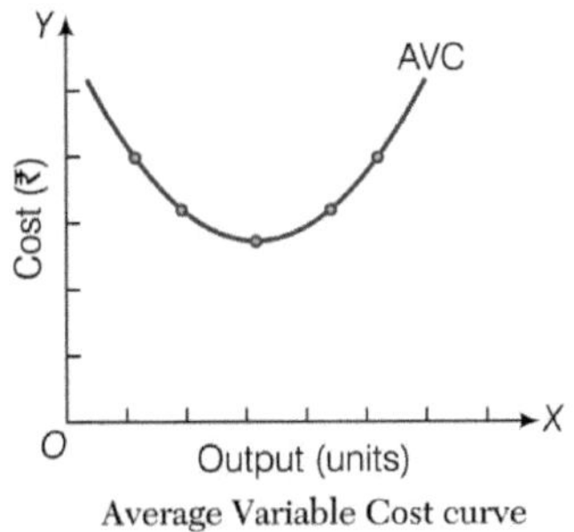

Average Variable Cost curve

AVC curve is always 'U' shaped showing the behaviour of declining cost in the initial stages and rising finally in the later stages.

5. **Marginal Cost** (MC) It is defined as addition made to total variable cost or total cost when one more unit of output is produced.

$$MC_{nth} = TC_n - TC_{n-1} \ Or \ TVC_n - TVC_{n-1}$$

Output (Units)	Total Variable Cost (₹)	Marginal Cost (₹)
0	0	—
1	10	10
2	18	8
3	24	6
4	28	4
5	34	6

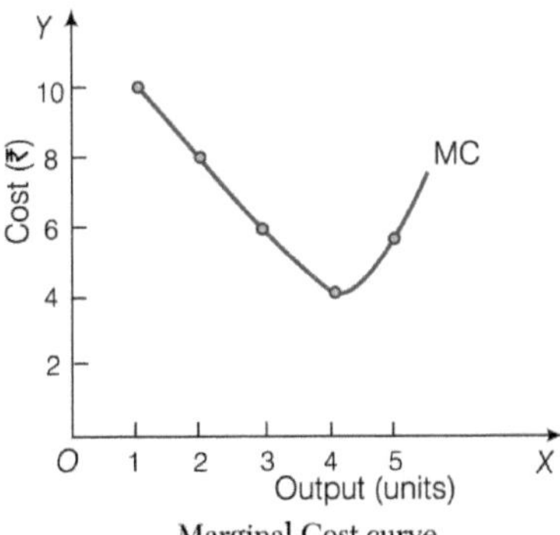

Marginal Cost curve

Marginal cost curve is also 'U' shaped indicating that Marginal cost falls in the beginning due to operation of law of increasing return and ultimately, it rises due to the operation of law of decreasing return. MC is addition to the variable cost as fixed cost remains constant.

Example 4. Complete the following table

Output (Units)	Average Fixed Cost (AFC) (₹)	Average Variable Cost (AVC) (₹)	Marginal Cost (MC) (₹)	Total Cost (TC) (₹)	Average Cost (AC) (₹)
1	...	...	18	...	...
2	36	16	14	...	...
3	24	...	...	120	...
4	18	18	...	...	...

Ans.

Output (Q) (Units)	TFC (₹)	AFC (₹)	AVC (₹)	MC (₹)	TC (₹)	AC (₹)	TVC (₹)
1	72	72	18	18	90	90	18
2	72	36	16	14	104	52	32
3	72	24	16	16	120	40	48
4	72	18	18	24	144	36	72

Formulae used

$$TC = TFC + TVC$$

$$TVC = AVC \times Q$$

$$AVC = TVC/Q$$

$$\text{Or} \quad AC - AFC$$

$$MC_{nth} = TVC_n - TVC_{n-1}$$

$$AFC = \frac{TFC}{Q}, \ TFC = AFC \times Q$$

Example 5. Complete the following table

Output (Units)	Total Cost (TC) (₹)	Average Fixed Cost (AFC) (₹)	Average Variable Cost (AVC) (₹)	Marginal Cost (MC) (₹)
0	36	—	—	—
1	...	...	...	18
2	...	...	...	14
3	...	...	16	...
4	...	...	...	24

Ans.

Output (Q) (Units)	TC (₹)	TFC (₹)	AFC (₹)	AVC (₹)	MC (₹)	TVC (₹)
0	36	36	—	—	—	0
1	**54**	36	**36**	18	18	18
2	**68**	36	18	16	14	32
3	**84**	36	12	16	**16**	48
4	**108**	36	9	18	24	72

Formulae used

$$TC = TFC + TVC,$$

$$TVC = AVC \times Q$$

$$AVC = TVC/Q \ or \ AC - AFC$$

$$MC_{nth} = TVC_n - TVC_{n-1}$$

$$AFC = \frac{TFC}{Q}$$

TFC = First value of TC at zero level of output

Relations between Cost Curves

There exists a close relationship between the various costs, which can be studied under following sub-heads

1. **Relationship between Average Cost (AC) and Marginal Cost (MC)**
   - When AC falls, MC is less than AC.

- When AC rises, MC is greater than AC.
- When AC is constant and minimum, MC is equal to AC.
- MC is always to the left of AC and cuts AC from its lowest point.

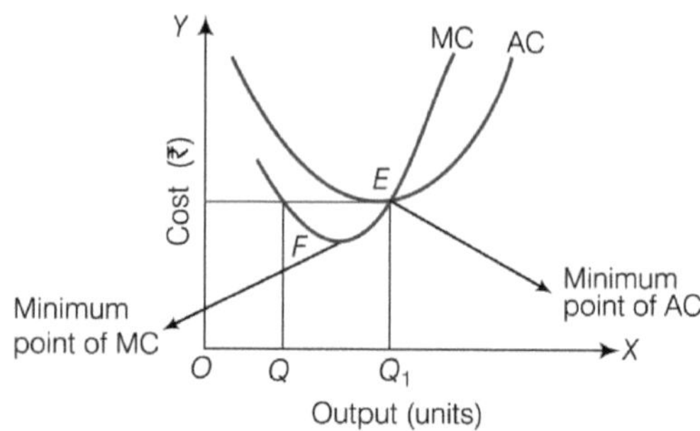

Diagrammatic representation of relationship between AC and MC

2. **Relationship between Marginal Cost (MC) and Average Variable Cost (AVC)**
   - When AVC is falling, AVC > MC.
   - When AVC is constant and minimum, AVC = MC.
   - When AVC is rising, AVC < MC.
   - MC curve cuts AVC curve at its lowest point.
   - Both AVC and MC curves are 'U' shaped.
   - Both AVC and MC curves start from same point.

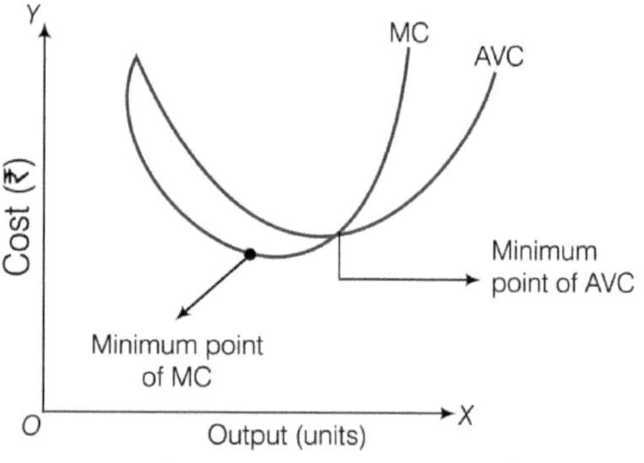

Diagrammatic representation of relationship between MC and AVC

3. **Relationship between Total Cost (TC) and Marginal Cost (MC)**
   - MC is estimated as the difference between TC of two successive units of output.
   $$MC_{nth} = TC_n - TC_{n-1}$$
   - When MC is diminishing, TC increases at a diminishing rate.
   - When MC is rising, TC increases at an increasing rate.
   - When MC reaches its lowest point, TC stop increasing at a decreasing rate, it represents the point of inflexion of TC curve.

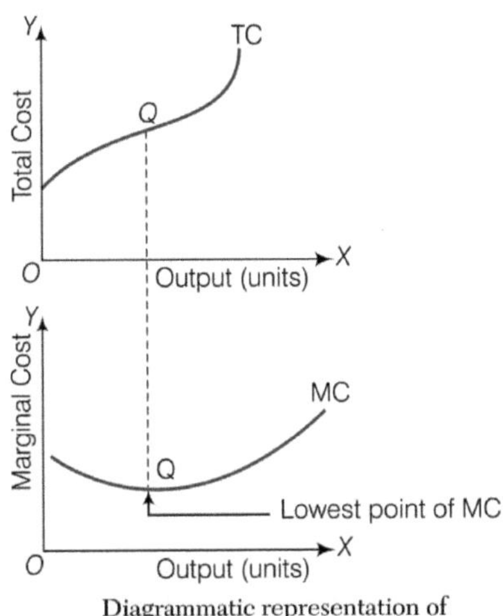

Diagrammatic representation of
relationship between TC and MC

4. **Relationship between TVC and MC** We know, MC is
addition to TVC when one more unit of output is
produced. So, TVC can be obtained as summation of
MC's of all the units produced.

If output is assumed to be perfectly divisible, then total
area under the MC curve will be equal to TVC.

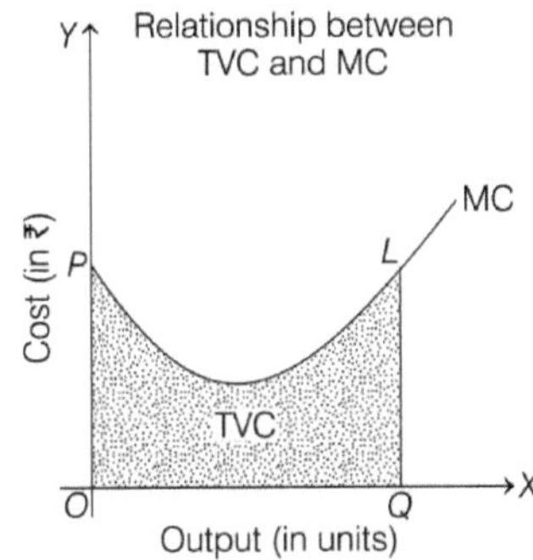

As seen in the diagram, at OQ level of output, TVC is
equal to the shaded area OPLQ in the diagram.

Concept of Revenue

Revenue is the money payment received from the sale of a
commodity.

In other words, the revenue of a firm is its sale receipts or
money receipts which is received from the sale of a product.
Revenue is different from the profit. Profit forms part of
revenue, i.e.

$$\text{Revenue} = \text{Costs} + \text{Profit}$$

Concept of revenue has three variants, viz Total Revenue
(TR), Average Revenue (AR) and Marginal Revenue (MR).

1. **Total Revenue** It is defined as the total or aggregate of
proceeds to the firm from the sale of different
commodities. It can be calculated by multiplying the
units of the sales with the price. Also, it is sum of total
marginal revenue. i.e.

$$TR = P \times Q \ or \ \Sigma MR$$

where,   TR = Total Revenue
           P = Price
           Q = Quantity
           MR = Marginal Revenue

2. **Average Revenue** It is revenue per unit of output sold.
It can be obtained by dividing total revenue by the
quantity sold.

In other words, it is the per unit revenue received from
the sale of one unit of a commodity, i.e. $AR = \dfrac{TR}{Q}$

where,   AR = Average Revenue
           TR = Total Revenue
           Q = Quantity

It is said that $AR = P$

As we know, $AR = \dfrac{TR}{Q}$ ...(a)

$$TR = P \times Q$$ ...(b)

(Here, P = Price, Q = Quantity or output sold)

Thus, $AR = \dfrac{P \times Q}{Q}$ [from equation (a) and (b)]

Hence, it is proved, AR = Price.

3. **Marginal Revenue** It is the addition to total revenue
by the sale of an additional unit of the commodity. i.e.

$$MR = TR_n - TR_{n-1} \quad Or \quad \dfrac{\Delta TR}{\Delta Q}$$

Where,   MR = Marginal Revenue
         TR = Total Revenue
         TR_{n-1} = Total Revenue from $(n-1)$ units
         TR_n = Total Revenue from n units
         ΔTR = Change in Total Revenue
         ΔQ = Change in Quantity

Example 6. In the given table, AR and output is given,
calculate TR and MR.

AR	Output
80	1
60	2
40	3
20	4

Ans.

AR	Output	TR = AR × Q	$MR_{n\text{th}} = TR_n - TR_{n-1}$
80	1	80	80
60	2	120	40
40	3	120	0

Relationship between TR, AR and MR

1. **Relationship between Revence Curves under Imperfect Competition** From the curves, following relationship is derived between TR and MR (at falling price)

   - TR increases at diminishing rate, when MR is diminishing but remains positive.
   - TR is maximum and constant, when MR is constant and zero.
   - TR decreases, when MR becomes negative.

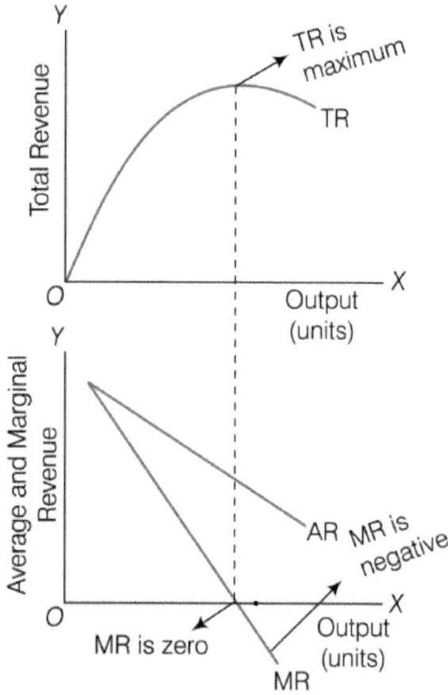

From the above curves, following relationship is derived between AR and MR

   - When AR is diminishing, AR > MR.
   - MR can be negative, but not AR.
   - Slope of AR is twice of slope of MR.

2. **Relationship between Revenue Curves Under Perfect Competition** This relationship is as follows

   - MR is merely an addition to TR when one more unit of output is sold.
   - In case, price is constant, then MR should also be constant and equal to AR. Both are parallel to X-axis.
   - Constant MR implies constant addition to TR when an additional unit of output is sold.
     This implies that TR will increase at constant rate, i.e. a straight line from origin.

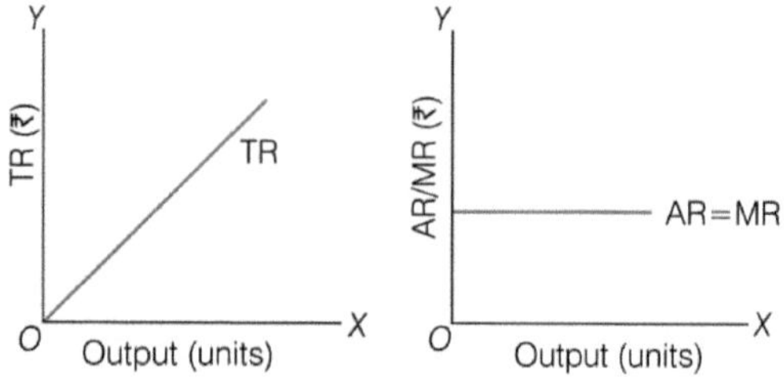

3. **General Relationship between the Revenue Concepts** This relationship is as follows

   - When TR increases at an increasing rate, MR and AR also increases.
   - When TR increases at a diminishing rate, MR falls but remains positive, AR increases to its maximum point and starts to fall.
   - When MR is zero, TR is constant and maximum.
   - When TR falls, MR becomes negative, AR falls but remains positive.
   - MR is equal to AR, at the maximum point of AR.

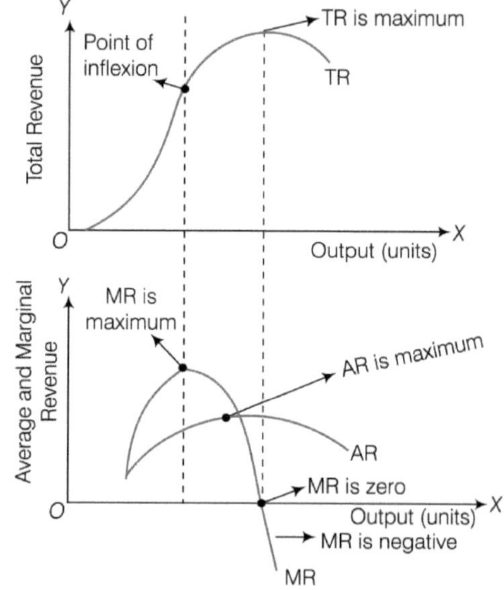

Firm's Revenue Curve in Different Markets

Generally, markets are of two types

- Perfectly competitive market
- Imperfectly competitive market

Again imperfect competition market includes three market forms, i.e.,

- Monopoly market Monopolistic market
- Oligopoly market

Firm's revenue curves are different in different markets, as discussed below

Revenue Curves under Perfect Competition

A firm under perfect competition is a price-taker. It cannot influence the market price, implying a constant AR for a firm corresponding to all levels of output.

Given the price, a firm under perfect competition can sell any amount of the commodity, it wishes to sell.

Marginal revenue, average revenue and price curve are the same and horizontally parallel to X-axis, i.e., we can say that under perfect competition, firm's AR and MR curves are perfectly elastic.

Firm's Revenue Status when Price is Fixed ($P = ₹\ 6$) (an imaginary schedule)

Output/ Sales (Units) (Q)	Average Revenue = Price (₹) $AR\ (P) = TR\ /\ Q$	Total Revenue (₹) $TR = AR \times Q$	Marginal Revenue (₹) $MR_{nth} = TR_n - TR_{n-1}$
1	6	6	6
2	6	12	6
3	6	18	6
4	6	24	6

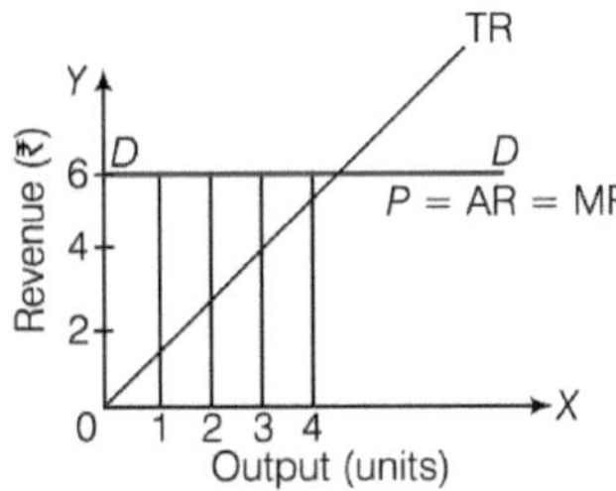

Firm's revenue curves under perfect competition

Revenue Curves under Imperfect Competition

It can be studied under various sub-heads which are as follows

1. **Revenue Curves under Monopoly** For a firm under monopoly, more of the commodity can be sold only at a lower price. This implies an inverse relationship between price of the commodity and demand for the firm's output. As a result, TR initially increases, reaches maximum and finally falls with increase in output.

   Hence, Average revenue and marginal revenue curves are downward sloping and negatively sloped, i.e. we can say that under monopoly, firm's AR and MR curves are inelastic.

Firm's Revenue Status when Price is set by the Producer to Sell more and more Units of Output (an imaginary schedule)

Output/ Sales (Units)(Q)	Average Revenue = Price (₹) $AR\ (P) = TR/Q$	Total Revenue (₹) $TR = AR \times Q$	Marginal Revenue (₹) $MR_{nth} = TR_n - TR_{n-1}$
1	9	9	9
2	8	16	7
3	7	21	5
4	6	24	3
5	5	25	1
6	4	24	−1
7	3	21	−3

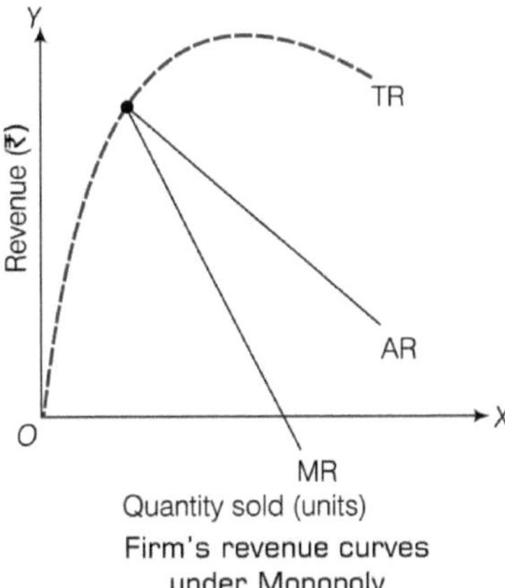

Firm's revenue curves under Monopoly

2. **Revenue Curves under Monopolistic Competition** For a firm under monopolistic competition, AR and MR curves are downward sloping and negatively sloped i.e., curves under monopolistic competition are similar to monopoly.

   In monopolistic situation, AR and MR curves are more elastic than in monopoly.

   It is because in a monopolistic competitive market, goods have close substitutes.

Firm's Revenue Status when Producers have Partial Control over Price (an imaginary schedule)

Output/ Sales (Units) (Q)	Average Revenue = Price (₹) $AR(P) = TR\ /\ Q$	Total Revenue (₹) $TR = AR \times Q$	Marginal Revenue (₹) $MR_{nth} = TR_n - TR_{n-1}$
1	9	9	9
2	8.5	17	8
3	8	24	7
4	7.5	30	6

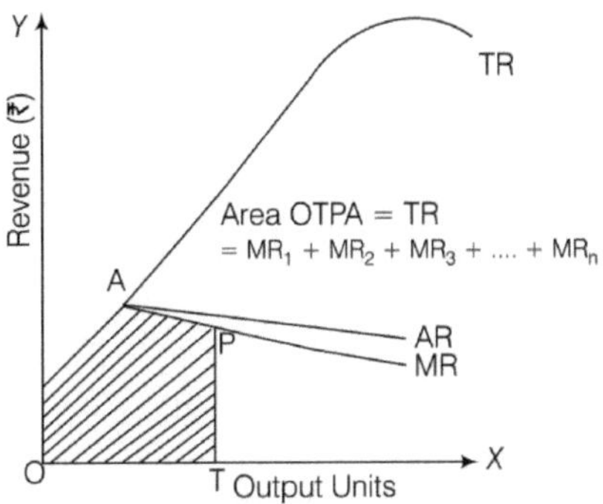

3. **Revenue Curves under Oligopoly** Under oligopoly, market revenue curves or demand curve are not clearly defined due to high degree of interdependence between the firms.

Chapter Practice

Objective Questions

• **Multiple Choice Questions**

1. Function showing relationship between input and output is known as ....
(a) Consumption function   (b) Investment function
(c) Production function   (d) Cost function

Ans. (c) Production function

2. What is 'production' in economics?
(a) Creation/Addition to the value of output
(b) Production of foodgrains
(c) Creation of services
(d) Manufacturing of goods

Ans. (a) Production in economics refers to adding value or creating something useful which has a market value.

3. When total product falls, then ....
(a) average product is equal to zero
(b) marginal product is equal to zero
(c) marginal product is negative
(d) average product continues to rise

Ans. (c) The movement in TP depends upon change in MP. So, when MP becomes negative, TP starts to diminish.

4. Average Product (AP) is at its maximum when
(a) MP > AP   (b) MP < AP
(c) MP = AP   (d) MP becomes negative

Ans. (c) Relationship between AP and MP
(i) AP increases as long as MP > AP.
(ii) AP decreases when MP < AP.
(iii) AP is maximum when AP = MP.

5. In which time period, all factors of production become variable and factors of production change with the change in level of production?
(a) Long period   (b) Market period
(c) Short period   (d) All of these

Ans. (a) Long period is a time period when producer changes both fixed and variable factors of production to change the level of production. There is no difference between fixed and variable factors in the long-run.

6. In the first stage of law of variable proportions, total product increases at an ....
(a) decreasing rate   (b) increasing rate
(c) constant rate   (d) Both (a) and (b)

Ans. (b) In the initial phase of production, all factors of production are highly efficient and hence, TP increases at an increasing rate with employment of each additional variable factor.

7. Increasing returns is applicable because of ....
(a) increased efficiency of variable factor
(b) fuller utilisation of fixed factor
(c) indivisibility of factors
(d) Both (a) and (b)

Ans. (d) Attainment of increasing returns to factor depends upon how the fixed factors are utilised along with the variable factors of production.

8. Law of variable proportion is valid when ....
(a) atleast one input is fixed and all other inputs are kept variable
(b) all factors are kept constant
(c) all inputs are varied in the same proportion
(d) None of the above

Ans. (a) atleast one input is fixed and all other inputs are kept variable

9. Which of the following curve is not 'U' shaped?
(a) AFC   (b) AVC
(c) MC   (d) AC

Ans. (a) AFC curve is rectangular hyperbola shaped in nature as TFC remains fixed for all levels of output including zero.

10. Payment made to outsiders for their goods and services are called ....
(a) Opportunity cost   (b) Real cost
(c) Explicit cost   (d) Implicit cost

Ans. (c) Explicit cost

11. When average cost curve is rising, then marginal cost curve ....
(a) must be decreasing   (b) must be constant
(c) must be rising   (d) Any of these

Ans. (c) MC curve lies above AC curve when AC is increasing thus, marginal cost also increases with increase in AC.

12. As output increases, average fixed cost curve ....
  (a) remains constant   (b) starts falling
  (c) starts rising   (d) None of these

Ans. (b) As output increases, AFC tends to fall continuously but it never becomes zero as TFC is always positive.

13. Area under MC curve is ....
  (a) total cost   (b) total fixed cost
  (c) total variable cost   (d) None of these

Ans. (c) TVC can be derived by adding each unit of MC, thus the area under MC curve is known as TVC.

14. Average Revenue is equal to ..... .
  (a) $\dfrac{\text{Total Revenue}}{\text{Quantity Sold}}$ (b) $\dfrac{\text{Average Revenue}}{2}$

  (c) $\dfrac{\text{Total Revenue}}{100}$ (d) $\dfrac{\text{Average Quantity}}{\text{Quantity Sold}} \times 2$

Ans. (a) $\dfrac{\text{Total Revenue}}{\text{Quantity Sold}}$

15. When the firm is producing 3 tonnes of sugar, it receives total revenue of ₹ 24. Raising production to 4 tonnes, increases total revenue to ₹ 28. Thus, marginal revenue is ....
  (a) ₹ 4   (b) ₹ 8
  (c) ₹ 28   (d) ₹ 52

Ans. (a) $MR = 28 - 24 = ₹ 4$

16. **Statement I** MC becomes zero when AC is at its minimum point.

  Statement II AC, AVC and MC curves always start from the same point.

  Alternatives
  (a) Statement I is correct and Statement II is incorrect
  (b) Statement II is correct and Statement I is incorrect
  (c) Both the statements are correct
  (d) Both the statements are incorrect

Ans. (b) Statement II is correct and Statement I is incorrect

17. **Statement I** Total revenue is the product of price per unit of output and units sold.

  Statement II Average revenue is the slope of marginal revenue.

  Alternatives
  (a) Statement I is correct and Statement II is incorrect
  (b) Statement II is correct and Statement I is incorrect
  (c) Both the statements are correct
  (d) Both the statements are incorrect

Ans. (a) Statement I is correct and Statement II is incorrect

18. If AR is ₹ 40 per unit from the sale of 3 goods and it is ₹ 30 per unit from the sale of 4 goods. Find the marginal revenue of 4th unit of goods.
  (a) ₹ 10   (b) ₹ 30
  (c) ₹ 40   (d) 0

Ans. (d) Total revenue from 3 goods sold, $TR_3 = AR \times Q$
$$= 40 \times 3 = ₹ 120$$
Total revenue from 4 goods sold, $TR_4 = AR \times Q$
$$= 30 \times 4 = ₹ 120$$
Marginal Revenue $(MR_4) = TR_4 - TR_3$
$$= 120 - 120 = 0$$

19. Choose the correct pair.

	Column I		Column II
A.	Overhead cost	(i)	Variable cost
B.	Total variable cost curve	(ii)	Starts from the point of TFC curve
C.	Marginal revenue	(iii)	Equal to Price when price is constant

  Codes
  (a) A–(i)   (b) B–(ii)
  (c) C–(iii)   (d) All the pairs

Ans. (c) C–(iii)

• Assertion-Reasoning MCQs

Direction (Q. Nos. 1 to 5) *There are two statements marked as Assertion (A) and Reason (R). Read the statements and choose the appropriate option from options the given below*
  (a) Both Assertion (A) and Reason (R) are true and Reason (R) is the correct explanation of Assertion (A)
  (b) Both Assertion (A) and Reason (R) are true, but Reason (R) is not the correct explanation of Assertion (A)
  (c) Assertion (A) is true, but Reason (R) is false
  (d) Assertion (A) is false, but Reason (R) is true

1. **Assertion** (A) Average product increases only when marginal product increases.

  Reason (R) Rate of change of marginal product is greater than rate of change in average product.

Ans. (d) Average product increases so long as marginal product is greater than average product.

2. **Assertion** (A) According to law of diminishing returns to factor, marginal physical product of labour decrease but remains positive.

  Reason (R) In the second stage of returns to factor, there is over utilisation of fixed factors.

Ans (a) Both Assertion (A) and Reason (R) are true and Reason (R) is the correct explanation of Assertion (A)

3. **Assertion** (A) Total variable cost curve is inversely 'S' shaped owing to law of variable proportions.

  Reason (R) In the initial stage of production, both fixed and variable factors are underutilised.

Ans. (a) Both Assertion (A) and Reason (R) are true and Reason (R) is the correct explanation of Assertion (A)

4. Assertion (A) During increasing returns to factor, total variable cost increases at a diminishing rate.

Reason (R) In the first phase of law of variable proportions, variable factors are highly efficient.

Ans. (a) Both Assertion (A) and Reason (R) are true and Reason (R) is the correct explanation of Assertion (A)

5. Assertion (A) A rational producer prefer producing in the second stage of law of variable proportion.

Reason (R) In the stage of diminishing returns, AP and MP both falls but AP lies above MP.

Ans. (b) A rational producer produces in the second phase as in this phase, marginal product decreases but remains positive.

• Case Based MCQs

1. **Direction** *Read the following text and answer question no. (i) to (vi) on the basis of the same.*

   Farmers in our country are mostly small and marginal. They produce for self-consumption and hardly have any surplus crop to sell in market. These farmers produce with the help of their family members. Also due to limited land holding at times, there are more labour working compared with what is actually required, this leads to disguised unemployment.

   Use of primitive tools and techniques further reduces the ability of these families to increase production.

   (i) In case of disguised unemployment, marginal product of labour is equal to
   (a) zero
   (b) positive
   (c) negative
   (d) Either (a) or (c)

Ans. (a) In case of disguised unemployment, marginal productivity of labour becomes zero. Thus, he/she does not contribute anything to output.

   (ii) In case of land, the 'law of returns to factor' is applicable in ....
   (a) short-run   (b) medium-run
   (c) long-run   (d) None of these

Ans. (a) short-run

   (iii) In the above situation, productivity was low due to ....
   (a) fixity of land
   (b) use of primitive tools and techniques
   (c) excessive use of variable factor
   (d) All of the above

Ans. (d) All of the above

   (iv) A rational producer should opt to produce in .... stage.
   (a) increasing-returns to scale
   (b) diminishing-returns to scale
   (c) constant returns to scale
   (d) None of the above

Ans. (b) diminishing-returns to scale

   (v) Which of the following is a variable factor of production in farming?
   (a) Farming land
   (b) Labour
   (c) Equipments
   (d) Both (b) and (c)

Ans. (d) Labour and equipments are variable factors as they vary directly with the level of output.

   (vi) **Assertion** (A) In case of disguised employment, total physical product becomes constant.

   Reason (R) When more people work at a place then required, additional workers does not contribute much to the output.

   Alternatives
   (a) Both Assertion (A) and Reason (R) are true and Reason (R) is the correct explanation of Assertion (A)
   (b) Both Assertion (A) and Reason (R) are true, but Reason (R) is not the correct explanation of Assertion (A)
   (c) Assertion (A) is true, but Reason (R) is false
   (d) Assertion (A) is false, but Reason (R) is true

Ans. (a) Both Assertion (A) and Reason (R) are true and Reason (R) is the correct explanation of Assertion (A)

2. **Direction** *Read the following text and answer question no. (i) to (vi) on the basis of the same.*

   Revenue is an important aspect of producer's behaviour. In indicates a firm's receipts from sales. In other words, it also indicates the demand for firm's goods and services. More sales usually indicates more revenue but higher sale depends upon the form of market and clasticity of demand. Firms have better control over price when demand is inelastic.

   (i) In which form of market, average revenue is inelastic?
   (a) Perfect competition   (b) Monopoly
   (c) Monopolistic   (d) None of these

Ans. (b) Monopoly

   (ii) Incremental revenue is always equal to price under .... market.
   (a) perfect competition   (b) monopoly
   (c) monopolistic   (d) None of these

Ans. (a) perfect competition

(iii) Average revenue under monopolistic competition is elastic due to

   (a) lower price   (b) greater choice
   (c) price control   (d) All of these

Ans. (b) greater choice

(iv) When average revenue is elastic, marginal revenue is

   (a) inelastic   (b) also elastic
   (c) perfectly elastic   (d) perfectly inelastic

Ans. (b) also elastic

(v) **Assertion** (A) Total revenue and profits are equal under the market with constant price.

Reason (R) When price becomes constant, additional revenue becomes equal to average revenue.

Alternatives

(a) Both Assertion (A) and Reason (R) are true and Reason (R) is the correct explanation of Assertion (A)

(b) Both Assertion (A) and Reason (R) are true, but Reason (R) is not the correct explanation of Assertion (A)

(c) Assertion (A) is true, but Reason (R) is false

(d) Assertion (A) is false, but Reason (R) is true

Ans. (d) Profit is the difference between revenue and cost thus, it's not always equal to each other.

(vi) .... curve represent the demand curve of a firm as mentioned in the given paragraph.

(a) Total revenue

(b) Average revenue

(c) Marginal revenue

(d) None of the above

Ans. (b) Average revenue

PART 2

Subjective Questions

• Short Answer (SA) Type Questions

1. Explain the concept of a production function. (NCERT)

Ans. It is the technological knowledge that determines the maximum levels of output that can be produced using different combinations of inputs.

If the technology improves, the maximum levels of output obtainable for different input combinations increase. Then we have a new production function.

e.g., A firm produce a product (Y) by using two inputs X_1 and X_2. Then production function can be expressed as

$$q_y = f(X_1 . X_2)$$

2. "Average product can never be zero while marginal product can be". Comment.

Ans. MP can become zero when production does not increase with increase in the number of variable factor. On the other hand, AP can never be zero as it is calculated on the basis of TP and variable units of input. Both TP and variable units cannot be zero which makes it impossible for AP to be zero. Hence, it is clear that MP can be zero, but AP will never be zero.

3. Explain the concepts of the short-run and the long-run. (NCERT)

Ans. **Short-run** Short-run refers to a period in which output can be changed by changing only variable factors.

In the short- run, fixed inputs like land, building, plant machinery etc, cannot be changed. It means, production can be raised by increasing only variable factors, but till the extent of fixed factors.

Long- run Long-run refers to a period in which output can be changed by changing all factors of production. In the long run, firm can change its factory size, techniques of production, purchase new plant machinery, patents etc.

4. Complete the following data

Units of Labour	Average Product (Units)	Marginal Product (Units)
1	8	—
2	10	...
3	...	10
4	9	...
5	...	4
6	7	...

Ans.

Units of Labour	Total Product (Units) (AP ×L)	Average Product (Units) (TP/L)	Marginal Product (Units) (TP$_n$ – TP$_{n-1}$)
1	8	8	—
2	20	10	12
3	30	10	10
4	36	9	6
5	40	8	4
6	42	7	2

5. State giving reasons, whether the following statements are true or false.

(i) When there are diminishing returns to a factor, total product first increases and then starts falling?

(ii) When marginal product falls, average product will also fall?

Ans. (i) False, this is because of decline in marginal product. Falling marginal product implies that total product continues to increase at a diminishing rate.

(ii) False, Average product can rise even when marginal product falls.

6. What is meant by returns to a factor? State the law of diminishing returns to a factor.

Ans. **Returns to a Factor** It refers to the behaviour of output when only one variable factor of production is increased in short-run and fixed factors remain constant.

Law of Diminishing Returns to a Factor It refers to a situation in which total output increases at a diminishing rate when more and more variable factor is combined with the fixed factor of production. In this situation, Marginal Product of the variable factor must be diminishing.

7. "Fixed cost of input is ignored in the study of the law of increasing return". Do you agree?

Ans. No, it is not correct. In fact, fixed cost plays an important role in deriving increasing returns from variable inputs.

A firm can leverage its fixed cost to derive better returns due to improved productivity of resources.

e.g. rent is paid every month for the factory space which is fixed cost.

By employing more labours, the production can be maximised and returns of paying rent as fixed cost can be increased. Hence, fixed cost is not ignored in the analysis of law of increasing returns to variable factor.

8. Define variable costs. Explain the behaviour of total variable cost as output increases.

Ans. Variable costs are those costs, which vary directly with the quantity of output produced.

Total variable cost increases with increase in output. Initially, it increases at decreasing rate. Eventually, it increases at an increasing rate.

9. A producer borrows money and opens a shop. The shop premises is owned by him. Identify implicit cost and explicit cost from this information. Also, explain.

Ans. In the above example, interest paid on borrowed money will be explicit cost, whereas, the imputed rent of the shop premises is implicit cost.

Explicit Cost These are those cash payments, which firms make to outsiders for their services and goods. e.g. wages, payment for raw material, rent, interest, etc.

Implicit Cost These are the costs of self-owned and self-employed resources. e.g. entrepreneur may utilise his own building for factory use, interest on self-capital, etc.

10. Complete the following table

Output (Q) (Units)	Total Variable Cost (TVC) (₹)	Average Variable Cost (AVC) (₹)	Marginal Cost (MC) (₹)
1	10	...	...
2	...	8	6
3	27	...	...
4	...	10	13

Ans.

Output (Q) (Units)	TVC (₹) (AVC×Q)	AVC (₹) (TVC/Q)	MC (₹) ($TVC_n - TVC_{n-1}$)
1	10	10	10
2	16	8	6
3	27	9	11
4	40	10	13

11. "Average revenue curve represents law of demand". Discuss.

Ans. Average revenue is determined by dividing total revenue by the quantity sold which indicates price of the commodity. Hence, average revenue curve shows the relationship between price of a commodity and quantity demanded.

It is downward sloping curve because to increase its sales, firms have to lower their prices. So, it possesses all the characteristics of the demand curve. Therefore, we can say that Average Revenue curve represents law of demand.

12. A firm can sell as many units of a good as it wants to sell at a given price. Prepare a schedule showing total revenue, average revenue and marginal revenue of such a firm.

Ans. $TR = AR \times Q$, $MR_{nth} = TR_n - TR_{n-1}$

Output/Sales (Units) (Q)	Average Revenue = Price (₹)	Total Revenue (₹) (AR ×Q)	Marginal Revenue (₹) ($TR_n - TR_{n-1}$)
1	5	5	5
2	5	10	5
3	5	15	5
4	5	20	5

13. Explain the relationship between AP and MP.

Ans. Relationship between AP and MP is stated below

(i) AP increases when MP is greater than AP.

(ii) AP is maximum when both MP and AP are equal.

(iii) AP decreases when MP is less than AP.

(iv) AP continues to be positive even when MP is zero or negative.

(v) AP may rise even when MP falls but lies above AP.

14. Explain the relationship between Marginal Cost and Average Cost using diagram.

Ans. Relationship between Marginal Cost (MC) and Average Cost (AC) is stated below

(i) When AC falls, MC is lower than AC.

(ii) When AC rises, MC is greater than AC.

(iii) When AC is constant and minimum, MC is equal to AC.

(iv) MC is always to the left of AC and cuts AC from its lowest point.

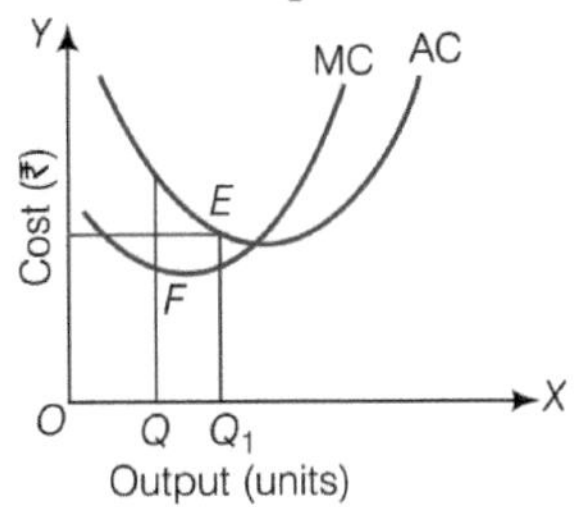

15. Why AC curve is 'U' shaped?

Ans. The main reason for this 'U' shaped AC curve is the operation of the law of variable proportion. We know as output increases, law of increasing return operates in the initial stages. At this stage, when a firm increases its output, it gets economies and the result is decline in average cost. After the point of optimum combination, economies turn into diseconomies and result in increase in output and average cost. This is the stage of law of diminishing returns.

16. Complete the following table

Output (Units)	Average Fixed Cost (AFC) (₹)	Marginal Cost (MC) (₹)	Total Cost (TC) (₹)
1	...	...	72
2	...	10	82
3	20	8	...
4	...	...	99
5	12	10	...

Ans.

Output (Q) (Units)	TFC (₹) (AFC ×Q)	AFC (₹) (TFC/Q)	TVC (₹) (AVC ×Q)	MC (₹) $(TVC_n - TVC_{n-1})$	TC (₹) (TFC + TVC)
1	60	**60**	12	**12**	72
2	60	**30**	22	10	82
3	60	20	30	8	**90**
4	60	**15**	39	9	99
5	60	12	49	10	**109**

17. State giving reasons, whether the following statements are true or false

(i) When Total Revenue is constant, Average Revenue will also be constant.

(ii) When Marginal Revenue falls to zero, Average Revenue becomes maximum.

(iii) Marginal Revenue is always the price at which the last unit of the commodity is sold.

(iv) When Marginal Revenue is positive and constant, Average Revenue and Total Revenue will both increase at constant rate.

Ans. (i) False, when Total Revenue is constant, Average Revenue will be diminishing.

(ii) False, when Marginal Revenue is zero, Average Revenue will be diminishing.

(iii) False, Marginal Revenue can never be the price at which the last unit of the commodity is sold. It simply refers to additional revenue, when an additional unit of output is sold.

(iv) False, because when Marginal Revenue is positive and constant, Total Revenue increases at constant rate but Average Revenue tends to be equal to Marginal Revenue.

18. Complete the following table.

Output (Units)	Price (₹)	Total Revenue (₹)	Marginal Revenue (₹)
4	9	36	—
5	...	...	4
6	...	42	...
7	6	...	...
8	...	40	...

Ans.

Output (Q) (Units)	Price (P) (₹) (TR/Q)	Total Revenue (TR) (₹) $(P \times Q)$	Marginal Revenue (MR) (₹) $(TR_n - TR_{n-1})$
4	9	36	—
5	8	40	4
6	7	42	2
7	6	42	0
8	5	40	– 2

19. Calculate total revenue from the following data

Output	Average Revenue
0	10
1	10
2	10
3	10
4	10
5	10

Ans.

Output	Average Revenue	Total Revenue
0	10	-
1	10	10
2	10	20
3	10	30
4	10	40
5	10	50

TR = AR X Q

20. Complete the following table

Price (₹)	Output (Units)	Total Revenue (₹)	Marginal Revenue (₹)
7	...	7	...
...	2	10	...
...	3	...	–1
1	...	...	– 5

Ans.

Price (P) (AR) (₹) (TR/Q)	Output (Q) (Units) (TR/P)	Total Revenue (TR) (₹) $(P \times Q)$	Marginal Revenue (MR) (₹) $(TR_n - TR_{n-1})$
7	1	7	7
5	2	10	3
3	3	9	– 1
1	4	4	– 5

21. Why the total revenue curve of a competitive firm faces a straight line passing through origin?

Ans. A competitive firm sells its output at the uniform price. The price or AR is constant and MR is also constant which is equal to AR.

The Total Revenue is the sum total of MR corresponding to different levels of output. Since, MR is constant, TR increases at a constant rate. Thus, TR curve is a straight line. It passes through the origin because when sale is zero, TR is also zero.

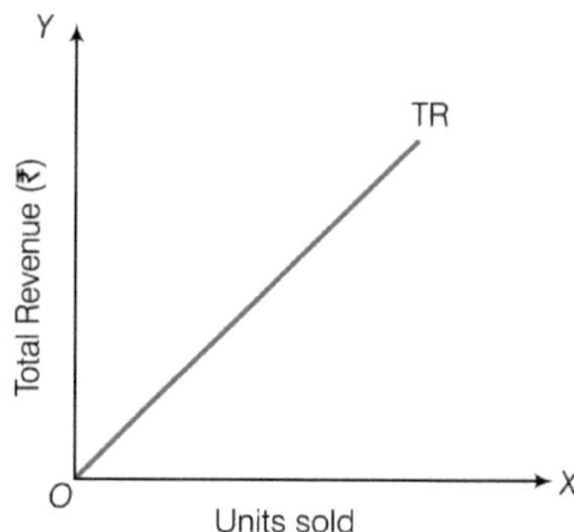

22. The following table gives the Average Product (AP) schedule of labour.

Find the Total Product (TP) and Marginal Product (MP) schedules. It is given that the Total Product is zero at zero level of labour employment.   **(NCERT)**

Labour	1	2	3	4	5	6
Average Product	2	3	4	4.25	4	3.5

Ans.

Units of Labour (L)	Average Product (AP)	Total Product (TP = AP/L)	Marginal Product $(MP_{nth} = TP_n - TP_{n-1})$
1	2.00	2	—
2	3.00	6	$6 - 2 = 4$
3	4.00	12	$12 - 6 = 6$
4	4.25	17	$17 - 12 = 5$
5	4.00	20	$20 - 17 = 3$
6	3.50	21	$21 - 20 = 1$

23. The following table gives the marginal product schedule of labour. It is also given that total product of labour is zero at zero level of employment.

Calculate the total and average product schedules of labour. **(NCERT)**

L	1	2	3	4	5	6
MP_L	3	5	7	5	3	1

Ans.

Labour (L)	MP of Labour (Units)	TP (Units)	AP (Units); $AP = \dfrac{TP}{L}$
1	3	3	3
2	5	$3+5=8$	4
3	7	$8+7=15$	5
4	5	$15+5=20$	5
5	3	$20+3=23$	4.60
6	1	$23+1=24$	4

• Long Answers (LA) Type Questions

1. State giving reasons, whether the following statements are true or false

(i) Average Variable Cost falls even when Marginal Cost is rising.

(ii) The difference between Total Cost and Total Variable Cost falls with increase in output.

(iii) As soon as Marginal Cost starts rising, Average Variable Cost also starts rising.

(iv) Average Cost falls only when Marginal Cost falls.

(v) The difference between Average Total Cost and Average Variable Cost is constant.

(vi) As output is increased, the difference between Average Total Cost and Average Variable Cost falls and ultimately becomes zero.

Ans. (i) True, Average Variable Cost can fall even when Marginal Cost is rising as minimum point of MC lies to the left of AVC.

(ii) False, because the difference between Total Cost and Total Variable Cost is equal to Total Fixed Cost which remains constant at all levels of output.

(iii) False, Average Variable Cost can fall even when Marginal Cost is rising.

(iv) False, Average Cost can fall even when Marginal Cost is rising.

(v) False, the difference between AVC and ATC is AFC which can never be constant. Since, AFC tends to decline with increase in output, the difference between ATC and AVC must reduce as output increases.

(vi) False, because as output increases, the difference between ATC and AVC falls but can never be zero. The difference is equal to AFC, which must remain positive, even when it is falling.

2. Discuss the causes of increasing returns to a factor.

Ans. Increasing returns to a factor occur because of the following factors

(i) **Fuller Utilisation of the Fixed Factor** In the initial stages, fixed factor remains underutilised. Its fuller utilisation is possible by adding additional units of the variable factor to total output and the Marginal Product of the variable factor tends to increase.

(ii) **Increased Efficiency of the Variable Factor** Additional application of the variable factor causes process based division of labour that raises efficiency of the factor. Accordingly, marginal productivity of the factor tends to rise.

(iii) **Better Coordination between the Factors** So long as fixed factor remains underutilised, additional application of the variable factor tends to improve. As a result, total output increases at an increasing rate.

3. Discuss the causes of diminishing returns to a factor.

Ans. Diminishing returns to a factor or the law of diminishing returns may be explained in terms of the following factors

(i) **Fixity of the Factor** It is the principal cause behind the law of diminishing returns.

As more and more units of the variable factor is combined with the fixed factor, the latter gets excessively utilised, leading to decrease in its productivity.

(ii) **Imperfect Factor Substitutability** Factors of production are imperfect substitutes of each other. e.g. more and more of labour cannot be continuously used in place of additional capital.

Accordingly, diminishing returns to the variable factor become inevitable.

(iii) **Poor Coordination between the Factors** Continuous increasing application of the variable factor alongwith fixed factors beyond a point, crosses the limit of ideal factor ratio.

This results in poor coordination between the fixed and variable factors.

4. Distinguish between

(i) Fixed Cost and Variable Cost with examples.　　　(ii) Average Cost and Marginal Cost with examples.

Ans. (i) Difference between Fixed Cost and Variable Cost

Basis	Fixed Cost	Variable Cost
Meaning	It does not change with change in quantity of output.	It changes with change in quantity of output.
Output	It remains the same whether output is zero or maximum.	It is zero when output is zero. It increases with increase in output and decreases with decrease in output.
Examples	Rent of building, licence fee, etc.	Cost of raw material, wages of casual labour, etc.

(ii) Difference between Average Cost and Marginal Cost

Basis	Average Cost	Marginal Cost
Meaning	It is the per unit cost of output.	It is the change in Total Cost when more and more additional unit of a commodity is produced.
Formula	$AC = TC/Q$	$MC_{nth} = TC_n - TC_{n-1}$ or $\Delta TC/\Delta Q$
Example	Production of 10 units is ₹ 70, then $AC = 70 \div 10 = ₹ 7$	For producing, 4 units of a commodity costs ₹170 and 5th unit costs ₹ 200. Then, $MC = 200 - 170 = ₹ 30$.

5. What are the total fixed cost, total variable cost and total cost of a firm? How are they related?　　　**(NCERT)**

Ans. Total Fixed Cost The cost which does not change with the change in output. Even when output is zero. In other words, fixed costs are the sum total expenditure on the purchase or hiring of fixed factors of production.

Total Variable Cost The cost which change with the change in output. In other words, variable costs are the expenditure incurred on the use of variable factors of production.

Total Cost Total cost is the sum total of total fixed cost and total variable cost at various level of output.

Relation among TFC, TVC and TC Cost Schedule Table

Output (Units)	TFC	TVC	TC = TFC + TVC
0	15	0	15+0=15
1	15	5	15+5=20
2	15	12	15+12=27
3	15	20	15+20=35
4	15	28	15+28=43
5	15	35	15+35=50
6	15	42	15+42=67

(i) TC = TFC + TVC.　　　　　　　　　　　　(ii) TFC is constant at all levels of output.

(iii) TVC increases as output increases.　　　　(iv) TC is parallel to TVC.

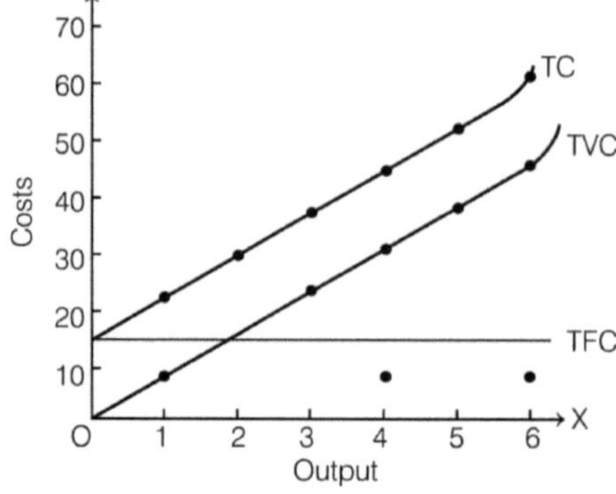

Multiple Choice Questions

1. Under the relationship between TP, MP and AP curves, MP becomes negative when
(a) TP increases   (b) TP decreases   (c) TP remain constant   (d) TP becomes zero

2. If the Average Product (AP) of a labour is 30 units of outputs, then find total product of 2 labours.
(a) 10 units of output   (b) 15 units of output   (c) 30 units of output   (d) 60 units of output

3. If the total product of 5 labours is 50 units of output and total product of 6 labours is 66 units of output, find Average Product (AP) of 6th unit of labour.
(a) 10 units of output   (b) 11 units of output   (c) 50 units of output   (d) 16 units of output

4. At the point of inflexion, the marginal product is ....
(a) increasing   (b) decreasing   (c) maximum   (d) negative

5. Which of the stages is relevant for a firm which aims at maximum economic efficiency in the law of variable proportion?
(a) Stage I   (b) Stage II   (c) Stage III   (d) Stage IV

6. Short-run supply curve of the firm is ..... .
(a) rising portion of MC curve
(b) rising portion of MC curve which lies above AVC curve
(c) rising portion of MC curve which lies above AFC curve
(d) entire MC curve

7. Cost function explain the relationship between
(a) income and expenditure   (b) input and output   (c) fixed cost and variable cost   (d) output and cost of production

Short Answer (SA) Type Questions

1. State giving reasons, whether the following statements are true or false
(i) When there are diminishing returns to a factor, total product always decreases?
(ii) Total Product will increase only when marginal product increases.

2. Giving reasons, state whenever the following statements are true or false
(i) Average product will increase only when marginal product increases.
(ii) With increase in level of output, average fixed cost goes on falling till reaches zero.
(iii) Under diminishing returns to factor, total product continues to increase till marginal product reaches zero.

3. Complete the following table

Output (Units)	Total Variable Cost (TVC) (₹)	Average Variable Cost (AVC) (₹)	Marginal Cost (MC) (₹)
1	...	12	...
2	20	...	...
3	...	10	10
4	40	...	...

4. Complete the following table

Output (Units)	Marginal Cost (MC) (₹)	Average Variable Cost (AVC) (₹)	Average Fixed Cost (AFC) (₹)	Average Cost (AC) (₹)
1	...	...	...	140
2	...	45	...	...
3	45	...	30	...
4	...	48	22.5	...
5	...	52	18	...

5. Why is average revenue always equal to price?

Long Answers (LA) Type Questions

1. (i) Draw average revenue and marginal revenue curves in a single diagram of a firm which can sell more units of a good only by lowering the price of that good. Explain.

(ii) Draw a single diagram of the average revenue and marginal revenue curves of a firm which can sell any quantity of the good at a given price. Explain.

2. (i) Complete the following table

Output (Units)	Price (₹)	Marginal Revenue (₹)	Total Revenue (₹)
1	...	10	10
2	...	4	...
3	...	...	15
4	...	− 3	...

(ii) Complete the following table

Output (Units)	Average Variable Cost (AVC) (₹)	Total Cost (TC) (₹)	Marginal Cost (MC) (₹)
1	...	60	20
2	18	...	...
3	...	...	18
4	20	120	...
5	22	...	...

Answers

Multiple Choice Questions

1. (b)   **2.** (d)   **3.** (b)   **4.** (c)   **5.** (b)   **6.** (b)   **7.** (d)

For Detailed Solutions

Scan the code

CHAPTER 02

Supply and Price Elasticity of Supply

In this Chapter...

- Supply
- Law of Supply
- Price Elasticity of Supply

Supply

Supply refers to the quantity of a commodity that a seller is willing and able to sell at a given price during a given period of time.

In other words, supply refers to whole quantity of goods that can be offered for sale at different possible prices.

It should be kept in mind that supply is a desired quantity, i.e., it is the quantity that the producers are willing to sell and not what they actually sell.

There are four components in supply

- Willingness of producer to sell
- Ability of producer to sell
- Price of the commodity
- Time period

Quantity Supplied refers to the amount of commodity offered for sale against specific price at a point of time. Supply for a commodity can be studied under two heads, which are as follows

1. **Individual Supply** It refers to the quantity of a particular commodity that an individual firm is willing and able to sell at a given price during a given period of time.

2. **Market Supply** It means the total quantity of a commodity that all the firms are willing and able to sell at a given price during a given period of time.

Determinants of Supply

Determinants are also known as factors which affect the supply of a commodity. These are as follows

1. **Price of Given Commodity** (P_X) There is a direct relationship between price of a commodity and its quantity supplied. Higher the price, higher the quantity supplied and vice-versa.

2. **Price of Related Goods** (P_R) The supply of a particular commodity is inversely related with the price of its substitute commodities, such as the supply of wheat will fall with rise in the price of rice, i.e. supply decreases and vice-versa.

   In case of complementary goods, supply is directly related with the price of complementary goods. With rise in price of petrol, supply of cars will rise, i.e. supply increases and vice-versa.

3. **Goal of the Firm** (G) If goal of the firm is to **maximise profits**, more quantity of the commodity will be offered only at a higher price. On the other hand, if goal of the firm is to **maximise sales**, more will be supplied even at the same price or same will be supplied even at a reduced price. Sales maximiser firm supplies greater quantity than a profit maximiser firm.

4. **Price of Factors of Production** (P_F) With the rise in the price of factors of production, the cost of production rises, which results in decrease in supply due to lesser profit margin and vice-versa.

5. **State of Technology** (T) New discoveries bring reduction in costs and increase in production. This will increase the level of supply also. A cost saving technology increases the supply.

6. **Number of Firms in the Industry** (N_F) Increase in the number of firms in the market implies increase in market supply and decrease in the number of firms implies decrease in market supply of a commodity.

7. **Expectation of Future Price** (E_X) If a firm expects a rise in the price of the commodity in near future, it will reduce the current market supply of the commodity and vice-versa.

8. **Government Policy** (G_P) The production of the commodity is discouraged, if heavy duty on its production is imposed. In this case, supply will decrease. In the same way, tax concessions encourage producers to increase supply. Also, subsidy offered by the government has a positive effect on supply. As subsidy on a product increases, supply also increases and vice-versa.

Note *The first five factors affect individual supply. All the factors taken together affect market supply.*

Supply Function

Supply function studies the functional relationship between supply of a commodity and its various determinants. It is expressed in the following equation

$$S_X = f(P_X, P_R, G, P_F, T, N_F, E_X, G_P)$$

where, S_X = Supply of commodity

f = Functional relations

P_X = Price of given commodity X

P_R = Price of related goods

G = Goal of the firm

P_F = Price of factors of production

T = State of technology

N_F = Number of firms in the industry

E_X = Business confidence/Expectation

G_P = Government's policy

Supply Schedule

It is a tabular presentation of various quantities of a commodity offered for sale, corresponding to different possible prices of that commodity. It shows the positive relationship between price and quantity supplied of a commodity.

Supply schedule has two aspects

1. **Individual Supply Schedule** Tabular presentation of various quantities that a seller is willing to sell at different possible prices during a given period of time is called individual supply schedule.

Individual Supply Schedule

Price (₹)	Quantity Supplied (Units)
1	100
2	200
3	300
4	400
5	500

From the above schedule, it is clear that as price rises, supply increases.

2. **Market Supply Schedule** Tabular presentation of various quantities that all the sellers are willing to sell at different possible prices during a given period of time is called market supply schedule.

Market Supply Schedule

Price (₹)	Quantity Supplied of Firm A	Quantity Supplied of Firm B	Market Supply (A + B) (Units)
1	10	5	$10 + 5 = 15$
2	20	10	$20 + 10 = 30$
3	30	15	$30 + 15 = 45$
4	40	20	$40 + 20 = 60$
5	50	25	$50 + 25 = 75$

(It has been assumed that market consists of only two firms).

Supply Curve

It is a graphical representation of supply schedule showing various quantities of a commodity offered for sale at different possible prices of that commodity.

It shows the positive relationship between price of a commodity and its quantity supplied. It is an upward sloping curve. Supply curve has two aspects

1. **Individual Supply Curve** Graphical representation of the relationship between price and individual supply of a commodity by an individual firm is called individual supply curve.

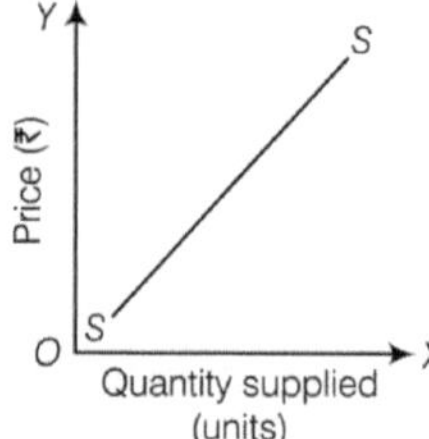

Individual supply curve

Individual supply curve slope upwards which shows that more of a commodity is supplied only at a higher price.

2. **Market Supply Curve** Graphical representation of the relationship between price and market supply of a commodity by all the firms is called market supply curve. Market supply curve is a horizontal summation of individual supply curves. It is also an upward sloping curve.

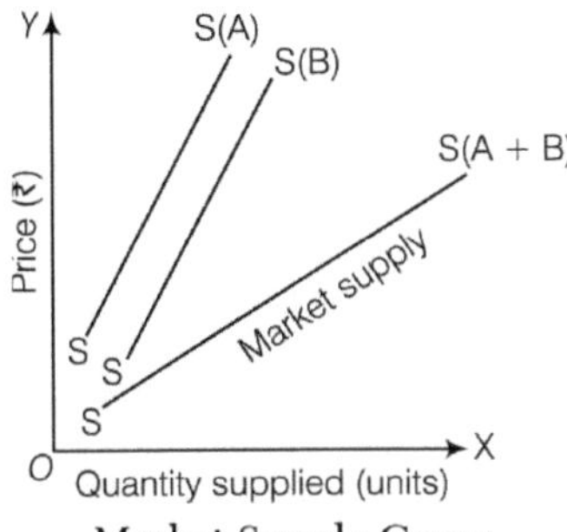

Market Supply Curve

Slope of Supply Curve

Slope of supply curve is measured by the ratio of change in price with respect to change in quantity. Mathematically, it is expressed as

$$\text{Slope of Supply Curve} = \frac{\Delta Y}{\Delta X} = \frac{\text{Change in Price } (\Delta P)}{\text{Change in Quantity } (\Delta Q)}$$

As the slope of supply curve is always positive, supply curve is upward sloping.

Below diagram shows the slope of supply curve

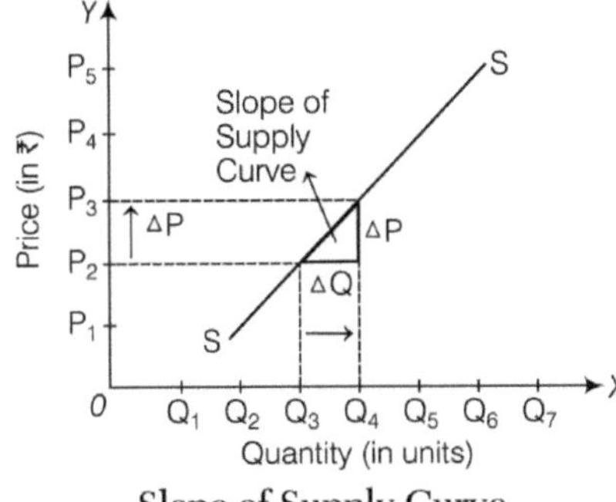

Slope of Supply Curve

Law of Supply

It states that keeping other determinants of supply constant, the quantity supplied decreases with the fall in price and increases with the rise in price.

Law of supply derives the relationship between price and quantity supplied.

According to this law, quantity supplied of a commodity is directly related to the price of a commodity. The quantity supplied decreases with the fall in price and vice-versa.

Law of supply is explained with the help of following schedule and diagram

Price (₹)	Quantity Supplied (Units)
10	100
15	200
20	300

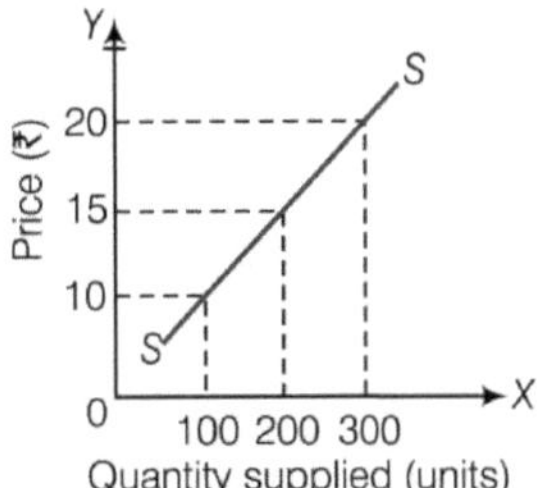

Supply curve moves upward from left to right. It shows positive relationship between price of given commodity and its quantity supplied. As price rises, quantity supplied also rises and vice-versa.

Assumptions of Law of Supply

Law of supply holds true when 'other factors remain constant.' Here 'other factors' is used to cover the following assumptions of law of supply

- There is no change in the price of the factors of production.
- There is no change in the techniques of production.
- There is no change in the goal of the firm.
- There is no change in the price of related goods.
- Investors have full confidence over business.

Causes for Application of 'Law of Supply'

Or

Why Does 'Law of Supply' Operate?

The following are the reasons for the operation of law of supply

1. **Profit Motive** As price rises, supplier's profit margin also rises. This increased profit motivates a supplier to supply more with increase in price.

2. **Change in the Number of Firms** High prices generally imply a higher profit margin, as discussed above. High margin of profit makes the particular business lucrative to new investors. As a result of this, the number of firms increases in the market, causing supply to rise simultaneously.

3. **Reduction in Stock** As price rises, the producers are willing to supply more from their accumulated stocks, causing stocks to deplete and supply to increase.

Exceptions to the Law of Supply

Certain goods which do not follow law of supply are

1. **Agricultural Goods** Law of Supply does not apply for agricultural goods, as their supply depends on climatic conditions and not on price.
2. **Perishable Goods** Perishable goods like fruits, vegetables, milk and milk products cannot be held for long. Therefore, suppliers are willing to supply these products, even when prices are less, because of the fear that they would become totally useless.
3. **Antique Goods, Rare Articles and Paintings** These goods are highly priced, but still their supply is limited, as supply here is affected by factors other than price. For example, the supply of Hussain's paintings cannot be increased even if buyers are willing to pay high price for it.
4. **Future Expectations regarding Prices** If prices are rising, but sellers anticipate that they would rise further in future, then they would not increase their supply now.
5. **Lack of Resources** In underdeveloped or backward economies, supply cannot be increased due to lack of resources.

Movement Along the Supply Curve or Change in Quantity Supplied

A movement along the supply curve is caused by changes in the price of the goods, other factors remaining constant. It is also called change in quantity supplied of the commodity. Here, we move on the same supply curve either up or down.

Movements along a supply curve can take the form of

1. **Extension or Expansion of Supply** When the quantity supplied increases with the rise in price, it is called expansion of supply. In this case, we move upward or rightward on the same supply curve.
   It is explained with the help of an imaginary schedule and diagram

Price (₹)	Quantity Supplied (Units)
1	10
2	20
3	30

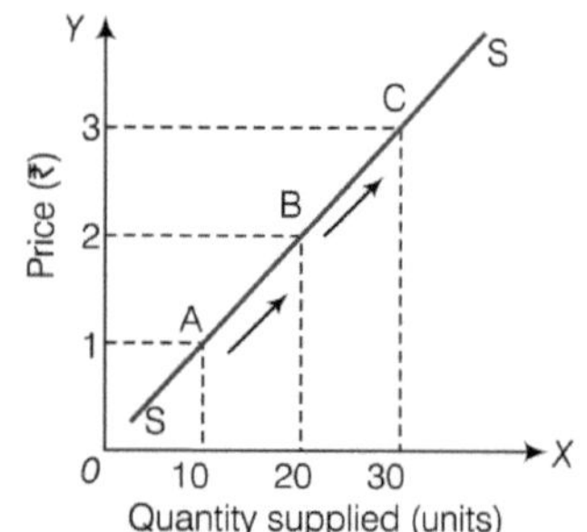

Extension of Supply (A → B → C)

Extension of supply is shown by a movement from point A to B to C on the same supply curve. More is supplied, in response to increase in own price of the commodity. So, when price increases from ₹ 1 to ₹ 2, quantity supplied increases from 10 to 20 and so on.

2. **Contraction of Supply** When the quantity supplied decreases with the fall in price, it is called contraction of supply. In this case, we move downward or leftward on the same supply curve. It is explained with the help of an imaginary schedule and diagram

Price (₹)	Quantity Supplied (Units)
3	30
2	20
1	10

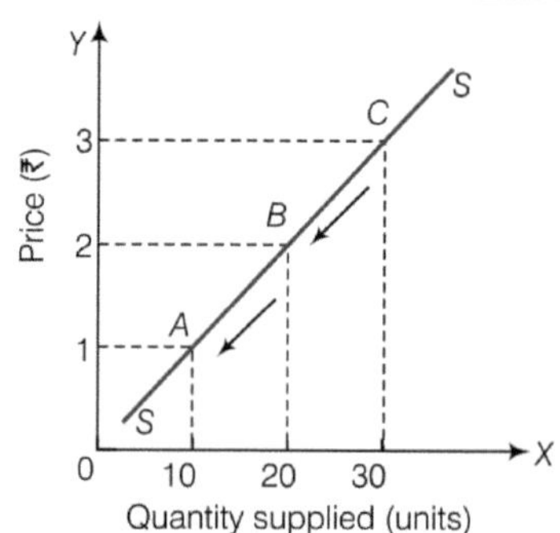

Contraction of Supply (C → B → A)

Contraction of supply is shown by a movement from point C to B to A on the same supply curve. Less is supplied in response to decrease in own price of the commodity.

So, when price decreases from ₹ 3 to ₹ 2, quantity supplied falls to 20 units from 30 units.

Shift in the Supply Curve or Change in Supply

Shift in supply curve shows the situation of increase or decrease in supply, even when, own price of the commodity remains constant.

Shift is caused by other factors like price of related commodities, state of technology, cost of production, government policy, number of firms in the industry, business confidence/expectation and goal of firm.

It is also called change in supply. In shift, a new supply curve is drawn.

Shift in supply curve can take the following two forms

1. **Increase in Supply** When supply of a commodity increases due to favourable changes in factors other than its price, it is called increase in supply. In this situation, supply curve shifts rightward.

It is explained with the help of an imaginary schedule and diagram

Price (₹)	Quantity Supplied (Units)
10	100
10	200

Increase in Supply (A → B)

At the same price, supply increases from 100 to 200 units. Accordingly, supply curve shifts rightward from SS to $S_1 S_1$ and the production shifts from point A to B (from old supply curve to new supply curve). Increase in supply may occur on account of the following factors

- Fall in the price of substitute goods.
- Rise in the price of complementary goods.
- Changes in the goals of producers to being sales maximisation.
- Fall in the price of factors of production.
- Improvements in technology.
- Increase in the number of firms in the market.
- Changes in government's policy, either by decreasing taxes or increasing subsidies.

2. **Decrease in Supply** When supply of a commodity decreases due to unfavourable changes in factors other than its price, it is called decrease in supply. In this situation, supply curve shifts leftward. It is explained with the help of an imaginary schedule and diagram

Price (₹)	Quantity Supplied (Units)
10	200
10	100

Decrease in Supply (B ← A)

At the same price, supply decreases from 200 to 100 units.

Accordingly, supply curve shifts leftward from SS to $S_1 S_1$, the production shifts from point A to B (from old supply curve to new supply curve).

Decrease in supply may occur on account of the following factors

- Rise in the price of substitute goods.
- Fall in the price of complementary goods.
- Changes in the goals of producers to being profit maximisation.
- Rise in the price of factors of production.
- Outdated technology.
- Decrease in the number of firms in the market.
- Changes in government policy, either by increasing taxes or decreasing subsidies.

Price Elasticity of Supply

It can be defined as a measure of the responsiveness of quantity supplied to change in the own price of the commodity.

It is also defined as the percentage change in the quantity supplied of a commodity divided by the percentage change in its price.

Price elasticity of supply is a pure number, it has no unit. Also, it is always positive as there exist a direct relation between own price and quantity supplied of a commodity.

Price Elasticity of Supply

$$(E_s) = \frac{\text{Percentage Change in Quantity Supplied}}{\text{Percentage Change in Price}}$$

Measurement of Price Elasticity of Supply: Percentage Change Method

According to this method, elasticity of supply is the ratio between 'percentage change in quantity supplied' and 'percentage change in price' of the commodity.

$$E_s = \frac{\text{Percentage Change in Quantity Supplied}}{\text{Percentage Change in Price}} \text{ or } \frac{\Delta Q}{\Delta P} \times \frac{P}{Q}$$

Here, Q = Initial quantity

P = Initial price

ΔQ = Change in quantity supplied

ΔP = Change in price

Example 1. The price elasticity of supply of commodities X and Y are equal. The price of X falls from ₹ 10 to ₹ 8 per unit and its quantity supplied falls by 16%. The price of Y rises by 10%. Calculate the percentage increase in its supply.

Ans. Price Elasticity of Supply of Commodity X

$$(E_s) = \frac{\text{Percentage Change in Quantity Supplied of X}}{\text{Percentage Change in Price of X}}$$

Percentage Change in Price of X

$$= \frac{\Delta P}{P} \times 100 = \frac{2}{10} \times 100 = 20\%$$

$$\therefore \quad E_s \text{ of X} = \frac{16}{20} = 0.8$$

According to the question, E_s of X $= E_s$ of Y

$$\therefore \qquad E_s \text{ of Y} = 0.8$$

Now, Price Elasticity of Supply of Commodity Y

$$(E_s) = \frac{\text{Percentage Change in Quantity Supplied of Y}}{\text{Percentage Change in Price of Y}}$$

$$0.8 = \frac{\text{Percentage Change in Quantity Supplied of Y}}{10}$$

$0.8 \times 10 =$ Percentage Change in Quantity Supplied of Y $= 8\%$

$\therefore$ Percentage change in quantity supplied of Y $= 8\%$

Example 2. The market price of a good changes from ₹ 5 to ₹ 20. As a result, the quantity supplied by a firm increases by 15 units. The price elasticity of firm's supply curve is 0.5. Find the initial and final output levels of the firm.

Ans. Initial price $(P) = ₹ 5$, New price $(P_1) = ₹ 20$

$$\Delta P = P_1 - P = 20 - 5 = 15$$

Change in quantity supplied $(\Delta Q) = 15$ units $E_s = 0.5$

Accordingly, $E_s = \dfrac{\Delta Q}{\Delta P} \times \dfrac{P}{Q} \Rightarrow 0.5 = \dfrac{15}{15} \times \dfrac{5}{Q}$

$$\therefore \qquad Q = 10 \text{ units}$$

i.e., initial quantity supplied $= 10$ units

$$\text{Final Output Level} = Q + \Delta Q$$
$$= (10 + 15) \text{ units} = 25 \text{ units}$$

Example 3. At the market price of ₹ 10, a firm supplies 4 units of output. The market price increases to ₹ 30. The price elasticity of the firm's supply is 1.25. What quantity will the firm supply at the new price?

Ans. Initial price $(P) = ₹ 10$

Initial quantity $(Q) = 4$ units

New price $(P_1) = ₹ 30$

Change in price $(\Delta P) = 30 - 10 = ₹ 20$ $E_s = 1.25$

Accordingly, $E_s = \dfrac{\Delta Q}{\Delta P} \times \dfrac{P}{Q} \Rightarrow 1.25 = \dfrac{\Delta Q}{20} \times \dfrac{10}{4}$

$$\therefore \qquad \Delta Q = 10 \text{ units}$$

New Level of Output $= Q + \Delta Q = (4 + 10) = 14$ units

Example 4. A firm earns a revenue of ₹ 50 when the market price of a good is ₹ 10. The market price increases to ₹ 15 and the firm now earns a revenue of ₹ 150. What is the price elasticity of the firm's supply curve?

Ans. Firm's revenue when price is ₹10 per unit $=$ ₹ 50

$$\therefore \quad \text{Quantity Sold} = \frac{50}{10} = 5 \text{ units}$$

Firm's revenue when price is ₹15 per unit $=$ ₹ 150

$$\therefore \quad \text{Quantity Sold} = \frac{150}{15} = 10 \text{ units}$$

$$P = 10, \ P_1 = 15, \ Q = 5$$
$$Q_1 = 10$$
$$\Delta P = P_1 - P = 15 - 10 = 5$$
$$\Delta Q = Q_1 - Q = 10 - 5 = 5$$

Accordingly, $E_s = \dfrac{\Delta Q}{\Delta P} \times \dfrac{P}{Q}$

$$= \frac{5}{5} \times \frac{10}{5} = 2$$

$\therefore$ $E_s = 2$, which implies elastic supply.

Degrees of Elasticity of Supply

There are five degrees of elasticity of supply as explained below

1. **Perfectly Inelastic Supply** $(E_s = 0)$ When supply of a commodity does not change, irrespective of any change in its price, it is called perfectly inelastic supply.
   In this condition, supply curve will be a straight line parallel to Y–axis.

   It can be explained with the help of following schedule and diagram

Price (₹)	Quantity Supplied (Units)
10	20
20	20
30	20

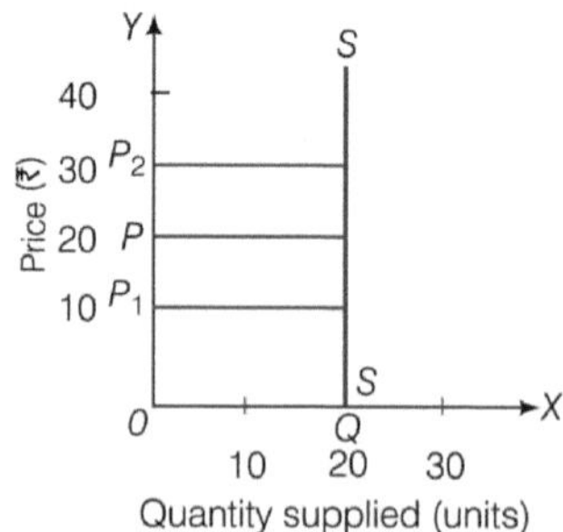

2. **Perfectly Elastic Supply** $(E_s = \infty)$ Supply of a commodity is said to be perfectly elastic when its supply expands or contracts to any extent without any change in the price. In this condition, supply curve will be a straight line parallel to X-axis. It can be explained with the help of following schedule and diagram

Price (₹)	Quantity Supplied (Units)
10	10
10	20
10	30

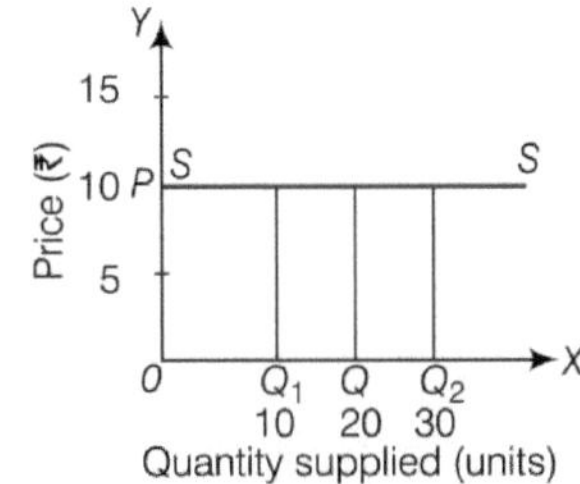

3. **Unit Elastic Supply** $(E_s = 1)$ If percentage change in supply is equal to percentage change in price, it is called unit elastic supply. In this case, the coefficient of E_s is equal to one. In this condition, supply curve is a straight line passing through the origin, irrespective of the angle that it makes or how flat or steep it is. It can be explained with the help of following schedule and diagram

Price (₹)	Quantity Supplied (Units)
10	20
20	40

4. **Inelastic or Less than Unit Elastic Supply** $(E_s < 1)$ When percentage change in quantity supplied is less than percentage change in price, it is called inelastic supply. In this condition, the straight line supply curve intersects the X-axis in its positive range (or cuts the X-axis/quantity axis). It can be explained with the help of following schedule and diagram

Price (₹)	Quantity Supplied (Units)
10	20
20	25

5. **Elastic or More than Unit Elastic Supply** $(E_s > 1)$ When percentage change in supply is more than the percentage change in price, it is called more than unit elastic supply.

In this condition, the straight line supply curve intersects the X-axis in its negative range (or cuts Y-axis/price axis).

It can be explained with the help of following schedule and diagram

Price (₹)	Quantity Supplied (Units)
10	20
11	40

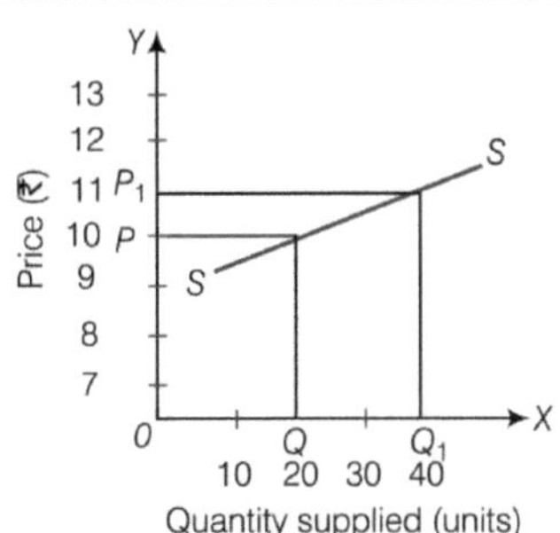

Factors affecting Elasticity of Supply

The factors which affect the elasticity of supply are

1. **Nature of Inputs Used** The elasticity of supply depends on the nature of inputs used for the production of a commodity. If commonly available inputs are used, supply will be elastic, but in case of scarcely available inputs, the supply will be inelastic.

2. **Risk Taking** If entrepreneurs are willing to take risk, the supply will be more elastic. On the other hand, if entrepreneurs are reluctant to take risk, the supply will be inelastic.

3. **Nature of Commodity** Perishable goods are relatively less elastic in supply than durable goods, because of limited shelf-life of perishables.

4. **Time Factor** Longer the time period, greater will be the elasticity of supply. Because over a long period of time, factors are easily adjustable and vice-versa.

5. **Technique of Production** In case of production of a commodity, supply will be less elastic if it involves the use of a complex and expensive technology. On the other hand, use of a simple technology facilitates quicker changes in output and supply.

6. **Cost of Production** Elasticity of supply is also influenced by cost of production. Supply will be less elastic in case, increase in production causes a substantial increase in cost of production and vice-versa.

Chapter Practice

Objective Questions

• Multiple Choice Questions

1. The supply of a commodity implies
(a) actual product of a good
(b) stock available for sale
(c) total existing stock of the good
(d) the amount of goods offered for sale at a different prices, per unit of time

Ans. (d) the amount of goods offered for sale at a different prices, per unit of time

2. Supply of a commodity is ...... concept.
(a) stock
(b) flow
(c) Both (a) and (b)
(d) wholesale

Ans. (b) The quantity of supply changes with time and thus, measured over a period of time. So, it is a flow concept.

3. The supply curve is usually
(a) upward rising
(b) downward sloping
(c) nothing definite can be said
(d) None of the above

Ans. (a) upward rising

4. The claim that other things being equal, the quantity supplied of a good rises when the price of good rises and vice-versa is known as
(a) Law of Economics
(b) Law of Supply
(c) Law of Demand
(d) All of these

Ans. (b) Law of Supply

5. The functional relationship between supply of a commodity and its various determinants is known as
(a) Supply function
(b) Change in supply
(c) Change in quantity supplied
(d) None of the above

Ans. (a) Supply function

6. When supply curve shifts to the right, there is ...... in supply.
(a) an increase
(b) expansion
(c) contraction
(d) decrease

Ans. (a) Rightward shift in supply indicates increase in quantity at the existing price leading to change in other factors known as increase in supply.

7. Increase or decrease in supply means
(a) change in supply due to change in its own price.
(b) change in supply due to change in factors other than its own price.
(c) Both (a) and (b)
(d) None of the above

Ans. (b) change in supply due to change in factors other than its own price.

8. Expansion in supply refers to a situation when the producers are willing to supply a
(a) larger quantity of the commodity at an increased price.
(b) larger quantity of the commodity due to increased taxation on that commodity.
(c) larger quantity of the commodity at the same price.
(d) larger quantity of the commodity at the decreased price.

Ans. (a) larger quantity of the commodity at an increased price.

9. Contraction of supply curve means
(a) upward movement along the supply curve
(b) downward movement along the supply curve
(c) rightward shift in supply curve
(d) leftward shift in supply curve

Ans. (b) downward movement along the supply curve

10. If a firm's supply increases due to application of improved technology, this is known as
(a) Expansion in supply
(b) Contraction in supply
(c) Increase in supply
(d) Increase in quantity supplied

Ans. (c) If the supply of a commodity increases due to other factors than its price, it is called 'increase in supply'. Causes of increase in supply are improvement in technology, increase in price of its complementary goods, decrease in taxation, decrease in price of its substitute goods, etc.

11. Elasticity of supply is defined as a measure of the responsiveness of quantity supplied of a good to change in
(a) price of concerned good (b) price of substitute good
(c) demand (d) None of these

Ans. (a) price of concerned good

12. A horizontal supply curve parallel to the quantity axis implies that the elasticity of supply is
(a) zero (b) infinite
(c) equal to one
(d) greater than zero but less than one

Ans. (b) infinite

13. When supply is perfectly inelastic, elasticity of supply is equal to
(a) − 1 (b) zero
(c) 1 (d) infinity

Ans. (b) zero

14. Statement I Supply and quantity supplied are one and the same thing.

Statement II Change in supply due to price is called as change in quantity supplied.

Alternatives
(a) Statement I is correct and Statement II is incorrect
(b) Statement II is correct and Statement I is incorrect
(c) Both the statements are correct
(d) Both the statements are incorrect

Ans. (b) Statement II is correct and Statement I is incorrect

15. Statement I Supply of precious goods is inelastic in nature.

Statement II Supply curve starting from Y-axis is elastic in nature.

Alternatives
(a) Statement I is correct and Statement II is incorrect
(b) Statement II is correct and Statement I is incorrect
(c) Both the statements are correct
(d) Both the statements are incorrect

Ans. (c) Both the statements are correct

16. Choose the correct pair.

	Column I		Column II
A.	Improvement in Technology	(i)	Upward Movement along Supply Curve
B.	Rise in Taxes	(ii)	Leftward Shift in Supply
C.	Supply Curve Passing through Origin	(iii)	Inelastic Supply

Codes
(a) A–(i) (b) B–(ii)
(c) C–(iii) (d) All of these

Ans. (b) B–(ii)

• Assertion-Reasoning MCQs

Direction *(Q. Nos. 1 to 5). There are two statements marked as Assertion (A) and Reason (R). Read the statements and choose the appropriate option from the options given below*
(a) Both Assertion (A) and Reason (R) are true and Reason (R) is the correct explanation of Assertion (A)
(b) Both Assertion (A) and Reason (R) are true, but Reason (R) is not the correct explanation of Assertion (A)
(c) Assertion (A) is true, but Reason (R) is false
(d) Both Assertion (A) and Reason (R) are false

1. Assertion (A) According to law of supply, as the cost of production increases producer increase selling price and accordingly supply of the good increases.

Reason (R) Increase in price of complementary goods, leads to increase in quantity supply.

Ans. (d) According to law of supply, other factors remain constant and thus movement happens along the supply curve only due to price of the commodity.

Price of complementary goods is considered as other factors and thus leads to change in supply and not quantity supplied.

2. Assertion (A) Extension in supply is caused by change in factors other than own price. This leads to movement along the supply curve.

Reason (R) Change in quantity supplied is an impact of change in other factors leading to shift in supply curve to the right.

Ans. (d) Extension of supply is caused by increase in price keeping other factors constant while change in quantity supplied is caused by change in price keeping other factors constant.

3. Assertion (A) Elasticity of supply curve passing through the origin always has elasticity equal to unity regardless of the angle it makes.

Reason (R) Slope of supply curve and elasticity of supply are directly proportional.

Ans. (c) Slope of supply curve and elasticity of supply are inversely proportional i.e., as slope increases, elasticity decreases and vice-versa.

4. Assertion (A) Elasticity of supply is higher for flatter curve compared with a steeper supply curve.

Reason (R) Percentage change of quantity is greater than that of change in price on a flatter supply curve.

Ans. (a) Both Assertion (A) and Reason (R) are true and Reason (R) is the correct explanation of Assertion (A)

5. Assertion (A) Supply of agricultural goods is less elastic in nature.

Reason (R) There are many natural constraints in an agricultural produce which restricts its supply.

Ans. (a) Both Assertion (A) and Reason (R) are true and Reason (R) is the correct explanation of Assertion (A)

• Case Based MCQs

1. Direction *Read the following case study and answer the question no. (i) to (vi) on the basis of the same.*

A tariff is a tax placed on the products of foreign countries sold in the United States. Assume, there is a 10% tax on foreign-made automobiles. Who would bear the incidence of this tax? Assume that a Japanese car and a similar American car each sell in the United States at a price of $25,000.

With the 10% tax on the Japanese car ($2,500), the Japanese company would like to raise the price of its car to $27,500. Whether it can do so or not depends on the price elasticity of demand for Japanese cars. If the demand for Japanese cars is relatively inelastic, the quantity demanded will fall very little at the price of $27,500. This means that buyers do not find Japanese and American cars to be close substitutes.

The incidence of the tax would be on the car buyers. On the other hand, if the demand for Japanese cars is relatively elastic, the quantity of Japanese cars demanded will fall considerably at the price of $27,500. This means that buyers will closely substitute between Japanese and American cars. The Japanese company will have to charge a price close to $25,000 in the United States to be able to compete.

The incidence of the tariff will be on the Japanese automobile companies. In technical language, a tariff on a foreign product that has very elastic demand is called an optimal tariff. The price of the foreign product rises very little in the United States. Most of the tariff is paid by the foreign company as reduced profits. The gain, of course, goes to the United States Government, who collects the money.

(i) What be the impact of tariff imposed on supply for Japanese cars?
(a) Supply will remain constant
(b) Supply will increase
(c) Supply will decrease (d) None of these

Ans. (c) Supply will decrease

(ii) Impact of tariff will be higher on supply of cars, if demand is ....
(a) less elastic   (b) more elastic
(c) perfectly elastic   (d) perfectly inelatic

Ans. (a) Impact of tariff will be higher when the supply is inelastic as in that case, quantity does not change by much even though price changes.

(iii) What will be the impact on the supply for American cars, if tariff is imposed on Japanese cars with low price elasticity of supply?
(a) Increase   (b) Decrease
(c) Remain constant   (d) May or may not increase

Ans. (c) Remain constant

(iv) With increase in taxes by the government, supply will fall due to ....
(a) increase in cost of production
(b) fall in investments
(c) Both (a) and (b)
(d) Neither (a) nor (b)

Ans. (a) increase in cost of production

(v) **Assertion** (A) A tariff has a lower impact on supply if the good is inelastic.

Reason (R) In case of inelastic supply, quantity doesn't change much due to change in its determinants.

Alternatives
(a) Both Assertion (A) and Reason (R) are true and Reason (R) is the correct explanation of Assertion (A)
(b) Both Assertion (A) and Reason (R) are true, but Reason (R) is not the correct explanation of Assertion (A)
(c) Assertion (A) is true, but Reason (R) is false
(d) Both Assertion (A) and Reason (R) are false

Ans. (a) Both Assertion (A) and Reason (R) are true and Reason (R) is the correct explanation of Assertion (A)

(vi) As per the above information, which of the following has an impact on the supply of the cars?
(a) Tariff
(b) Consumer's preferences
(c) Elasticity of supply   (d) All of the above

Ans. (d) All of the above

2. Direction *Read the following case study and answer the question no. (i) to (vi) on the basis of the same.*

Year 2020 has seen many ups and downs in terms of production activities and demand in the whole country. Not only India, the entire world has suffered in a big way due to the outbreak of Corona Virus Pandemic. Since, this Pandemic started in November 2019 in China till Present time our trading relation with China has also been affected, not only this due to boarder conflict as well.

India is now facing the problem of deflationary gap and heading towards a negative growth rate. Government of India has also announced a relief package to help revive the economic condition of the vulnerable groups.

Slowly and gradually impact has been seen on the market as India's fuel demand is increased during September 2020.

(i) What was the impact of lockdown in India on supply of essential items?
(a) Remain constant
(b) Increased
(c) Decreased
(d) Can't be determined

Ans. (b) During the lockdown, government focused upon supplying essential goods to all people leading to rise in supply of goods.

(ii) What will be impact on supply of fuel if demand increase?
(a) Increase　　　　(b) Decrease
(c) Remain constant
(d) Depends upon availability of fuel in the international market.

Ans. (d) Depends upon availability of fuel in the international market.

(iii) With increase in supply of essentials goods, its supply curve will ....
(a) shift to the right　　(b) shift to the left
(c) move upward　　　(d) move downward

Ans. (a) Increase in supply causes a rightward shift in the supply curve.

(iv) **Assertion** (A) With the announcement of relief packages by the government, supply of essential commodities will further increase.

Reason (R) Essential goods are necessity of life thus given priority by the government.

Alternatives
(a) Both Assertion (A) and Reason (R) are true and Reason (R) is the correct explanation of Assertion (A)
(b) Both Assertion (A) and Reason (R) are true, but Reason (R) is not the correct explanation of Assertion (A)
(c) Assertion (A) is true, but Reason (R) is false
(d) Both Assertion (A) and Reason (R) are false

Ans. (b) Relief packages were meant for supplying essentials to all people and thus leads to rise in supply.

(v) If the fuel prices increase, it will lead to..........in supply of essential goods.
(a) increase　　　　(b) decrease
(c) remain constant　(d) Either (a) or (b)

Ans. (d) Impact of fuel price is not clear on supply as it depends upon the nature of commodity sold.

(vi) Elasticity of supply of essential commodities are
(a) highly inelastic　　(b) elastic
(c) perfectly inelastic　(d) perfectly elastic

Ans. (a) highly inelastic

PART 2
Subjective Questions

• Short Answer (SA) Type Questions

1. Explain, how technological progress is a determinant of supply of a good by a firm.

Ans. Technological progress tends to lower the Marginal and Average Costs of production, because better technology facilitates higher output with the same inputs.

Accordingly, producers are willing to supply more at the existing price, as a result, supply of producer increases.

2. Explain, how input prices are a determinant of supply of a good by a firm.

Ans. In case of increase in input price, cost of production tends to rise. Accordingly, producers will supply less of the commodity at its existing price as there is a decrease in producer's profit.

On the other hand, in case of fall in the prices of inputs, the cost of production tends to fall, leading to an increase in producer's profit. This induces him to increase his supply.

3. Using diagram and schedule, explain the law of supply.

Ans. The law of supply states that other things being equal, quantity supplied increases with the increase in price and decreases with the decrease in price of a commodity.

It can be explained with the help of following schedule and diagram

Price (₹)	Quantity Supplied (Units)
10	100
20	200
30	300

The supply schedule shows the positive relationship between price and quantity supplied. This is in accordance with the law of supply.

SS is the supply curve sloping upward. It shows a positive relationship between price and quantity supplied of a commodity. When price increases from ₹ 10 to ₹ 20, quantity supplied increases from 100 to 200 units.

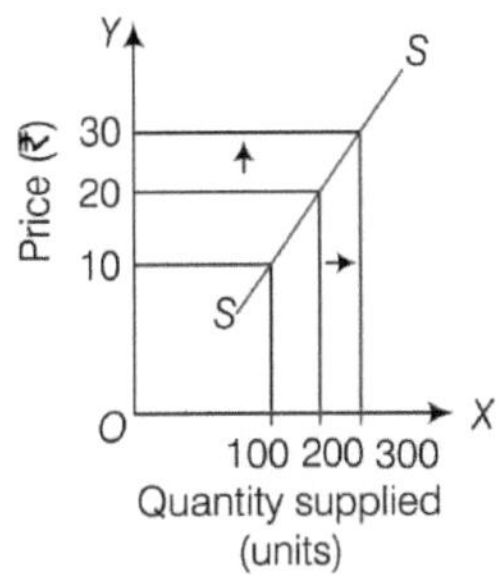

4. (i) Explain the effect of rise in input prices on supply of a commodity.

   (ii) Explain the effect of fall in prices of inputs on the supply of a good.

Ans. (i) In case of increase in input price, marginal cost tends to rise. Accordingly, producers will supply less of the commodity at its existing price because of a fall in their profits.

   (ii) In case of fall in input price, marginal cost will decline. Accordingly, producer will supply more of the commodity at its existing price because of increase in their profits.

5. State any three causes of rightward shift in supply curve.

Ans. Causes of rightward shift in supply curve are as follows (any three)

   (i) Fall in the price of substitute goods.

   (ii) Fall in the price of factors of production.

   (iii) Improvement in technology.

   (iv) Increase in the number of firms in the market.

   (v) Rise in the price of complementary goods.

6. Explain the situation of zero elasticity of supply with the help of a diagram.

Ans. It refers to a vertical straight line supply curve showing constant supply.

It is shown in the given figure

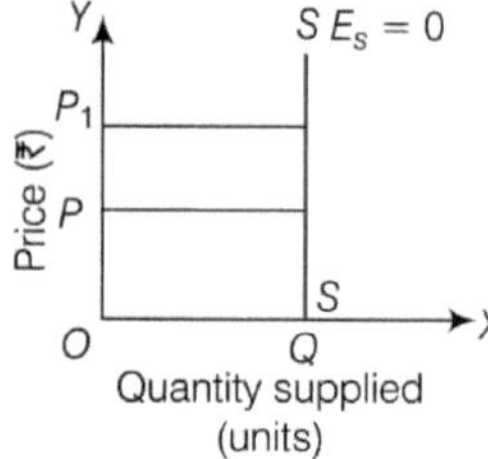

In such a situation, it is assumed that supply is constant, whatever the changes in price.

7. A firm supplies 10 units of a good at a price of ₹ 5 per unit. Price Elasticity of Supply is 1.25. What quantity will the firm supply at a price of ₹ 7 per unit?

Ans. Given, $E_s = 1.25$, $P = ₹\ 5$

$$P_1 = ₹\ 7, \quad Q = 10$$
$$Q_1 = ?,$$
$$\Delta P = P_1 - P = 7 - 5 = 2$$

Price Elasticity of Supply $(E_s) = \dfrac{\Delta Q}{\Delta P} \times \dfrac{P}{Q}$

$$1.25 = \dfrac{\Delta Q}{2} \times \dfrac{5}{10}, \quad \Delta Q = 1.25 \times 4 = 5$$

Q_1 = Actual Quantity + Change in Quantity
$$= Q + \Delta Q = 10 + 5$$
$$Q_1 = 15 \text{ units}$$

8. A firm supplies a certain quantity of a good at a price of ₹ 10 per unit. When price changes to ₹ 9 per unit, the firm supplies 10 units less. Price elasticity of supply is 1. What is the quantity supplied before price change?

Ans. $P = ₹\ 10,\ P_1 = ₹\ 9$

$\Delta P = 9 - 10 = (-)₹\ 1 \Rightarrow Q = ?,\ \Delta Q = -10 \Rightarrow E_s = 1$

Now, Price Elasticity of Supply $(E_s) = \dfrac{\Delta Q}{\Delta P} \times \dfrac{P}{Q}$

$$1 = \dfrac{-10}{-1} \times \dfrac{10}{Q} \Rightarrow Q = 100$$

∴ Quantity supplied before price change = 100 units

9. Explain any two factors that cause a shift of supply curve.

Ans. Two factors that cause a shift of supply curve are

   (i) **Change in Technology** Technological improvement tends to lower the marginal and average costs of production because better technology facilitates higher output with the same inputs. Accordingly, producers are willing to supply more at the existing price. This implies a rightward shift in supply curve and vice-versa.

   (ii) **Change in Input Price** Input price may increase or decrease. In case of increase in input price, marginal and average costs tend to rise. Accordingly, producers will supply less of the commodity at its existing price. This implies a leftward shift in supply curve and vice-versa.

10. Price of commodity A is ₹ 10 per unit and Total Revenue at this price is ₹ 1,600. When its price rises by 20%, total Revenue increases by ₹ 800. Calculate its price elasticity of supply.

Ans. Given, $P = ₹\ 10,$

$$P_1 = 10 + 20\% \text{ of } 10$$
$$= 10 + 2 = ₹\ 12$$

Initial Total Revenue = ₹ 1,600

New Total Revenue $= 1,600 + 800 = ₹\ 2,400$

When, $P = ₹\ 10,\ Q = 1,600 \div 10 = 160$

When, $P_1 = ₹\ 12,\ Q_1 = 2,400 \div 12 = 200$

Now, $P = ₹\ 10,\ P_1 = ₹\ 12$

$$\Delta P = 12 - 10 = ₹\ 2,$$
$$Q = 160,\ Q_1 = 200$$
$$\Delta Q = 200 - 160 = 40$$

Price Elasticity of Supply $(E_s) = \dfrac{\Delta Q}{\Delta P} \times \dfrac{P}{Q}$

$$= \dfrac{40}{2} \times \dfrac{10}{160}$$
$$= \dfrac{5}{4} = 1.25$$

∴ Price Elasticity of Supply
$$(E_s) = 1.25 \text{ (more than unit elastic)}$$

11. When the price of a good rises from ₹ 20 per unit to ₹ 30 per unit, the revenue of the firm producing this good rises from ₹ 100 to ₹ 300. Calculate price elasticity of supply.

Ans. Given,

Price (₹)	Total Revenue (TR) (₹)
20	100
30	300

$$\text{Quantity Supplied } (Q) = \frac{\text{TR}}{P} = \frac{100}{20} = 5$$

$$Q_1 = \frac{300}{30} = 10$$

So,
$$P = 20$$
$$Q = 5$$
$$P_1 = 30$$
$$Q_1 = 10$$
$$\Delta P = P_1 - P = 30 - 20 = 10$$
$$\Delta Q = Q - Q = 10 - 5 = 5$$

$$\text{Price Elasticity of Supply } (E_s) = \frac{\Delta Q}{\Delta P} \times \frac{P}{Q} = \frac{5}{10} \times \frac{20}{5}$$

$$E_s = 2 \text{ (more than unit elastic)}$$

12. At a price of ₹ 5 per unit of a commodity A, total revenue is ₹ 800. When its price rises by 20%, total revenue increases by ₹ 400. Calculate its price elasticity of supply.

Ans. Given, $P = ₹ 5$, Initial Total Revenue $= ₹ 800$

$P_1 = 5 + 20\%$ of $5 = 5 + 1 = ₹ 6$

New Total Revenue $= 800 + 400 = ₹ 1,200$

$$Q = 800 \div 5 = 160$$
$$Q_1 = 1,200 \div 6 = 200$$
$$\Delta Q = Q_1 - Q = 200 - 160 = 40$$
$$\Delta P = P_1 - P = 6 - 5 = ₹ 1$$

$$\text{Price Elasticity of Supply } (E_s) = \frac{\Delta Q}{\Delta P} \times \frac{P}{Q}$$

$$= \frac{40}{1} \times \frac{5}{160} = \frac{5}{4} = 1.25$$

$$\therefore \qquad E_s = 1.25 \text{ (more than unit elastic)}$$

13. Commodities X and Y have equal Price Elasticity of Supply. The supply of X rises from 400 units to 500 units due to a 20% rise in its price. Calculate the percentage fall in supply of Y if its price falls by 8%.

Ans. Given, E_s of X = E_s of Y

$$Q_X = 400, \ Q'_X = 500$$

Percentage change in price of X = 20%

Percentage change in price of Y = 8%

$$\Delta Q_X = Q'_X - Q_X$$

$$= 500 - 400 = 100 \text{ units}$$

Price Elasticity of Supply of X

$$(E_s) = \frac{\text{Percentage Change in Quantity Supplied}}{\text{Percentage Change in Price}}$$

$$= \frac{\dfrac{\Delta Q_X}{Q_X} \times 100}{20} = \frac{\dfrac{100}{400} \times 100}{20} = \frac{25}{20} = 1.25$$

Price Elasticity of Supply of Y

$$(E_s) = \frac{\text{Percentage Change in Quantity Supplied}}{\text{Percentage Change in Price}}$$

$$1.25 = \frac{\text{Percentage Change in Quantity Supplied}}{8}$$

$$[\because E_s \text{ of } X = E_s \text{ of } Y]$$

$$\therefore \text{Percentage fall in quantity supplied of Y}$$
$$= 1.25 \times 8 = 10\%$$

14. When the price of a commodity rises from ₹ 10 to ₹ 11 per unit, its quantity supplied rises by 100 units. Its price elasticity of supply is 2. Calculate its quantity supplied at the increased price.

Ans. Given, $P = ₹ 10$

$$P_1 = ₹ 11$$
$$\Delta P = 11 - 10 = ₹ 1$$
$$Q = ?$$
$$\Delta Q = 100 \text{ units}, \quad E_s = 2$$

Price Elasticity of Supply

$$(E_s) = \frac{\Delta Q}{\Delta P} \times \frac{P}{Q} \ or \ 2 = \frac{100}{1} \times \frac{10}{Q},$$

$$Q = \frac{100 \times 10}{2} = 500$$

$\therefore$ Quantity supplied at the increased price

$$(Q_1) = Q + \Delta Q = 500 + 100 = 600 \text{ units}$$

15. Consider a market with two firms. The following table shows the supply schedules of the two firms. The SS_1 column gives the supply schedule of firm 1 and the SS_2 column gives the supply schedule of firm 2. Compute the market supply schedule.

(NCERT)

Price (₹)	SS_1 (Units)	SS_2 (Units)
0	0	0
1	0	0
2	0	0
3	1	1
4	2	2
5	3	3
6	4	4

Ans.

Market Supply Schedule

Price (₹)	SS_1 (Units)	SS_2 (Units)	Market Supply $= SS_1 + SS_2$ (Units)
0	0	0	0
1	0	0	0
2	0	0	0
3	1	1	2
4	2	2	4
5	3	3	6
6	4	4	8

16. Consider a market with two firms. In the following table, columns labelled as SS_1 and SS_2 give the supply schedules of firm 1 and firm 2, respectively. Compute the market supply schedule. **(NCERT)**

Price (₹)	SS_1 (kg)	SS_2 (kg)
0	0	0
1	0	0
2	0	0
3	1	0
4	2	0.5
5	3	1
6	4	1.5
7	5	2
8	6	2.5

Ans.

Market Supply Schedule

Price (₹)	SS_1 (kg)	SS_2 (kg)	Market Supply $= SS_1 + SS_2$ (kg)
0	0	0	0
1	0	0	0
2	0	0	0
3	1	0	1
4	2	0.5	2.5
5	3	1	4
6	4	1.5	5.5
7	5	2	7
8	6	2.5	8.5

• Long Answer (LA) Type Questions

1. Explain how changes in prices of other products influence the supply of a given product.

Ans. As resources have alternative uses, the quantity supplied of a commodity depends not only on its price, but also on the prices of other commodities.

Increase in the prices of substitute goods makes them more profitable in comparison to the given commodity.

As a result, the firm shifts its limited resources from production of the given commodity to production of other goods. e.g. increase in the price of wheat will induce the farmer to use land for cultivation of wheat in place of rice.

Decrease in price of substitute good will shift the supply curve to the right and vice-versa.

In case of complementary goods, if price of one good increases, then supply of its complementary good also increases, conveying a direct relationship. So, rise in the price of car, will cause the supply of petrol to also rise and the supply curve shifts to the rightward ad vice-versa.

2. Explain the meaning of increase in supply and increase in quantity supplied with the help of a schedule.

Ans. **Increase in Supply** When supply of a commodity increases due to favourable changes in factors other than price, it is called increase in supply.

In this situation, supply curve shifts to the right side. It can be explained with the help of an imaginary schedule

Price (₹)	Quantity Supplied (Units)
10	100
10	200
10	300
10	400

As, it is clear from the above schedule that supply is increasing at constant prices.

Increase in Quantity Supplied When supply of a commodity increases due to increase in price of a commodity and other factors remaining constant, it is called increase in quantity supplied. In this situation, supply curve moves upward. It can be explained with the help of an imaginary schedule

Price (₹)	Quantity Supplied (Units)
10	100
20	200
30	300
40	400

Here, we can see that quantity supplied is rising with rise in prices.

3. (i) Distinguish between change in supply and change in quantity supplied. Which of these causes a shift of supply curve?

  (ii) Distinguish between movement along the supply curve and shift in the supply curve with the help of a suitable diagram.

Ans. (i) Difference between change in supply and change in quantity supplied

Basis	Change in Supply	Change in Quantity Supplied
Reason	It is caused by change in determinants other than own price of the commodity.	It is caused only by change in own price of the commodity, other determinants remaining constant.
Determinants	These include price of related goods, number of firms in the industry, goal of the firm, price of factors of production, state of technology, business confidence, government's policy.	Change in own price of the commodity is the only cause.
Representation	Diagrammatically, it is shown as a rightward and leftward shift in supply curve.	Diagrammatically, it is shown as a downward and upward movement on the same supply curve.

(ii) Difference between movement along the supply curve and shift in the supply curve

Basis	Movement Along the Supply Curve	Shift in the Supply Curve
Movement	It represents expansion and contraction of supply due to change in the price of a concerned commodity.	It occurs due to factors other than price of a concerned commodity.
Effect	When price increases, there is an upward movement $(a \rightarrow b)$ along the supply curve showing increase in quantity supplied and when price decreases, there is a downward movement $(b \rightarrow a)$ along the supply curve showing decrease in quantity supplied as shown in figure A.	When other factors change in a positive direction, the supply curve shifts to the right, $(a \rightarrow b)$ showing increase in supply and when changes occur in the negative direction, the supply curve shifts to the left $(a \rightarrow c)$ showing a decrease in supply, as shown in figure B.
Graph	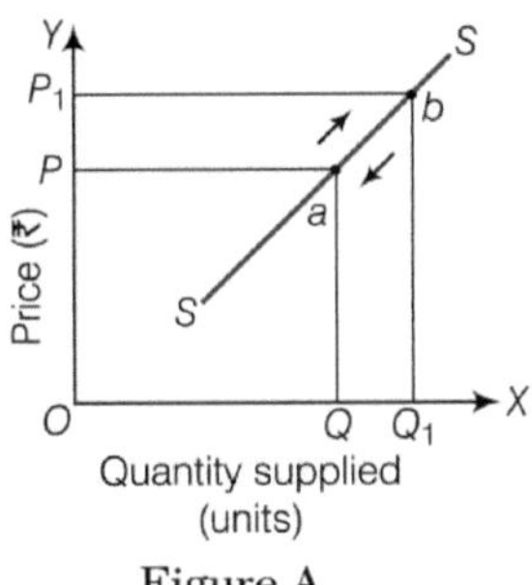	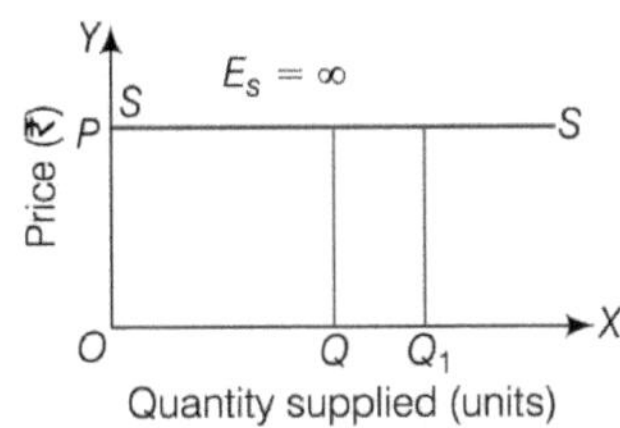

Figure A   Figure B

4. Using diagrams, explain various degrees of price elasticity of supply.

Ans. The various degrees of price elasticity of supply are given below

  (i) **Perfectly Elastic Supply** In this case, a slight change in price causes infinite change in quantity supplied. The supply curve SS is parallel to X-axis and $E_s = \infty$, as shown in the figure

(ii) **Perfectly Inelastic Supply** It is a situation where the quantity supplied remains unchanged, whatever be the changes in price. Hence, the supply curve is parallel to Y-axis and $E_s = 0$, as shown in the figure

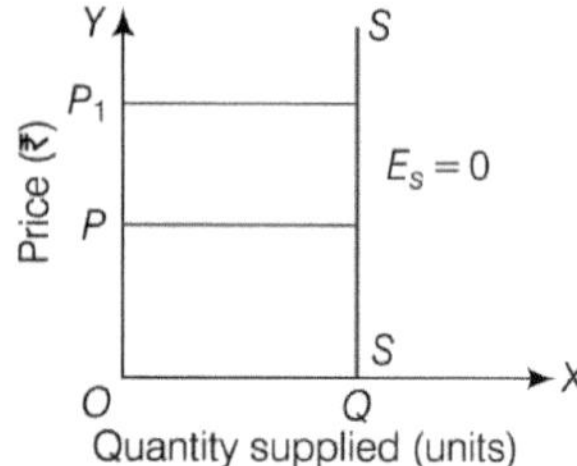

(iii) **Unitary Elastic Supply** In this case, percentage change in quantity supplied is exactly equal to percentage change in price. Hence, the supply curve is a straight line originating from the origin and sloping upward and $E_s = 1$, as shown in the figure

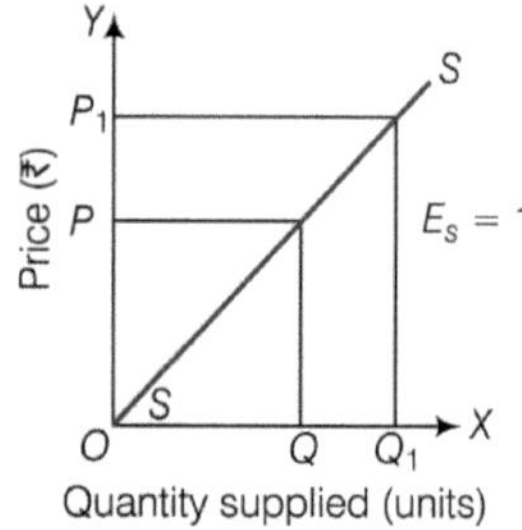

(iv) **More than Unitary Elastic Supply** In this situation, percentage change in quantity supplied is greater than the percentage change in price.
An upward sloping straight line supply curve originates from Y-axis and $E_s > 1$, as shown in the figure

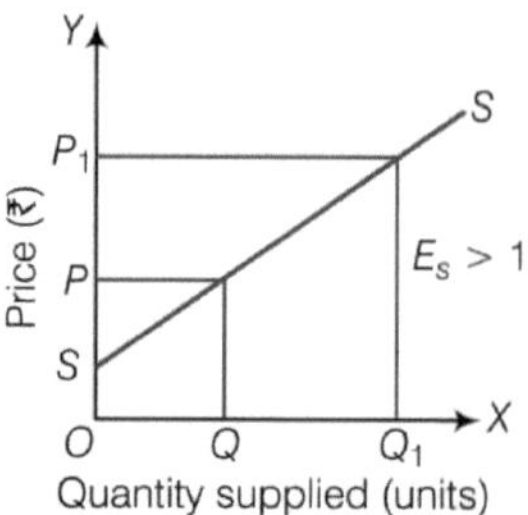

(v) **Less than Unitary Elastic Supply** In this situation, percentage change in quantity supplied is less than percentage change in price. An upward sloping straight line supply curve originates from X-axis and $E_s < 1$, as shown in the figure

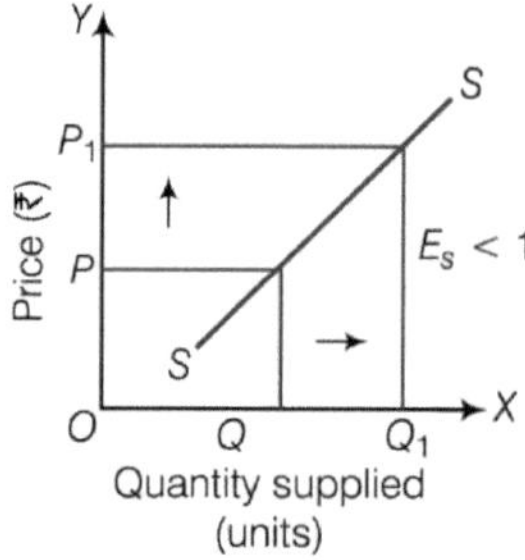

Chapter Test

Multiple Choice Questions

1. Supply schedule shows ...... relationship between price and quantity supplied of a commodity.
(a) positive (b) inverse (c) negative (d) opposite

2. Which the following shows relationship between the price of a commodity and quantity supplied graphically?
(a) Supply statement (b) Supply schedule (c) Supply curve (d) All of these

3. A firm will supply more quantity of a commodity at same price or even at a reduced price, if the firm wants to
(a) maximise profit (b) maximise social welfare (c) maximise sales (d) maximise wealth

4. A supply curve will shift leftward due to
(a) increase in supply (b) increase in quantity supplied (c) decrease in supply (d) decrease in quantity supplied

Short Answer (SA) Type Questions

1. 'Developing countries have constraints'. Do you agree?

2. A new technique of production reduces the marginal cost of producing stainless steel. How will this affect the supply curve of stainless steel utensils?

3. 'A loss-making firm has inelastic supply'. Do you agree? If yes, why?

4. Total Revenue at a price of ₹ 4 per unit of a commodity is ₹ 480. Total Revenue increases by ₹ 240 when its price rises by 25%. Calculate its price elasticity of supply.

5. Total Revenue is ₹ 400 when the price of the commodity is ₹ 2 per unit. When price rises to ₹ 3 per unit, the quantity supplied is 300 units. Calculate the price elasticity of supply.

Long Answer (LA) Type Questions

1. (i) There are three identical firms in a market. The following table shows the supply schedule of firm. Compute the market supply schedule.

Price (₹)	SS_1 (Units)
0	0
1	0
2	2
3	4
4	6
5	8
6	10
7	12
8	14

(ii) A firm earns a revenue of ₹ 50 when the market price of a good is ₹ 10. The market price increases to ₹ 15 and the firm now earns a revenue of ₹ 150. What is the price elasticity of the firm's supply curve?

2. (i) The market price of a good changes from ₹ 5 to ₹ 20. As a result, the quantity supplied by a firm increases by 15 units. The price elasticity of the firm's supply curve is 0.5. Find the initial and final output levels of the firm.

(ii) At the market price of ₹ 10, a firm supplies 4 units of output. The market price increases to ₹ 30. The price elasticity of the firm's supply is 1.25. What quantity will the firm supply at the new price?

Answers

Multiple Choice Questions

1. (a)   *2. (c)*   *3. (c)*   *4. (c)*

For Detailed Solutions

Scan the code

CHAPTER 03

Forms of Market and Price Determination

In this Chapter...

- Concept of Market
- Perfect Competition
- Market Equilibrium

Concept of Market

Market may be defined as an arrangement of establishing effective relationship between buyers and sellers of the commodities.

It is a complex set of activities by which potential buyers and sellers are brought in contact with each other for the purchase and sale of a commodity.

In other words, market refers to a place where buyers and sellers of a particular commodity meet and exchange goods or services at a particular price, during a given time period. It should be remembered that in economics, the term 'market' refers not necessarily to a place, but always to a commodity. So, there exist a market for cars, a market for clothes, etc.

Forms of Market

Market may assume different forms depending on the factors like number of buyers, sellers, nature of the product bought and sold, barriers to entry and exit of firms, degree of price control, etc.

On the basis of the given factors, there are two main forms of market

- Perfect competition
- Imperfect competition

  It can be further bifurcated as

  (a) Monoply   (b) Monopolistic competition

  (c) Oligopoly

Note *As per scope of syllabus, we will discuss only perfect competition in detail.*

Perfect Competition

It is a form of market where there are very large number of buyers and sellers of a commodity, exchanging homogeneous products at a price fixed by the market.

Pure Competition It is a market form in which there are very large number of buyers and sellers, presence of a homogeneous product and free entry or exit of firms, i.e., it follows some characteristics of perfect competition.

Features of Perfect Competition

Perfect competitive market exhibits the features given below

1. **Very Large Number of Buyers and Sellers** There are very large number of buyers and sellers in the market due to which no individual buyer or seller can influence the price of the commodity in the market.

   Any change in the output supplied by a single firm will not affect the total output of the industry, as it is very small according to the market size. It is due to this reason, that firm under perfect competition is said to be **price taker**.

   Similarly, any change in the demand pattern of one buyer would not affect the market demand because of his insignificant share in the total demand of the commodity.

2. **Homogeneous Product** Firms in this market sell homogeneous product. Homogeneity of a product implies that one unit of the product is a perfect substitute for another, i.e. there is no difference in the products in any form.

3. **Free Entry and Exit of Firms** In a perfectly competitive market, there are no barriers to entry or exit of firms. Entry or exit may take time, but firms have

freedom to move in and out of an industry, without any government intervention.

4. **Perfect Knowledge** Firms have all the knowledge about the product market and the factor market. Buyers also have perfect knowledge about the product market.

5. **Perfect Mobility of Factors of Production** The factors of production can move easily from one firm to another. Workers can also move between jobs and places.

6. **Absence of Transportation Cost** To insure uniform price in the market, it is assumed that goods can be easily transported from one place to another without any additional transportation cost or that the transportation cost of all the firms are identical.

Demand Curve under Perfect Competition

Under perfect competition, demand curve of the firm is perfectly elastic ($E_d = \infty$). It means that the firm can sell any amount of the commodity at the prevailing price.

Firm's demand curve is indicated by a horizontal straight line parallel to X-axis. This shows that the firm has to accept the price as determined by the forces of market supply and market demand.

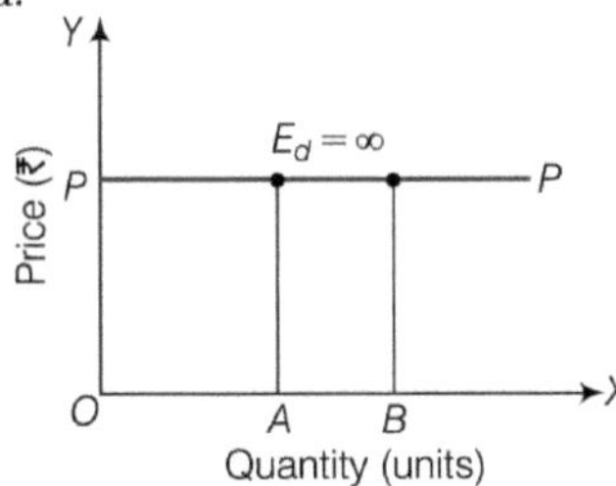

The above figure shows that at the given price OP, the firm can sell any quantity of the commodity it produces. Price remains constant which is determined by the market whether quantity demanded is OA or OB or even zero.

Determination of Market Equilibrium under Perfect Competition

Under perfect competition, market equilibrium is determined at the point where market demand and market supply for the industry as a whole are equal to each other, which gives the price of individual firms as given, and hence AR and MR curves of the firms coincide with each other and additional revenue (MR) is the price charged for the previous unit.

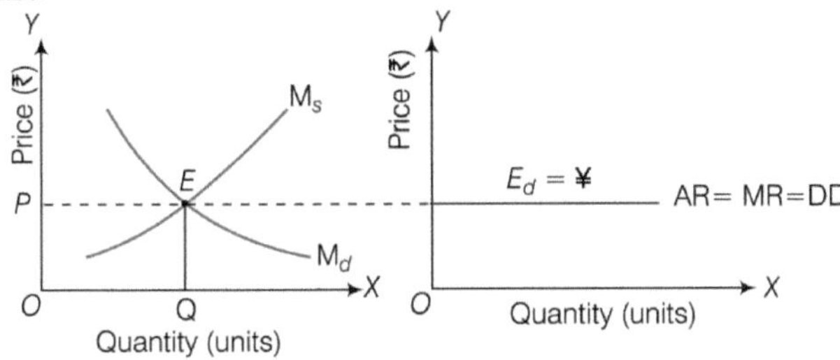

Demand curve and market equilibrium under perfect competition

Where,

M_s = Market supply, E = Equilibrium point,

M_d = Market demand, P = Equilibrium price,

  Q = Equilibrium quantity

Note *In perfect competition, Price = Average Revenue = Marginal Revenue because of a constant price prevailing in the market.*

Effect on Equilibrium due to Change in Demand
When there is increase in demand, demand curve shifts to the right, leading to rise in equilibrium price and quantity and decrease in demand causes a leftward shift in demand curve, leading to fall in equilibrium price and quantity.

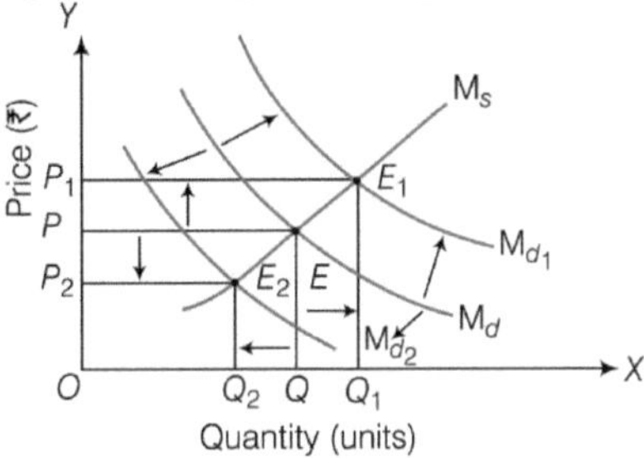

In short,

Effect of	On Price	On Quantity
Increase in demand	Increase	Increase
Decrease in demand	Decrease	Decrease

Effect on Equilibrium due to Change in Supply
When there is increase in supply, supply curve shifts to the right, leading to fall in equilibrium price and rise in equilibrium quantity and decrease in supply causes a leftward shift in the supply curve, leading to rise in equilibrium price and fall in equilibrium quantity.

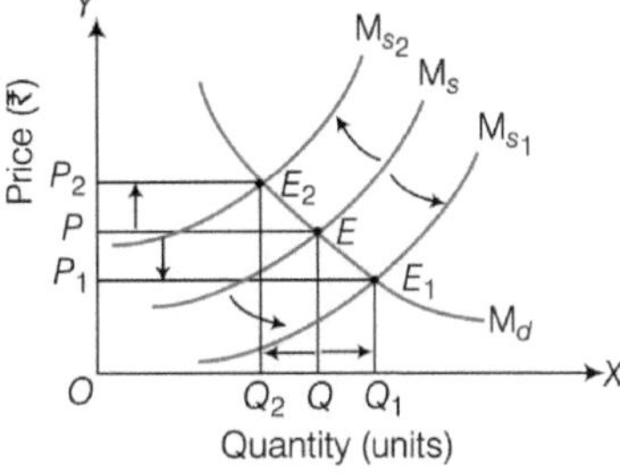

In short,

Effect of	On Price	On Quantity
Increase in supply	Decrease	Increase
Decrease in supply	Increase	Decrease

Impact on Market Equilibrium of Free Entry and Exit

In the long-run, free entry and exit of firms take place under perfect competition. Firms will earn only normal profit in the long-run. It is assumed that all firms in market are identical.

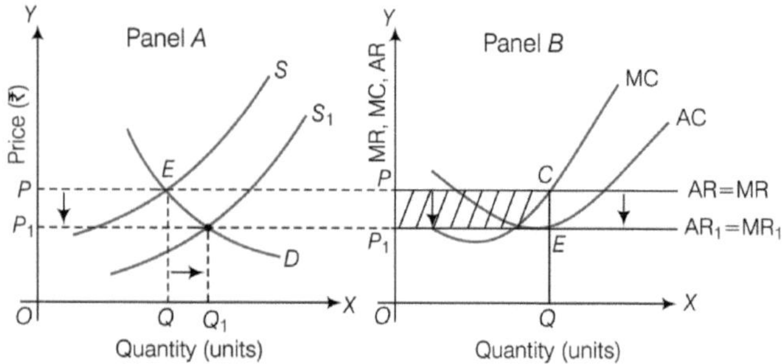

Long-run equilibrium of perfect competition

Above diagram states that as there is short-run profit equal to the shaded area of panel B, new firm will enter the market hence market price fall as supply rises and profit will be wiped out in the long-run. Similarly, loss in short-run will be wiped out by exit of existing firms. Let us understand this under different situations

- If the firm is earning supernormal profits in the short-run, it will attract new firms in the long-run till the supernormal profits are wiped away (it occurs when $P > AC$).
- If the firms are incurring losses in the short-run, some of them will leave the industry in the long-run till normal profits are earned (it occurs when $P < AC$).
- If price is equal to the minimum AC of the firms, each firm will be earning normal profit (it occurs when $P = AC$).

Thus, with free entry and exit of firms, equilibrium is always there, where price is equal to minimum AC.

Market Equilibrium

It is a situation of the market in which demand for a commodity is exactly equal to its supply corresponding to a particular price. Market equilibrium leads to equilibrium price and equilibrium quantity.

The price at which the quantity demanded and supplied are equal is known as **equilibrium price**, while the quantity demanded and supplied at an equilibrium price is known as **equilibrium quantity**.

The following are the assumptions of market equilibrium

- Demand curve should always has a negative slope.
- Supply curve should always has a positive slope.

Determination of Equilibrium Price and Quantity

In a market, market equilibrium is determined by the forces of

1. **Market Demand** It refers to the sum total of demand of a commodity by all the buyers in the market.
2. **Market Supply** It refers to the sum total of supply of a commodity by all the firms in the market.

In a market, the equilibrium price and quantity are determined by the interaction of the demand and supply curves in the market.

This has been explained with the help of an imaginary schedule and diagram

Price ($\r"mathrm{₹}$)	Demand (Units)	Supply (Units)	
1	500	100 ⎤	Excess demand
2	400	200 ⎦	
3	300	300	Equilibrium $(D = S)$
4	200	400 ⎤	Excess supply
5	100	500 ⎦	

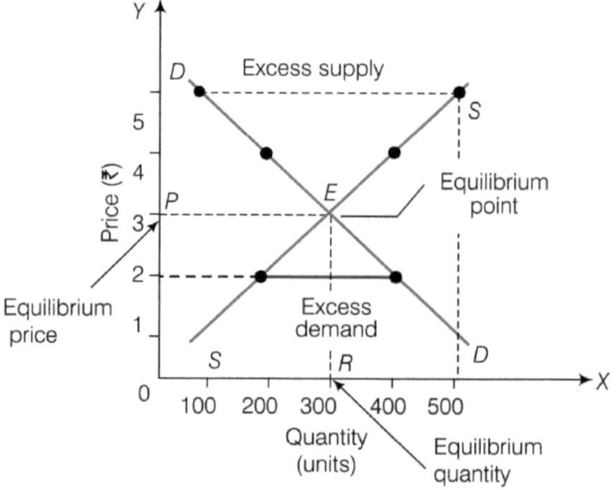

Determination of equilibrium price and quantity under perfect competition

In the above schedule and diagram, demand and supply are equal only at the price of ₹ 3.00, so it will be equilibrium price.

At this price, 300 units are demanded and supplied. So, equilibrium quantity is 300 units. Also, it is clear that equilibrium price is determined at the point, where demand and supply curves intersect each other.

Also, recept one equilibrium quantity, there will be either excess demand or excess supply.

Excess demand means market demand exceeds market supply of a commodity at a given price while **Excess supply** means market supply of a commodity is more than the market demand for a commodity at a given price.

Change in Demand and its Effect on Equilibrium Price

1. **Increase in Demand** Supply curve remaining unchanged, if there is increase in demand, demand curve and equilibrium point will shift to the right. As a result, equilibrium quantity and equilibrium price both will increase.

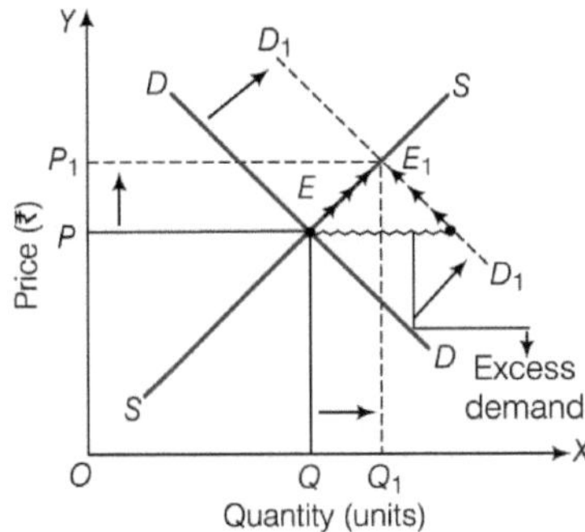
Increase in Demand

In the given diagram, actual demand curve DD and actual supply curve SS intersect at point E (i.e., equilibrium point). At this point, OP is equilibrium price and OQ is equilibrium quantity. Now, with the increase in demand, new demand curve becomes $D_1 D_1$.

So, equilibrium point shifts from E to E_1 and OP_1 is new equilibrium price and OQ_1 is the new equilibrium quantity.

2. **Decrease in Demand** Supply curve remaining unchanged, if there is a decrease in demand, demand curve and equilibrium point will shift to the left. As a result, equilibrium quantity and equilibrium price both will decrease.

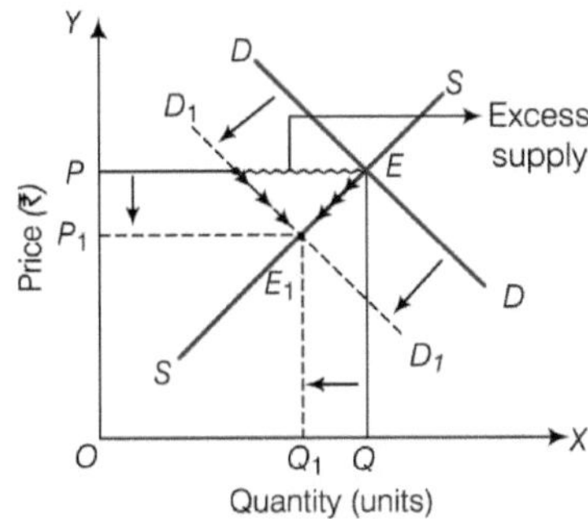
Decrease in Demand

In the given diagram, actual demand curve DD and actual supply curve SS intersect at point E (i.e. equilibrium point). At this point, the equilibrium price is OP and equilibrium quantity is OQ.

Now, due to decrease in demand, new demand curve is formed at $D_1 D_1$. It shows that price declines from OP to OP_1 because the demand has decreased from OQ to OQ_1.

Change in Supply and its Effect on Equilibrium Price

1. **Increase in Supply** Demand curve remaining unchanged, if there is increase in supply, supply curve and equilibrium point will shift rightwards. As a result, equilibrium price will decrease but equilibrium quantity will increase.

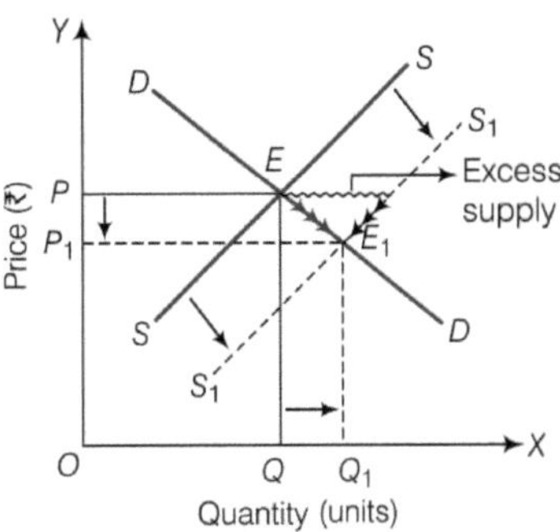
Increase in Supply

In the given diagram, actual demand curve DD and actual supply curve SS intersect at point E (i.e. equilibrium point). At this point, the equilibrium price is OP and equilibrium quantity is OQ.

Now, due to increase in supply, new supply curve is formed at $S_1 S_1$. It shows that price declines from OP to OP_1 and quantity increases from OQ to OQ_1.

2. **Decrease in Supply** Demand curve remaining unchanged, if there is decrease in supply, supply curve and equilibrium point will shift leftwards. As a result, equilibrium price will increase and equilibrium quantity will decrease. In the given diagram, actual demand curve DD and actual supply curve SS intersect at point E (i.e., equilibrium point).

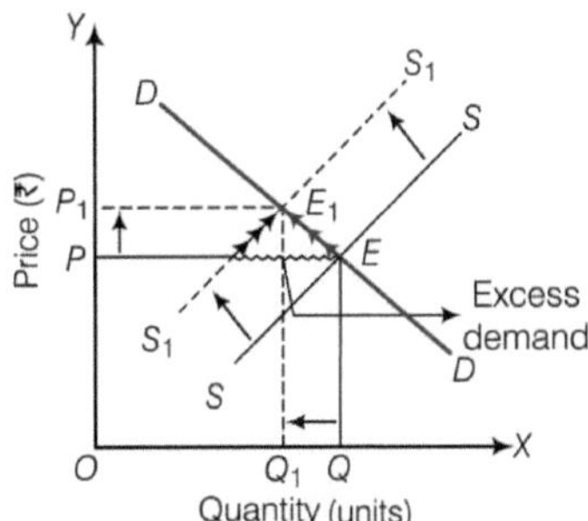
Decrease in Demand

At this point, OP is the equilibrium price and OQ is the equilibrium quantity.

Now, due to decrease in supply, new supply curve $S_1 S_1$ is formed. It cuts demand curve at new equilibrium point E_1. At this point, new equilibrium price increases to OP_1 and the equilibrium quantity reduces to OQ_1.

Simultaneous Change in both Demand and Supply

There may be the cases when demand and supply change simultaneously. There may be simultaneous increase in demand and supply or there may be simultaneous decrease in demand and supply.

Different situations are discussed as under

1. **When Both Demand and Supply Increase in the Same Proportion** Different situations are discusses as under When increase in demand is equal to increase in supply, the price will remain the same and the equilibrium output will increase.

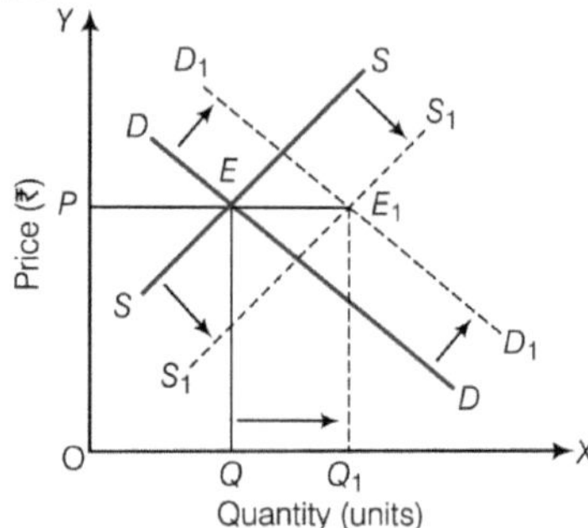

In the given diagram, actual demand curve DD and actual supply curve SS intersect at point E, (i.e., equilibrium point).

At this point, OP is the equilibrium price and OQ is equilibrium output.

Now, demand increases to D_1D_1 and supply increases to S_1S_1, such that both increases are equal. The new curves intersect each other at point E_1. It shows that equilibrium price remains the same because increase in demand and supply are in the same proportion. However, equilibrium quantity increases from OQ to OQ_1.

2. **When Increase in Supply is Less than Increase in Demand** If the increase in demand is more than the increase in supply, both equilibrium price and quantity will increase.

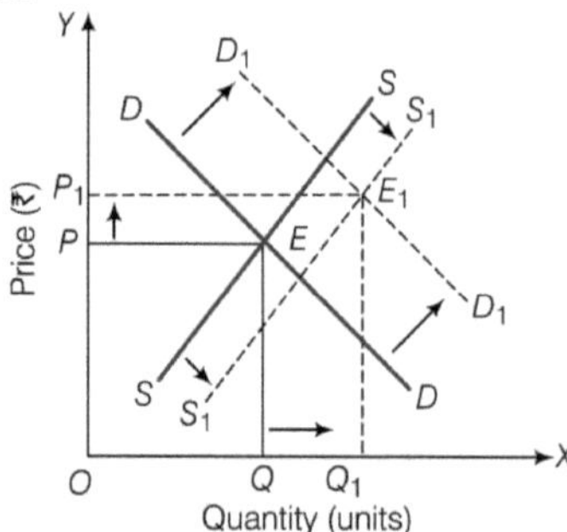

Increase in supply is less than increase in demand

In the given diagram, actual demand curve DD and actual supply curve SS intersect at point E (i.e., equilibrium point). At this point, OP is the equilibrium price and OQ is equilibrium output.

Now, demand increases to D_1D_1 and supply increases to S_1S_1, but the increase in demand is greater than the increase in supply. The new curves intersect each other at point E_1. It shows that price has increased to OP_1, and quantity demanded and supplied has increased to OQ_1.

3. **When Increase in Supply is More than Increase in Demand** If the increase in supply is more than the increase in demand, equilibrium price falls and equilibrium quantity goes up.

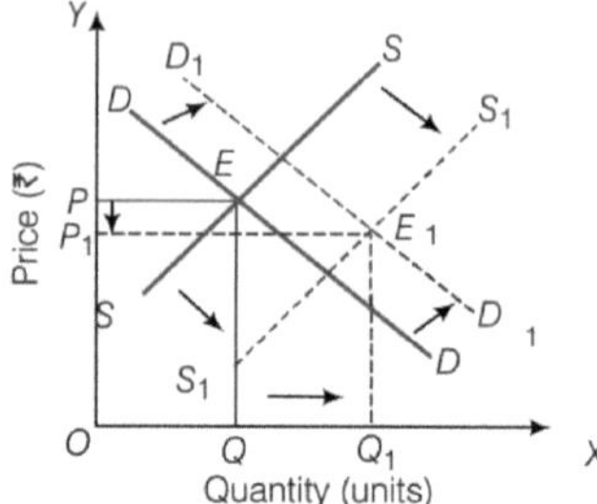

Increase in supply is more than increase in demand

In the above diagram, actual demand curve DD and actual supply curve SS intersect at point E (i.e., equilibrium point). At this point, OP is the equilibrium price and OQ is equilibrium quantity.

Now, demand increases to D_1D_1 and supply increases to S_1S_1, but the increase in supply is greater than the increase in demand. The new curves intersect each other at point E_1. It shows that price has decreased to OP_1 and the quantity demanded and supplied has increased to OQ_1.

4. **When Both Demand and Supply Decrease in the Same Proportion** When decrease in supply is equal to decrease in demand, equilibrium price will remain the same, but equilibrium output will decrease.

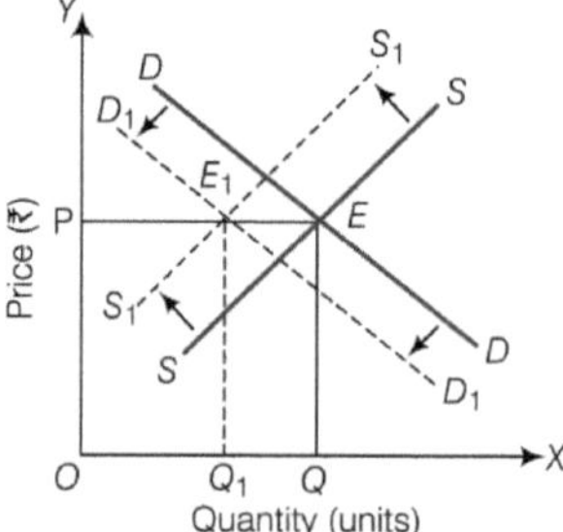

Demand and supply decrease in the same proportion

In the above diagram, actual demand curve DD and actual supply curve SS intersect at point E (i.e., equilibrium point). At this point, OP is equilibrium price and OQ is equilibrium quantity.

Now demand decreases to D_1D_1 and supply decreases to S_1S_1. The new curves intersect each other at point E_1. It shows that equilibrium price remains constant because both demand and supply have decreased in the same proportion. However, equilibrium quantity decreases to OQ_1.

5. **When Decrease in Demand is More than the Decrease in Supply** If decrease in demand is more than the decrease in supply, the equilibrium price and output both will fall.

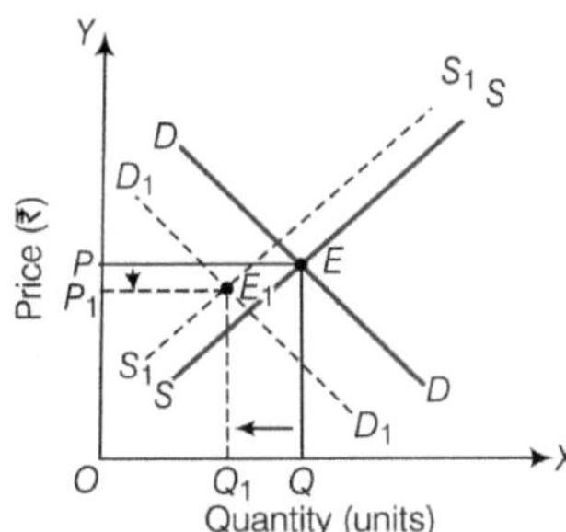

Decrease in demand is more than the decrease in supply

In the given diagram, actual demand curve DD and actual supply curve SS intersect at point E (i.e. equilibrium point). At this point, OP is equilibrium price and OQ is equilibrium quantity.

Now, demand decreases to $D_1 D_1$ and supply decreases to $S_1 S_1$, but decrease in demand is more than that of supply. The new curves intersect each other at point E_1 which is the new equilibrium point.

Thus, the equilibrium price reduces to OP_1 and quantity demanded and supplied will decrease to OQ_1.

6. **When Decrease in Demand is Less than the Decrease in Supply** If decrease in demand is less than the decrease in supply, equilibrium price will rise and equilibrium quantity will fall.

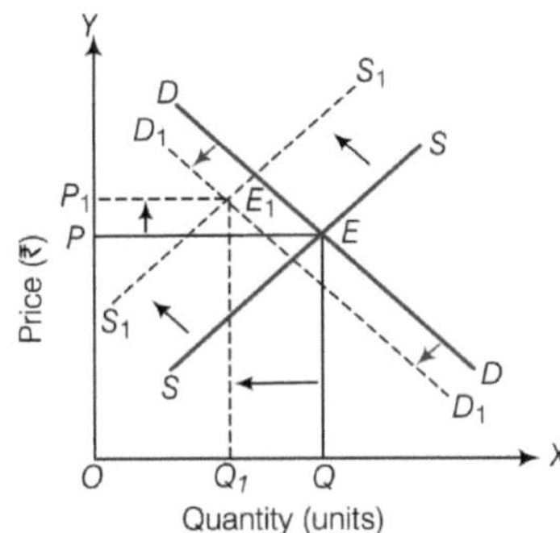

Decrease in demand is less than the decrease in supply

In the given diagram, actual demand curve DD and actual supply curve SS intersect at point E (i.e., equilibrium point). At this point, OP is equilibrium price and OQ is equilibrium quantity.

Now, demand decreases to $D_1 D_1$ and supply decreases to $S_1 S_1$, but decrease in demand is less than that of supply. The new curves intersect each other at point E_1 which is the new equilibrium point.

Thus, the equilibrium price increases from OP to OP_1 and quantity demanded and supplied will decrease from OQ to OQ_1.

7. **When Increase in Demand is Equal to Decrease in Supply** If the increase in demand is equal to decrease in supply, its equilibrium price will increase sharply and equilibrium quantity will remain the same.

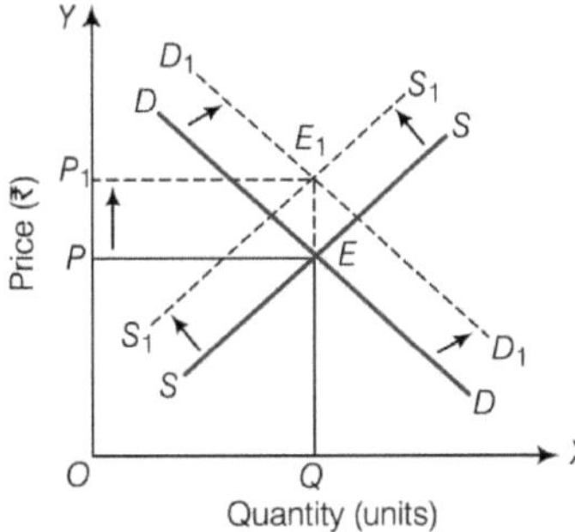

In the given diagram, actual demand curve DD and actual supply curve SS intersect at point E (i.e., equilibrium point). At this point, OP is equilibrium price and OQ is equilibrium quantity.

Now, demand increases to $D_1 D_1$ and supply decreases to $S_1 S_1$. New demand and supply curves intersect each other at point E_1.

The equilibrium price has risen from OP to OP_1 and equilibrium quantity remains the same at OQ units. Thus, equilibrium price increases sharply when increase in demand is equal to decrease in supply.

8. **When Decrease in Demand is Equal to Increase in Supply** If the demand for a commodity decreases and its supply increases in the same proportion, its equilibrium price will fall sharply and equilibrium quantity will remain the same.

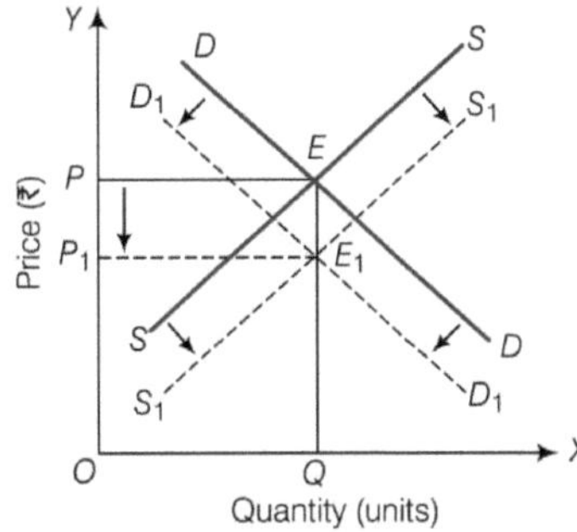

Decrease in demand is equal to increase in supply

In the given diagram, actual demand curve DD and actual supply curve SS intersect at point E (i.e., equilibrium point). At this point, OP is equilibrium price and OQ is equilibrium quantity.

Now, demand decreases to $D_1 D_1$ and supply increases to $S_1 S_1$. New demand and supply curves intersect each other at point E_1. It is the new point of equilibrium.

The equilibrium price falls from OP to OP_1 and equilibrium quantity remains the same at OQ units.

Thus, equilibrium price declines sharply when decrease in demand is equal to increase in supply.

Special Cases which affect Equilibrium Price

There are some special cases also, which affects the equilibrium price and quantity

1. **Change in Supply when Demand is Perfectly Elastic** In this case, price will remain constant, only quantity will increase with rise in supply and vice-versa.

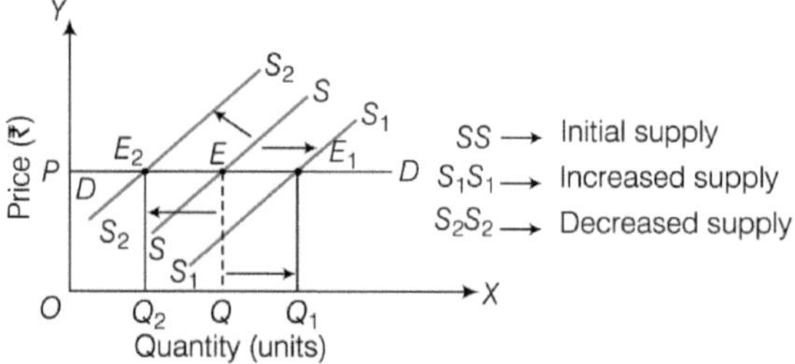

Change in supply when demand is perfectly elastic

2. **Change in Supply when Demand is Perfectly Inelastic** In this case, quantity will remain unchanged, only price will increase with fall in supply and vice-versa.

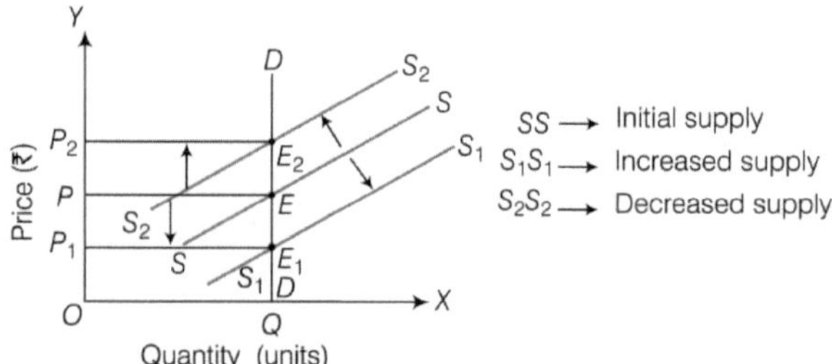

Change in supply when demand is perfectly inelastic

3. **Change in Demand when Supply is Perfectly Elastic** In this case, price will remain constant, quantity will increase with the increase in demand and vice-versa.

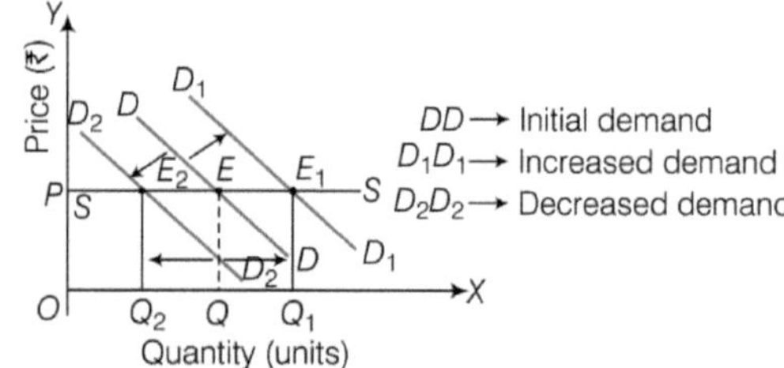

Change in demand when supply is perfectly elastic

4. **Change in Demand when Supply is Perfectly Inelastic** In this case, quantity will remain unchanged, only price will rise with rise in demand and vice-versa.

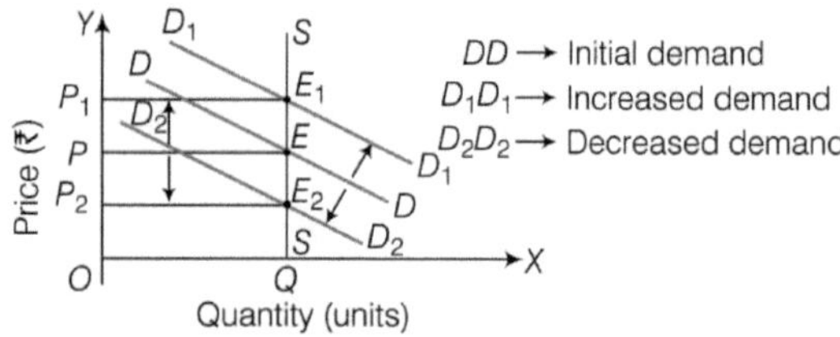

Change in demand when supply is perfectly inelastic

Simple Applications of Demand and Supply

There are following applications of demand and supply

1. **Price Ceiling** Ceiling means maximum limit. Price ceiling means maximum price of a commodity that the sellers can charge from the buyers.

   Often the government fixes this price much below the equilibrium market price of a commodity, so that it becomes within the reach of the poorer sections of the society. It is resorted to protect the interest of the consumer.

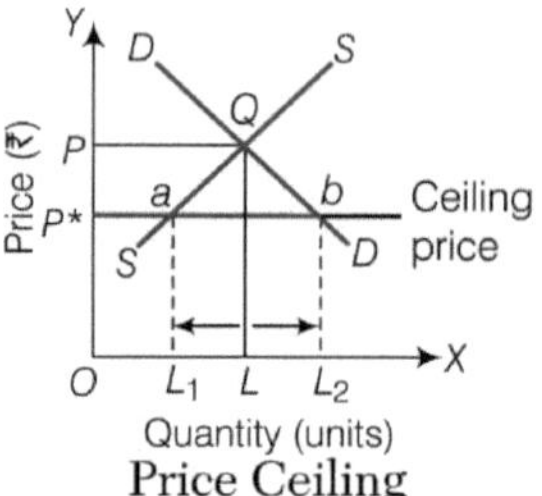

Price Ceiling

Equilibrium price $= OP$

Equilibrium quantity $= OL$

Ceiling price $= OP*$

Excess demand $= ab = L_1 L_2$

Excess demand may be fulfilled by

- Rationing
- First-cum-first serve basis

  It leads to black marketing.

2. **Price Floor** Floor means the lowest limit. Price floor means the minimum price fixed by the government for a commodity in the market to protect the interest of the producers.

   It seems paradoxical, but is true that the government in most countries fixes floor price for most agricultural products, food grains in particular. In fact, floor price invariably implies support price as well.

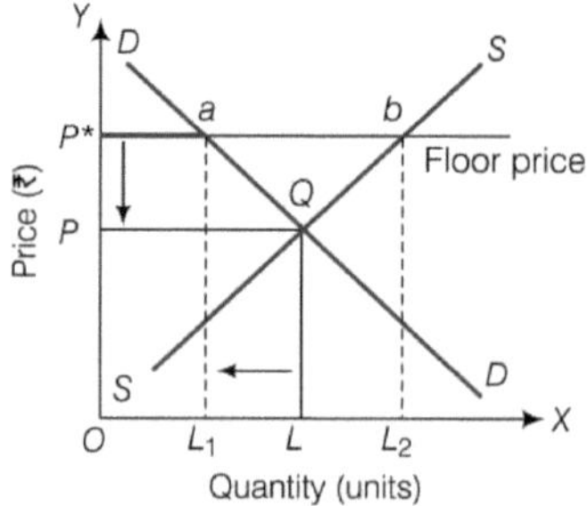

Price Floor

Equilibrium price $= OP$

Equilibrium quantity $= OL$

Floor price $= OP*$

Excess supply $= ab = L_1 L_2$

Generally, government buys the excess supply at this price.

3. **Viable Industry** An industry is said to be inviable condition, if corresponding to the minimum price, there is some demand in the market.

   In such industries, demand and supply curves coincide in the positive quadrant.

   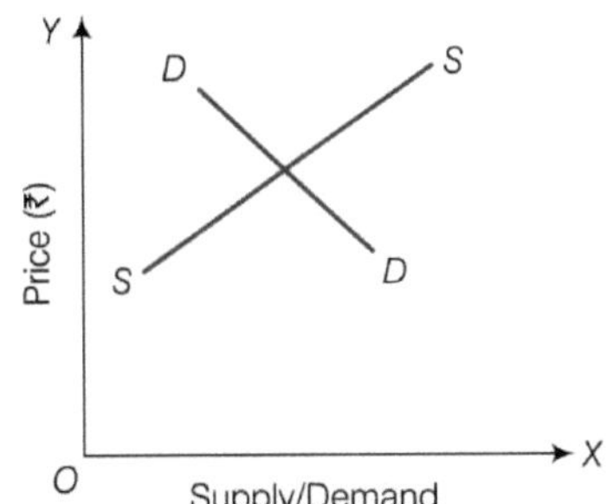

4. **Non-viable Industry** A non-viable industry is one which will not produce the product in an economy.

   It may be because cost of the product is too high and the consumers are not willing to pay a price that will cover the cost,

   e.g. commercial aircraft is a non-viable industry in India. In this case, demand and supply curve will not intersect in the positive quadrant.

   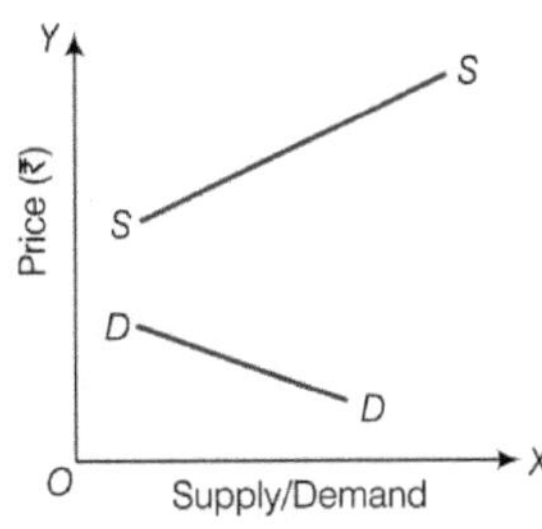

5. **Rationing** If there is shortage of certain goods, the government introduces rationing for distribution of commodity to consumers especially weaker sections of the society. Rationing ensures the availability of the commodity to the poor consumers, who would not have received the commodity in free marketing of the commodity. Rationing implies restriction on quantity which can be bought and consumed by the consumer.

6. **Black Marketing** It is a situation in which the controlled commodity is sold at a price higher than the price fixed by the government illegally under the desk. The reason arising for this situation are
   - Presence of such consumers who are willing to pay more than the ceiling price.
   - Presence of excessive influential and wealthy consumers in large numbers.

Chapter Practice

Objective Questions

• Multiple Choice Questions

1. In perfect competition, as the firm is a price taker, the ...... curve is a horizontal straight line.
(a) marginal cost
(b) total cost
(c) total revenue
(d) marginal revenue

Ans. (d) marginal revenue

2. Which of the following is not an essential condition of pure competition?
(a) Large number of buyers and sellers
(b) Homogeneous product
(c) Freedom of entry and exit
(d) Absence of transport cost

Ans. (d) Absence of transportation cost is a feature/assumption of perfect competition and not pure competition.

3. An increase in supply with demand remaining the same bring about ....
(a) an increase in equilibrium quantity and decrease in equilibrium price
(b) an increase in equilibrium price and decrease in equilibrium quantity
(c) decrease in both equilibrium price and quantity
(d) None of the above

Ans. (a) an increase in equilibrium quantity and decrease in equilibrium price

4. An increase in demand with unchanged supply leads to ....
(a) rise in equilibrium price and fall in equilibrium quantity
(b) fall in both equilibrium price and quantity
(c) rise in both equilibrium price and quantity
(d) fall in equilibrium price and rise in equilibrium quantity

Ans. (c) rise in both equilibrium price and quantity

5. If price is forced to stay below equilibrium price...... .
(a) excess supply exists
(b) excess demand exists
(c) Either (a) or (b)
(d) Neither (a) nor (b)

Ans. (b) When the market price is fixed below the equilibrium price, it is known as price flooring. Price floor leads to excess demand as there are less suppliers who are willing to supply at the existing price.

6. Equilibrium price may be determined through ....
(a) only demand
(b) only supply
(c) Both demand and supply
(d) None of the above

Ans. (c) Both demand and supply

7. ...... is a situation of the market in which demand for a commodity is exactly equal to its supply corresponding to a particular price.
(a) Consumer equilibrium
(b) Producer equilibrium
(c) Market equilibrium
(d) Balance of trade

Ans. (c) Market equilibrium

8. If the market supply is less than the market demand of a commodity at a given price, it is called
(a) Excess supply
(b) Excess demand
(c) Deficit demand
(d) Market supply

Ans. (b) Excess demand

9. If there is shortage of certain goods, the government introduces ...... for distribution of commodity to consumers.
(a) planning
(b) marketing
(c) rationing
(d) financing

Ans. (c) rationing

10. Nature of goods under pure competition is ....
(a) homogeneous
(b) heterogeneous
(c) both (a) and (b)
(d) neither (a) nor (b)

Ans. (a) homogeneous

11. Choose the correct statement from given below
(a) If a firm charge lower price under perfect competition, it faces losses.
(b) If a firm charge higher price under perfect competition, it faces losses.

(c) Individual firms under perfect competition, sell insignificant proportion in the market.

(d) All of the above

Ans. (d) All of the above

12. What is the implication of perfect knowledge under perfect competition?

(a) Losses in long-run

(b) No seller can charge a different price than market price

(c) Both (a) and (b)

(d) Neither (a) nor (b)

Ans. (b) No seller can charge a different price than market price

13. Which of the following is the closest example of perfect competition in Indian market?

(a) Aircraft industry   (b) Manufacturing

(c) Agriculture   (d) None of these

Ans. (c) Agriculture

14. **Statement I** When demand and supply changes in the same direction, equilibrium quantity always remains constant.

Statement II If demand is perfectly elastic, there will be no impact of change in supply on the equilibrium price.

Alternatives

(a) Statement I is correct and Statement II is incorrect

(b) Statement II is correct and Statement I is incorrect

(c) Both the statements are correct

(d) Both the statements are incorrect

Ans. (b) Statement II is correct and Statement I is incorrect

15. Choose the correct pair.

	Column I		Column II
A.	No Possible Market Equilibrium	(i)	Viable Industry
B.	Equilibrium with Equality of Market Forces	(ii)	Non-viable Industry
C.	Price Ceiling	(iii)	Black Marketing
D.	Price Flooring	(iv)	Rationing

Codes

(a) A–(i)   (b) B–(ii)

(c) C–(iii)   (d) D–(iv)

Ans. (c) C–(iii)

• Assertion-Reasoning MCQs

Direction *(Q. Nos. 1 to 4) There are two statements marked as Assertion (A) and Reason (R). Read the statements and choose the appropriate option from the options given below*

(a) Both Assertion (A) and Reason (R) are true and Reason (R) is the correct explanation of Assertion (A)

(b) Both Assertion (A) and Reason (R) are true, but Reason (R) is not the correct explanation of Assertion (A)

(c) Assertion (A) is true, but Reason (R) is false

(d) Both Assertion (A) and Reason (R) are false

1. **Assertion** (A) Industry is a price maker under perfectly competitive market.

Reason (R) Individual firms are too small according to the market size that they sell at the given price.

Ans. (a) Both Assertion (A) and Reason (R) are true and Reason (R) is the correct explanation of Assertion (A)

2. **Assertion** (A) Market based economies are more efficient as they work as the basis of free play of demand and supply.

Reason (R) Invisible hands of demand and supply automatically adjusts the market towards equilibrium.

Ans. (a) Both Assertion (A) and Reason (R) are true and Reason (R) is the correct explanation of Assertion (A)

3. **Assertion** (A) Price ceiling is a direct government action of fixing the market price above equilibrium price.

Reason (R) In non-viable industries, government intervenes to resort market as equilibrium price cannot be determined by market forces of demand and supply.

Ans. (d) Price ceiling is the direct action of the government to set the market price below equilibrium price. No equilibrium is possible in case of non-viable industries.

4. **Assertion** (A) Controlled price mechanism system prevails in socialistic an communist countries where the government has exclusive rights on production, distribution and consumption.

Reason (R) The central authority has to decide upon the various commodities which the economy should product with the available resources when market mechanism fails to give desirable result.

Ans. (a) Both Assertion (A) and Reason (R) are true and Reason (R) is the correct explanation of Assertion (A)

• Case Based MCQs

1. **Direction** *Read the following text and answer the question no. (i) to (vi) on the basis of the same.*

Under perfect competition, there are a large number of sellers selling homogenous product. Each seller sells quite an insignificant portion of total market supply that none of them can influence the price in the market. Both buyers and sellers do not have any trade union or association.

The price of the commodity under perfect competition is determined by the forces of demand and supply of the product. Every seller accepts the price as determined by the market. No individual firm can influence this price. It has to decide how much quantity of the commodity it wants to sell. It is because of this, that the seller under perfect competition is a price taker.

(i) Under which form of market, a firm sells homogeneous goods?
(a) Perfect competition
(b) Monopoly
(c) Monopolistic competition
(d) Both (a) and (b)

Ans. (a) Perfect competition

(ii) Average revenue curve under perfect competition is perfectly elastic due to ....
(a) large number of sellers
(b) homogeneous goods
(c) freedom of entry andexit
(d) All of the above

Ans. (a) large number of sellers

(iii) A perfectly competitive firm can earn only normal profits in long-run due to ....
(a) large number of sellers   (b) homogenous goods
(c) freedom of entry and exit (d) All of these

Ans. (c) freedom of entry and exit

(iv) What will happen to an individual seller if he decides to charge a lower price than the market?
(a) Earn higher profits
(b) Suffer losses
(c) Earn super normal profit in long-run
(d) Either (a) or (b)

Ans. (b) A seller is very small according to the market. So, if an individual seller charges a lower price, he will suffer loss as it can't serve the entire market.

(v) **Assertion** (A) A firm under perfect competition will suffer loss if it charges a price lower than the market price.

Reason (R) Individual firms under perfectly competitive market sells very insignificant proportion and thus cannot serve the entire market.

Alternatives
(a) Both Assertion (A) and Reason (R) are true and Reason (R) is the correct explanation of Assertion (A)
(b) Both Assertion (A) and Reason (R) are true, but Reason (R) is not the correct explanation of Assertion (A)
(c) Assertion (A) is true, but Reason (R) is false
(d) Both Assertion (A) and Reason (R) are false

Ans. (a) Both Assertion (A) and Reason (R) are true and Reason (R) is the correct explanation of Assertion (A)

(vi) Firms under perfect competition earns normal profit in long-run, which of the following conditions gets satisfied in long-run?
(a) TR=TVC   (b) AR=TVC
(c) AR=AC   (d) TR=AC

Ans. (c) Normal profit is the situation where revenue and cost becomes equal thus, equality of AR and AC indicates the same point.

2. **Direction** *Read the following text and answer the question no. (i) to (vi) on the basis of the same.*

As one example of demand and supply analysis, let us assume we have a product in which government has imposed an additional tax of ₹ 1.00 per unit. The tax is charged to the seller. For every ₹ 1 of sales, assume that the seller must pay ₹ 0.07 to the government. (Notice that consumers do not pay sales taxes. You have not paid any sales tax money to any government agency. The store pays the sales tax to the government.)

From the point of view of the seller, this is an additional cost of production. In addition to all other costs, the seller must also pay the sales tax.

(i) What will be the impact of increase on tax?
(a) Demand will decrease   (b) Supply will decrease
(c) Both demand and supply will decrease
(d) Supply will remain constant

Ans. (b) Increase in taxes leads to increase in cost of production that further leads to fall in supply of the commodity.

(ii) How will this tax impact the market price of the good concerned?
(a) Market price will increase
(b) Market price will remain constant
(c) Market price will decrease
(d) None of the above

Ans. (a) Due to imposition of tax, the market price of the commodity rises above the equilibrium price.

(iii) How will the tax impact demand and supply curves?
(a) Demand curve will shift to left, supply curve will shift to left
(b) Demand curve will shift to left, supply curve will shift to right
(c) Demand curve will remain unchanged, supply curve will shift to left
(d) Supply curve will remain unchanged, demand curve will shift to left

Ans. (c) Increase in taxes leads to fall in supply thus, supply curve shifts leftwards.

(iv) What will be the impact of above change on equilibrium quantity, if demand is perfectly inelastic?
(a) Increase   (b) Decrease
(c) Remain constant
(d) Either increase or decrease

Ans. (c) When demand is perfectly inelastic, it has no impact on the quantity thus, equilibrium quantity remains unchanged.

(v) **Assertion** (A) Tax imposed by the government increases the market price above equilibrium price.

Reason (R) Imposition of tax leads to the situation of dis-equilibrium in the market of the good.

(a) Both Assertion (A) and Reason (R) are true and Reason (R) is the correct explanation of Assertion (A)

(b) Both Assertion (A) and Reason (R) are true, but Reason (R) is not the correct explanation of Assertion (A)

(c) Assertion (A) is true, but Reason (R) is false

(d) Both Assertion (A) and Reason (R) are false

Ans. (b) Imposition of tax leads to increase in cost of production of the producers, keeping the equilibrium price constant, it decreases the profit of the producers and fall in supply.

(vi) In the above situation, assume that the government offers a subsidy to the economically weaker section of the society. What is the likely impact on the equilibrium position due the following step?

(a) Equilibrium price will fall

(b) Equilibrium demand will increase

(c) It will lead to disequilibrium in the market

(d) None of the above

Ans. (c) Both tax and subsidy leads to dis-equilibrium as it impacts free play of market forces of demand and supply.

PART 2
Subjective Questions

• Short Answer (SA) Type Questions

1. Explain the implications of 'perfect knowledge about market 'under perfect competition.

Ans. Perfect knowledge means that both buyers and sellers are fully informed about the market price. Therefore, no firm is in a position to charge a different price and no buyer will pay a higher price. As a result, a uniform price prevails in the market. In case of perfect competition, buyers and sellers have perfect knowledge of the market.

2. Why can a firm not earn abnormal profits under perfect competition in the long-run? Explain.

Ans. There is freedom of entry and exit of firms under perfect competition. In situations of abnormal profits, new firms will be induced to join the industry. This increases market supply and lowers market price to finally wipe out abnormal profits. So, a firm cannot earn abnormal profits under perfect competition in the long-run.

3. Explain the implications of freedom of entry and exit of the firms under perfect competition.

Ans. A firm can enter or leave the industry any time. Because of free entry and exit, firms in the long-run can earn only normal profits (TR = TC or AR = AC). In case extra normal profits are earned in the short-run, new firms will join the industry.

Market supply will increase and market price will fall. Extra profits will be wiped out. In case of extra normal losses or abnormal losses, some of the existing firms will leave the industry. Market supply will decrease. Hence, market price will increase and extra normal losses will be wiped out. So, we can say that firms under perfect competition can earn only normal profits in the long-run.

4. Explain the conditions of perfect competition. Why is the demand curve facing a firm under perfect competition is perfectly elastic?

Ans. The main conditions of perfect competition are

(i) Large number of buyers and sellers

(ii) Homogeneous product

(iii) Perfect knowledge

(iv) Perfect mobility of factors of production

(v) Free exit and entry of the firms

(vi) No transport cost

When goods are purchased across different buyers, demand curve of a firm is perfectly elastic ($E_d = \infty$) because even the slightest change in price will cause an infinite change in demand. Because of this feature, it is also referred to be an imaginary market form.

5. Explain, how in the long-run, equilibrium with free entry and exit, firms under perfect competition earn zero abnormal profits.

Ans. A perfectly competitive firm in the long-run can earn normal profits only. In case an industry is showing supernormal profits (TR > TC or AR > AC) in short-run, new firms will join the industry leading to increase in supply and will shift market supply curve to the right. Accordingly market price will be reduced and supernormal profits will be wiped out.

In case of negative abnormal profits (losses) in the short-run when (TR < TC or AR < AC) some of the existing firms will leave the industry. Accordingly, supply will fall and market supply curve will shift to the left forcing the price to move up till the situation of zero normal profit is reached.

6. "Is a firm under perfect competition a price taker, or a price maker?" Justify your answer.

Ans. A firm under perfect competition is a price taker because of the following reasons

(i) A firm under perfect competition is contributing such a small fragment to the market supply that total supply schedule remains unaffected by any change in individual firm's supply.

(ii) All firms are selling homogeneous product. Accordingly, even partial control over price is not possible.

(iii) If any firm tries to fix its own price, it won't succeed. Higher price would drive the buyers to a large number of other sellers. Lower price would bring so many buyers to a firm that it cannot cope with the demand.

7. Explain the changes that will take place when in a market, the demand for a good is greater than supply at the prevailing price.

Ans. If at a prevailing price, quantity demanded is more than quantity supplied, then supplier will be motivated to increase the price of the commodity due to which demand decreases, till it reaches at the equilibrium price where quantity demanded is equal to quantity supplied.

8. In the case of luxury items like diamond, decrease in demand decreases equilibrium price. Do you agree?

Ans. No, this is not correct. The price of luxury items like diamond does not fall even if there is a decrease in demand. These items indicate social status of rich class due to which the price remains high, irrespective of change in demand.

9. Discuss the effects of simultaneous increase in demand and supply on equilibrium price.

Ans. (i) When demand increases more than supply, equilibrium price increases.

(ii) When demand and supply increase equally, equilibrium price remains constant.

(iii) When supply increases more than demand, equilibrium price falls.

10. Suppose the price at which equilibrium is attained in the figure given below is above the minimum average cost of the firms constituting the market. Now, if we allow for free entry and exit of firms, how will the market price adjust to it? **(NCERT)**

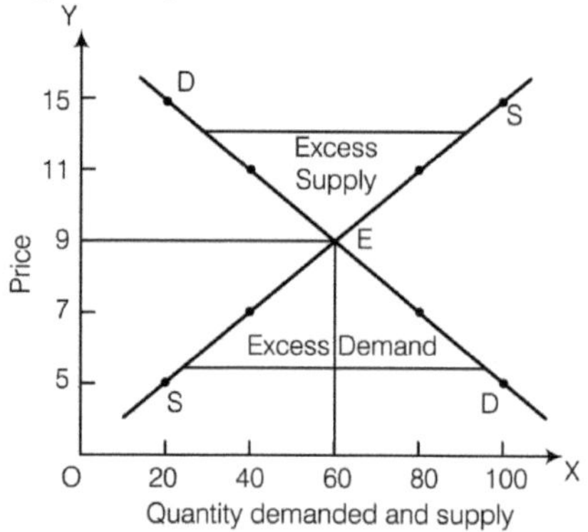

Ans. The equilibrium price is ₹ 9 in the above figure which is above the minimum of average cost. It implies that firm is earning supernormal profit. This situation attracts new firms, the industry supply of output also increases. New firms will continue to enter the industry which leads the price to fall until it becomes equal to minimum average cost. At this stage firms starts earning normal profit.

11. Increase in demand often causes a rise in price, but it is not always true. Explain.

Ans. Other things being equal, the increase in demand for a commodity should cause increase in price. But if other things are not equal, then this relationship may not hold true. e.g. if there is an equal increase in supply, the price may not increase. In fact, if the increase in supply is more than increase in demand, the price may fall.

12. How decisions are taken by the consumer and producer in a coordinated market?

Ans. The decisions of the consumers in the market are expressed through market demand schedule and market demand curve. The decisions of the producers are expressed through market supply schedule and market supply curve.

The decisions of consumers and producers are coordinated by the interaction of market demand and market supply. This is known as price mechanism, which determines equilibrium in the market.

13. Market for a good is in equilibrium. There is an increase in demand for this good. Explain the chain of effects of this change.

Or

By the given equilibrium in the market, explain the chain of effects of increase of demand for a good.

Ans. Equilibrium refers to the situation in which market demand is equal to market supply. The given diagram shows a situation of increase in demand. The demand curve shifts to the right from DD to D_1D_1. Equilibrium point shifts from E to E_1. Consequently, equilibrium price rises from OP to OP_1 and equilibrium quantity increases from OQ to OQ_1.

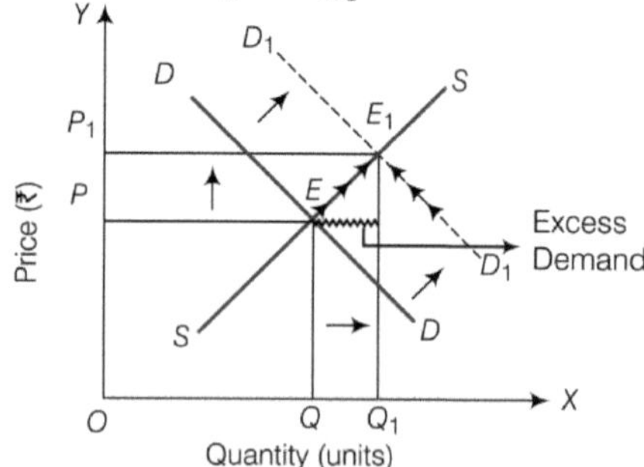

14. Explain why the equilibrium price of a commodity is determined at that level of output at which its demand equals its supply.

Ans. Equilibrium is a point when at a given price, quantity demanded is equal to quantity supplied and equilibrium can be attained only at that point. If at a given price, supply is more, it will show excess supply and if demand is more, it will show excess demand. In either case, there will be movement in price and hence quantities, i.e. these are not stable points. Only at equilibrium price, the quantity demanded is equal to quantity supplied and there is no tendency to change from this point.

15. Using supply and demand curves, show how an increase in the price of shoes affects the price of a pair of socks and the number of pairs of socks bought and sold. **(NCERT)**

Ans. Shoes and socks are complementary goods. An increase in the price of shoes will cause a decrease in demand of socks. It will lead to excess supply. This leads to competition among sellers, which reduces the price. Fall in price leads to decrease in supply and rise in demand. These changes continue till supply and demand become equal at a new equilibrium price. As a result there is a decrease in demand of both shoes and socks.

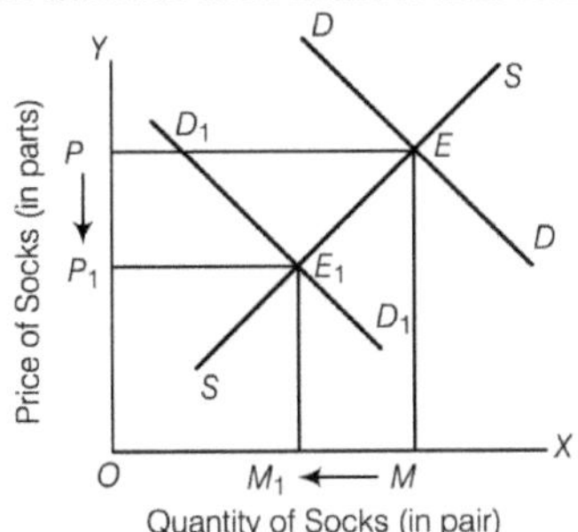

● Long Answer (LA) Type Questions

1. Equilibrium price of an essential medicine is too high. Explain what possible steps can be taken to bring down the equilibrium price, but only through the market forces. Also explain the series of changes that will occur in the market.

Ans. If the equilibrium price of an essential medicine is too high, then its price can be reduced by opting two ways

(i) Increase the supply of the commodity.

(ii) Government should provide such essential medicines on subsidised rates.

But as per the question, option (i) would be most appropriate. Changes that will occur in the market are described below using graph

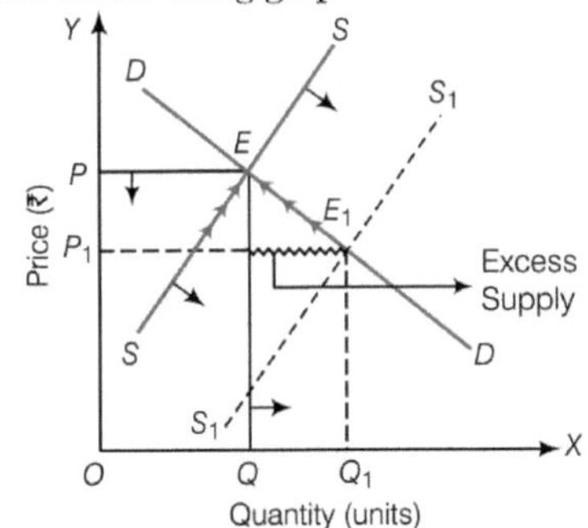

In the given figure, it is clearly depicted that due to increase in supply, the supply curve shifts to the right from SS to S_1S_1. The new supply curve S_1S_1 intersects the demand curve at point E_1. The equilibrium price decreases from OP to OP_1 and quantity increases from OQ to OQ_1.

Thus, it is clear that by increasing the supply of the medicines, its equilibrium price can be brought down as by doing so, competition will be increased among the producers and consequently, they would be forced to sell their output at lower cost.

2. (i) Explain the effect of increase in income of buyers of normal commodity on its equilibrium price.

(ii) How does the equilibrium price of a normal commodity change when income of its buyers falls? Explain the chain of effects.

Ans. (i) For a normal commodity, increase in income of the consumers means increase in its demand. Accordingly, demand curve shifts rightward and both equilibrium price and equilibrium quantity tends to increase.

In the given diagram, actual demand curve DD and actual supply curve SS intersect at point E (i.e. equilibrium point). When income of the buyer increases, the demand for normal good also rises and demand curve shifts rightward from DD to D_1D_1.

As a result, equilibrium price and quantity both are increased from OP to OP_1 and OQ to OQ_1.

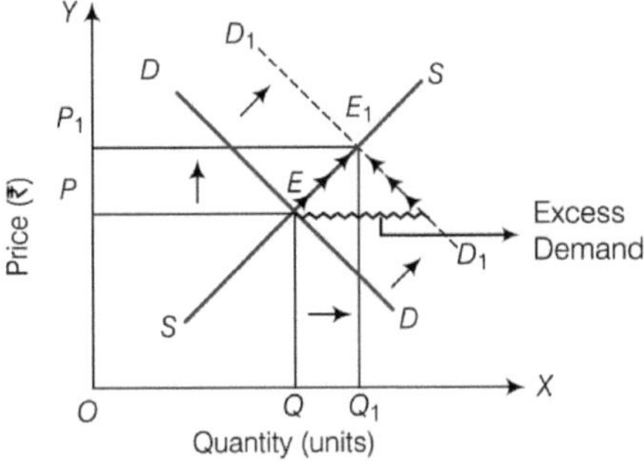

(ii) For a normal commodity, decrease in income of the buyers means decrease in its demand. Accordingly, demand curve shifts leftward and both equilibrium price and equilibrium quantity tend to decrease.

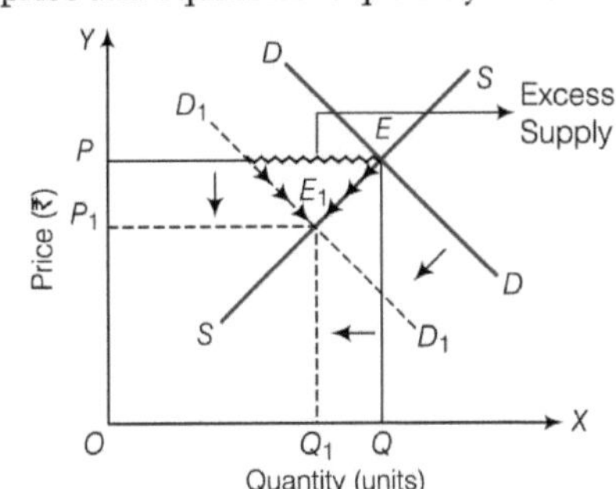

In the given diagram, actual demand curve DD and actual supply curve SS intersect at point E (i.e. equilibrium point). When income of the buyer decreases, the demand for normal good also falls and demand curve shifts leftward from DD to D_1D_1. As a result, equilibrium price and quantity both are decreased from OP to OP_1 and OQ to OQ_1.

3. Market for a good is in equilibrium. There is simultaneous increase in both demand and supply of the good. Explain its effect on market price.

Ans. There can be three situations in this respect which are as follows

(i) **Increase in Demand is Greater than Increase in Supply** From the given figure, it is clear that the rightward shift in demand curve from DD to D_1D_1 is proportionately more than the rightward shift in supply curve from SS to S_1S_1. The new equilibrium point is E_1. Equilibrium price rises from OP to OP_1 and equilibrium quantity rises from OQ to OQ_1. Increase in quantity is greater than increase in price.

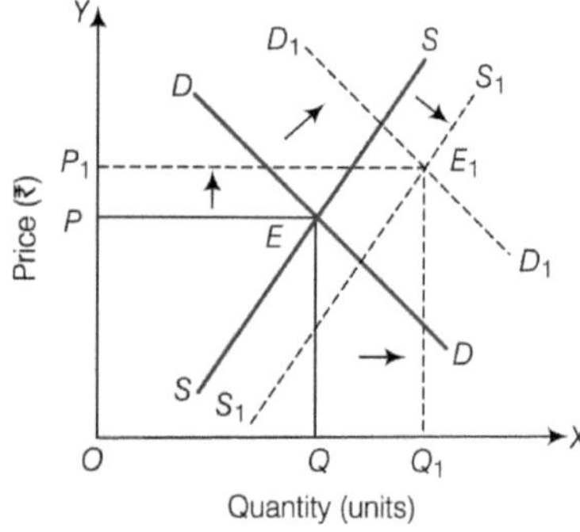

(ii) **Increase in Demand is Exactly Equal to Increase in Supply** From the given figure, it is clear that the rightward shift in demand curve from DD to D_1D_1 is proportionately equal to the rightward shift in supply curve from SS to S_1S_1. The new equilibrium point is E_1. Equilibrium price remains the same but equilibrium quantity rises from OQ to OQ_1.

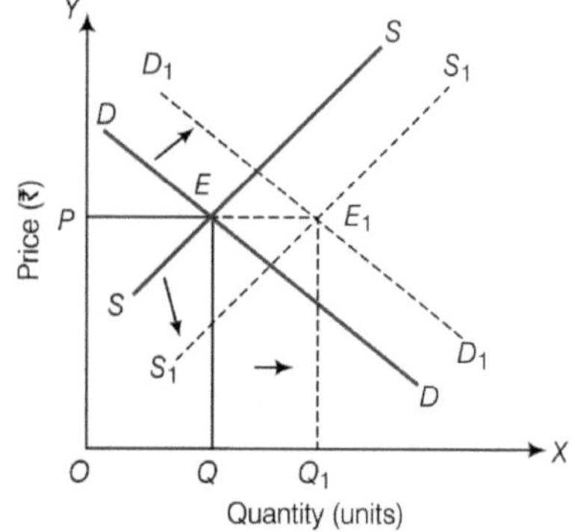

(iii) **Increase in Demand is Lesser than Increase in Supply** From the given figure, it is clear that rightward shift in demand curve from DD to D_1D_1 is proportionately less than the rightward shift in supply curve from SS to S_1S_1. The new equilibrium point is E_1. Equilibrium price falls from OP to OP_1 and equilibrium quantity rises from OQ to OQ_1. Increase in quantity is greater than decrease in price.

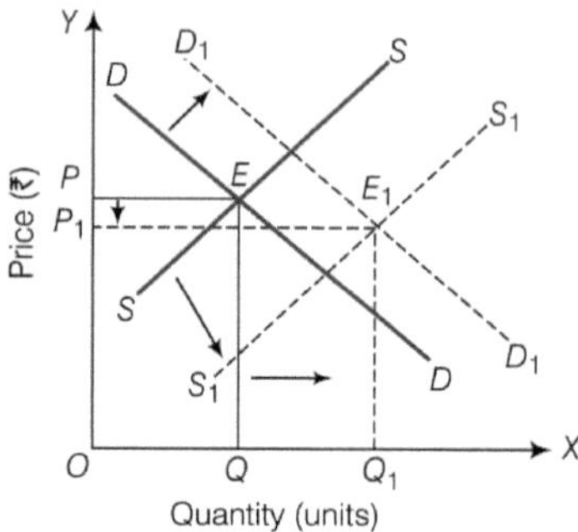

4. (i) Suppose the demand for jeans increases. At the same time, because of an increase in the price of cotton, the supply of jeans decreases. How will it affect the price and quantity sold of jeans?

(ii) Explain and illustrate with the help of a diagram, the effect of change in supply on the equilibrium price of a commodity.

Ans. (i) Increase in market demand for jeans along with the decrease in supply of jeans should raise the price of jeans and the quantity sold will decline.

In the given figure, when demand increases to D_1D_1 and supply decreases to S_1S_1, price increases from OP to OP_1 and but quantity remains the same at OQ. Becuase the propotionate increase in demand equals propotionate decrease in supply.

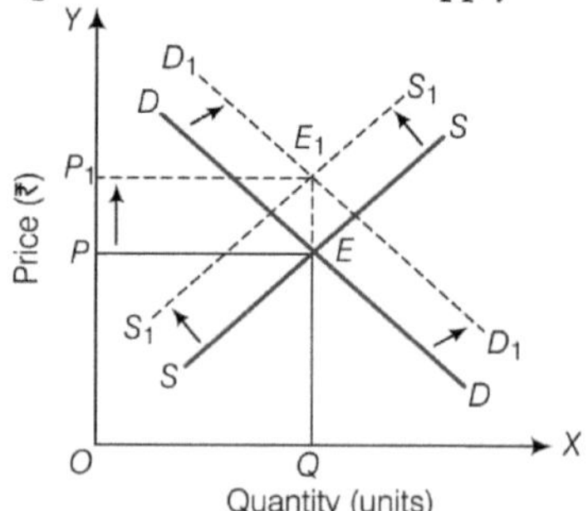

Increase in demand is equal to decrease in supply

(ii) Demand remaining constant, increase in supply means fall in equilibrium price and decrease in supply means increase in equilibrium price.

There is inverse relationship between equilibrium price and change in supply as shown in the given figure.

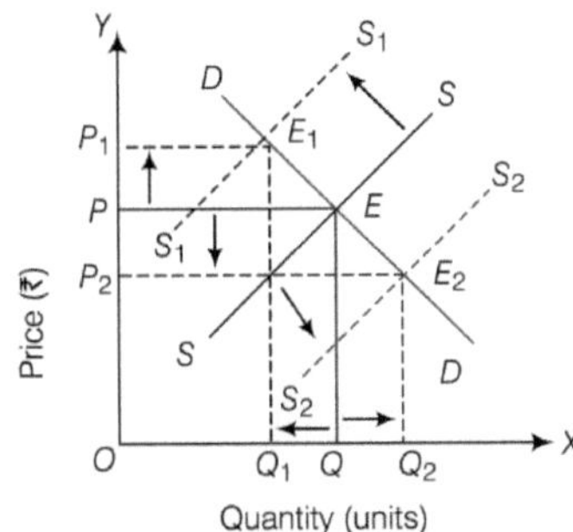

DD is initial demand curve, SS is initial supply curve, OP is initial equilibrium price, OQ is initial equilibrium quantity. Due to increase in supply, supply curve shifts to the right shown by S_2S_2 and equilibrium price falls to OP_2. With a fall in supply, shown by S_1S_1 equilibrium price rises to OP_1.

5. (i) X and Y are complementary goods. Explain the sequence of effects of a fall in the price of X on the equilibrium price and quantity of Y.

(ii) With the help of a diagram, explain the effect of decrease in demand of a commodity on its equilibrium price and quantity.

Ans. (i) In case of complementary goods, when the price of X falls, demand for commodity Y increases. As a result, demand curve of commodity Y will shift towards right but supply curve remains constant. Due to increase in demand of commodity Y, there will be excess demand. Therefore, supplier will be motivated to increase the price of commodity Y. The equilibrium price and quantity would tend to increase.

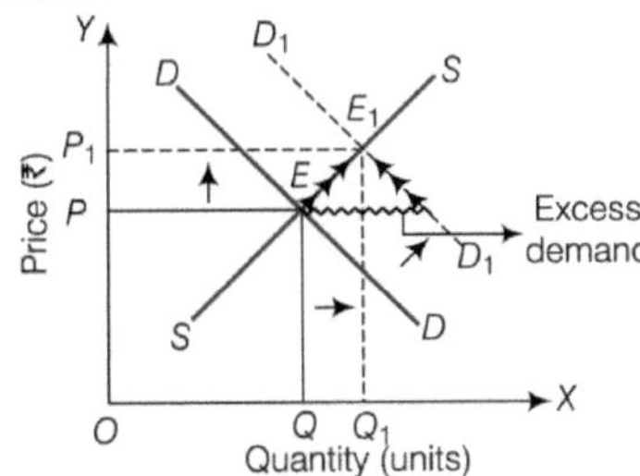

(ii) Effect of decrease in demand of a commodity on equilibrium price and quantity is discussed below

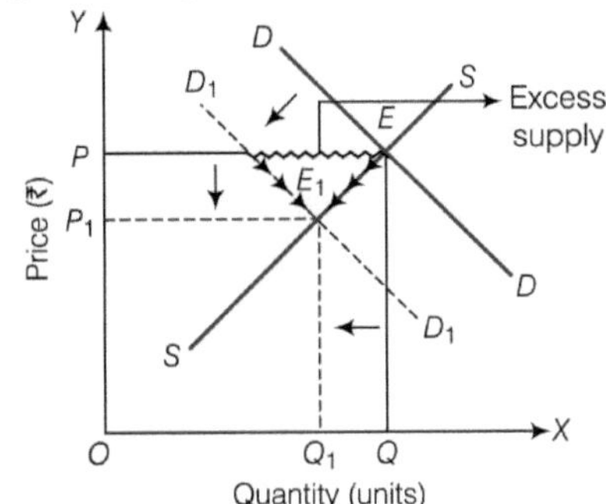

In the given figure, DD and SS are the initial demand curve and supply curve respectively. E is the initial equilibrium point, OQ is the equilibrium quantity and OP is the equilibrium price. Decrease in demand implies a shift in demand curve to the left. It is indicated by D_1D_1. This sets in the following chain of effects. Decrease in demand implies that less is demanded at the existing price. Given the supply, price of the commodity will tend to decrease from OP to OP_1. Fall in price will cause extension of demand and contraction of supply. Here, equilibrium quantity also decreases from OQ to OQ_1.

6. Consider the following demand and supply functions for a good

Quantity demanded $= 160 - 2p$

Quantity supplied $= -40 + 2p$

(i) Calculate the equilibrium price and quantity.

(ii) Find out a price at which there is excess demand.

(iii) Find out a price at which there is excess supply.

Ans. (i) Quantity Demanded $= 160 - 2p$

Quantity Supplied $= -40 + 2p$

Equilibrium is attained at a point where market demand is equal to market supply, i.e.

Quantity Demanded $=$ Quantity Supplied

Hence, $160 - 2p = -40 + 2p$

$160 + 40 = 2p + 2p$

$200 = 4p, \ p = \dfrac{200}{4} = 50$

Hence, equilibrium price $= ₹\ 50$

Equilibrium quantity will be,

Quantity Demanded $=$ Quantity Supplied

$= 160 - 2p = 160 - 2 \times 50$

$= 160 - 100 = ₹\ 60$

(ii) At any price below the equilibrium price there will be excess demand. Let us take at price ₹ 20

At $p = ₹\ 20$

Quantity Demanded $= 160 - 2p$

$= 160 - 2 \times 20 = 160 - 40 = ₹\ 120$

Quantity Supplied $= -40 + 2p$

$= -40 + 2 \times 20 = -40 + 40 = 0$

Quantity Demanded $>$ Quantity Supplied (excess demand)

Also it can be concluded that at ₹ 20 there will be no supply of the commodity, hence between $20 < p < 50$, there will be excess demand.

(iii) At any price above equilibrium, there will be excess supply. Let us take at price ₹ 80

Quantity Demanded $= 160 - 2p$

$= 160 - 2 \times 80 = 160 - 160 = 0$

Quantity Supplied $= -40 + 2p$

$= -40 + 2 \times 80 = -40 + 160 = 120$

Quantity demanded $<$ Quantity supplied (excess supply). Also, it can be concluded that at $p = ₹\ 80$, demand will be zero, hence there will be excess supply between $50 < p < 80$.

Mulitple Choice Questions

1. Under what condition, equilibrium price will increase and equilibrium quantity will decrease?
   (a) Increase in supply
   (b) Decrease in supply
   (c) Increase in demand
   (d) Decrease in demand

2. If in an industry, demand and supply will not intersect in positive quadrant, then it is called
   (a) Illegal industry
   (b) Viable industry
   (c) Non-viable industry
   (d) Sick industry

3. What is the impact of change in supply on market equilibrium when demand is perfectly inelastic?
   (a) Both equilibrium price and equilibrium quantity will change
   (b) Both equilibrium price and equilibrium quantity will not change
   (c) Equilibrium price remains same and equilibrium quantity will change
   (d) Equilibrium price will change and equilibrium quantity remains same

4. Which of the following is not an assumption of perfect competition?
   (a) Perfect mobility of factors   (b) Asymmetric information
   (c) Huge selling cost   (d) All of these

5. Elasticity of demand of average revenue curve under perfect competition is ....
   (a) elastic   (b) perfectly elastic
   (c) inelastic   (d) perfectly inelastic

Short Answer (SA) Type Questions

1. Under perfect competition, firms can sell any quantity at the existing price, then why firms are reluctant to reduce the price in order to capture the entire market?

2. Explain 'large number of buyers and sellers' as a feature of perfectly competitive market.

3. Show the determination of equilibrium price with the help of schedule.

4. Why price remains unaffected when supply curve is perfectly elastic and demand curve shifts?

5. How is the wage rate determined in a perfectly competitive labour market?

Long Answer (LA) Type Questions

1. How is price determined under perfect competition? Explain briefly.

2. Market for a good is in equilibrium. There is simultaneous decrease in both demand and supply of the good. Explain its effect on market price.

Answers

Multiple Choice Questions

   1. (b)   *2. (c)*   *3. (d)*   *4. (c)*   *5. (b)*

For Detailed Solutions
Scan the code

Practice Paper 1*
(Solved)

Instructions

Time : 2 Hours
Max. Marks : 40

1. There are 14 questions in the question paper. All questions are compulsory.
2. Question no. 1-5 are Case Based MCQs. Each question carries 1 mark.
3. Question no. 6-9 and 10 are Short Answer Type Questions. Each question carries 3 mark.
4. Question no. 11-14 are Long Answer Type Questions. Each question carries 5 marks.
5. There is no overall choice. However, internal choices have been provided in some questions. Students have to attempt only one of the alternatives in such question.

*** As exact Blue-print and Pattern for CBSE Term II exams is not released yet. So the pattern of this paper is designed by the author on the basis of trend of past CBSE Papers. Students are advised not to consider the pattern of this paper as official, it is just for practice purpose.**

Section A
Statistics for Economics

Case Based MCQ ($1 \times 5 = 5$ Marks)

Analyse the following case study graphs carefully and answer the question no. 1 to 5 on the basis of the same.

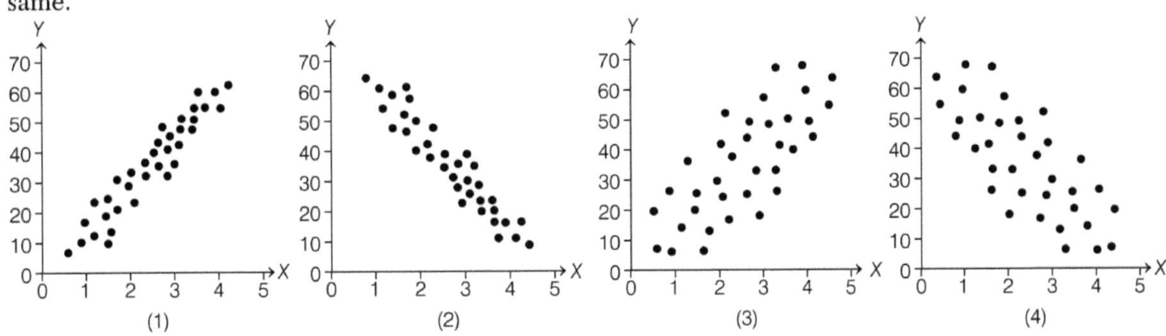

(1)   (2)   (3)   (4)

1. Coefficient of correlation has how many degrees?

(a) 4   (b) 5   (c) 3   (d) 6

2. Figure 3 represents .... correlation.

(a) positive   (b) perfect positive   (c) negative   (d) perfect negative

3. What will be the degree of coefficient of correlation if R_{xy} is 0.75?

(a) High degree of positive correlation   (b) Moderate degree of positive correlation

(c) Low degree of positive correlation   (d) Perfect positive correlation

4. Karl Pearson's coefficient of correlation can be calculated using ....
(a) assumed mean   (b) median   (c) Both (a) and (b)   (d) None of these

5. If the degree of correlation is 0.03, the series show .... degree of .... correlation.
(a) high, positive   (b) low, positive   (c) high, negative   (d) low, negative

Short Answer (SA) Type Questions (3 Marks)

6. "Correlation is preferred to covariance as a measure of association." Explain

Or

"There are some pre-requisites of a good index number." Defend.

7. Calculate standard deviation from the following data

Values	10	15	25	20	30	40	50	10

8. Calculate simple average of price relative from the following data

Commodity	Unit	Weight	Price (₹) 2014	Price (₹) 2015
A	kg	3	3.00	4.00
B	quintal	4	3.50	4.00
C	dozen	2	1.50	2.00
D	kg	1	2.50	3.00

Or

Compute Laspeyre's index from the following data

Commodity	Base Year Price (₹)	Base Year Quantity	Current Year Price (₹)	Current Year Quantity
A	10	30	12	50
B	8	15	10	25
C	6	20	6	30
D	4	10	6	20

9. The following information is given regarding series X and Y. Compute coefficient of correlation.

	X	Y
Number of items	15	15
Standard Deviation	3.01	3.03

Sum of Product of Deviations of X and Y series from their respective means 120

Section B
Introductory Microeconomics

Short Answer (SA) **Type Question** (3 Marks)

10. "There exists a unique relationship between Average Variable Cost (AVC) and Marginal Cost (MC)." Comment.

Or

Do you agree with the view that TP increases even when MP is decreasing?

Long Answer (LA) **Type Questions** (5 Marks)

11. (i) Can Marginal Revenue (MR) be negative? Explain your answer with the help of example.

(ii) Total Revenue (TR) of a firm, dealing in a particular commodity, initially was ₹ 15,000. It reduces to ₹ 13,500. Also, AR increases from ₹ 150 to ₹ 270. Find the change in market demand for that commodity.

Or

State whether the following statements are true or false. Give reasons for your answer.

(i) When Marginal Revenue (MR) is constant and not equal to zero, then Total Revenue (TR) will also be constant.

(ii) As soon as Marginal Cost (MC) starts rising, Average Variable Cost (AVC) also starts rising.

(iii) Total Product (TP) always increases whether there is increasing returns or diminishing returns to a factor.

12. Explain the effect of decrease in supply when

(i) demand is perfectly elastic   (ii) demand is perfectly inelastic

13. State the law of supply, the assumptions on which it is based and exceptions to the law of supply.

Or "Law of variable proportion in terms of marginal product gives another law known as law of diminishing marginal product." Explain this law by giving schedule and graph.

14. (i) How a firm is a price taker in perfect competition?

(ii) Why does it earns only normal profits in long-run?

Or

At a given price of a commodity there is 'excess supply'. Is this the equilibrium price? If not, how will the equilibrium price be reached?

Answers

1. (b) 5

2. (a) positive

3. (a) High degree of positive correlation

4. (a) assumed mean

5. (b) low, positive

6. Both, correlation coefficient and covariance measure the degree of linear relationship between two variables, but correlation coefficient is generally preferred to covariance. It is due to the following reasons

    (i) The correlation coefficient has no unit.

    (ii) The correlation coefficient is independent of origin as well as of scale.

    (iii) The correlation coefficient suggests cause and effect relationship between different variables.

Or Pre-requisites of an ideal index number are as follows

    (i) It should be a composite calculation i.e., consider every type of items.

    (ii) It should facilitate international comparision.

    (iii) It should be rigidly defined.

7. Let assumed mean be $(A) = 30$

Calculation of Standard Deviation

Values (X)	$d = X - A$	d^2
10	-20	400
15	-15	225
25	-5	25
20	-10	100
30	0	0
40	10	100
50	20	400
10	-20	400
$n = 8$	$\Sigma d = -40$	$\Sigma d^2 = 1,650$

where, $\Sigma d^2 = 1,650$, $n = 8$, $\Sigma d = -40$

$$\text{Standard Deviation } (\sigma) = \sqrt{\frac{\Sigma d^2}{n} - \left(\frac{\Sigma d}{n}\right)^2}$$

$$\Rightarrow \quad \sigma = \sqrt{\frac{1,650}{8} - \left(\frac{-40}{8}\right)^2} = \sqrt{206.25 - (-5)^2} = \sqrt{206.25 - 25} = \sqrt{181.25} = 13.463$$

8.

Commodity	Weight (W)	Price in 2014 (P_0)	Price in 2015 (P_1)	$I\left(\dfrac{P_1}{P_0} \times 100\right)$
A	3	3.00	4.00	$\dfrac{4.00}{3.00} \times 100 = 133.33$
B	4	3.50	4.00	$\dfrac{4.00}{3.50} \times 100 = 114.28$
C	2	1.50	2.00	$\dfrac{2.00}{1.50} \times 100 = 133.33$

Commodity	Weight (W)	Price in 2014 (P_0)	Price in 2015 (P_1)	$I\left(\dfrac{P_1}{P_0}\times 100\right)$
D	1	2.50	3.00	$\dfrac{3.00}{2.50}\times 100 = 120$
$n = 4$	$\Sigma W = 10$			$\Sigma I = 500.94$

Simple Average of Price Relative Method, $P_{01} = \dfrac{\Sigma I}{n} = \dfrac{500.94}{4} = 125.235$

Or

Construction of Price Index Number

Commodity	P_0	q_0	P_1	q_1	$P_0 q_0$	$P_0 q_1$	$P_1 q_0$	$P_1 q_1$
A	10	30	12	50	300	500	360	600
B	08	15	10	25	120	200	150	250
C	06	20	06	30	120	180	120	180
D	04	10	06	20	40	80	60	120
					580	960	690	1,150

Laspeyre's method $P_{01} = \dfrac{\Sigma P_1 q_0}{\Sigma P_0 q_0} \times 100 \Rightarrow \dfrac{690}{580} \times 100 = 118.965$

9. We are given that,

Number of items $(n) = 15$

Standard Deviation of X $(\sigma_X) = 3.01$

Standard Deviation of Y $(\sigma_Y) = 3.03$

Sum of products of deviations of X and Y from their respective means $(\Sigma xy) = 120$

Coefficient of Correlation $(r) = \dfrac{\Sigma xy}{n \cdot \sigma_X \cdot \sigma_Y} = \dfrac{120}{15 \times 3.01 \times 3.03} = \dfrac{120}{136.80} = 0.88$

It is a indicative of high degree of positive correlation.

10. Relationship between AVC and MC

(i) AVC and MC starts from same point and are 'U' shaped. (ii) When MC < AVC, AVC falls.

(iii) MC = AVC, at the minimum point of AVC. (iv) When MC > AVC, AVC rises.

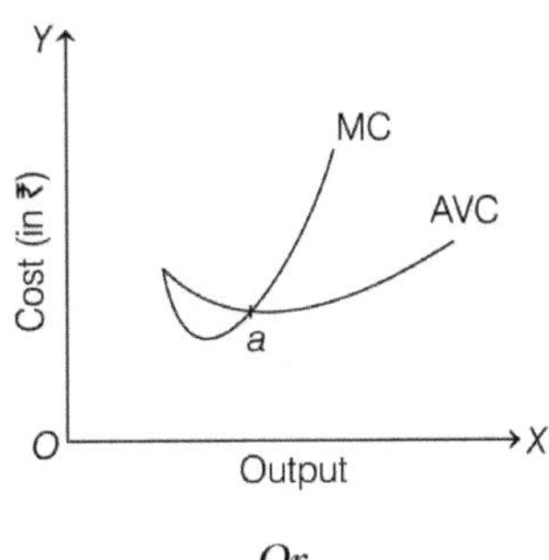

Or

Yes, TP increases even when MP is decreasing, because MP is an addition to TP. When MP is decreasing, only an addition to TP is decreasing i.e. TP continues to increase, though at a diminishing rate. TP starts declining only when MP becomes negative.

11. (i) Yes, Marginal Revenue (MR) can be negative. It can be negative only when average revenue is decreasing or when the price is declining as under monopoly and monopolistic competition. This can be explained by the following example

When price $= ₹ 20$, output $= 50$

Total revenue of 50 units $(\text{TR}_{50}) = P \times Q = 20 \times 50 = ₹ 1,000$

When price fall to $₹ 19$, output $= 51$

Total revenue of 51 units $(\text{TR}_{51}) = P \times Q = 19 \times 51 = ₹ 969$

$$\text{MR}_{51} = \text{TR}_{51} - \text{TR}_{50} = 969 - 1,000 = ₹ (31)$$

i.e., Marginal Revenue (MR) is negative.

(ii) $\text{TR} = ₹ 15,000, P(= \text{AR}) = ₹ 150$

$$\text{TR} = P \times Q \Rightarrow Q = \frac{\text{TR}}{P} = \frac{15,000}{150} = 100 \text{ units}$$

When $\text{TR} = ₹ 13,500, P(= \text{AR}) = ₹ 270$

$$\text{TR} = P \times Q \Rightarrow Q = \frac{\text{TR}}{P} = \frac{13,500}{270} = 50 \text{ units}$$

Change in market demand $= 50 - 100 = -50$ units

i.e., market demand falls by 50 units

Or

(i) **False**, because when Marginal Revenue (MR) is constant, Total Revenue (TR) is increasing at a constant rate, only when marginal revenue is zero, total revenue is constant.

(ii) **False**, Average Variable Cost (AVC) can fall even when Marginal Cost (MC) starts rising. See Average Variable Cost (AVC) and Marginal Cost (MC) corresponding to output range (MQ) in the diagram.

(iii) **True**, because in a situation of increasing returns to a factor, marginal product tends to rise accordingly, Total Product (TP) should be increasing at an increasing rate. Under diminishing returns to a factor, Marginal Product (MP) tends to fall. Falling Marginal Product (MP) implies that Total Product (TP) should be increasing, though at a decreasing rate.

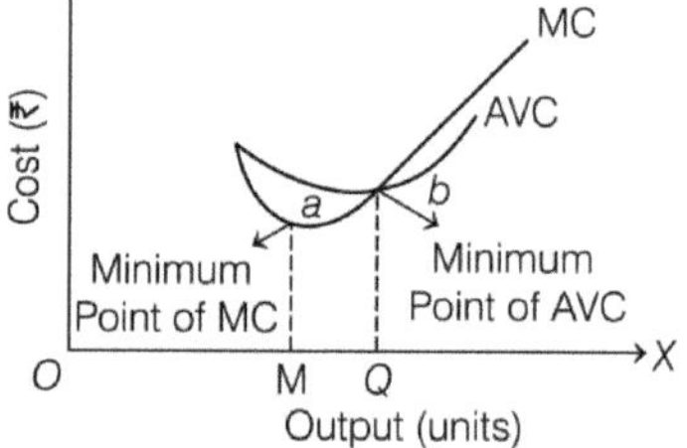

12. The effect of decrease in supply when

(i) **Demand is Perfectly Elastic** Decrease in supply of commodity does not cause any change in its price in case demand for the commodity is perfectly elastic. Only equilibrium quantity tends to change.

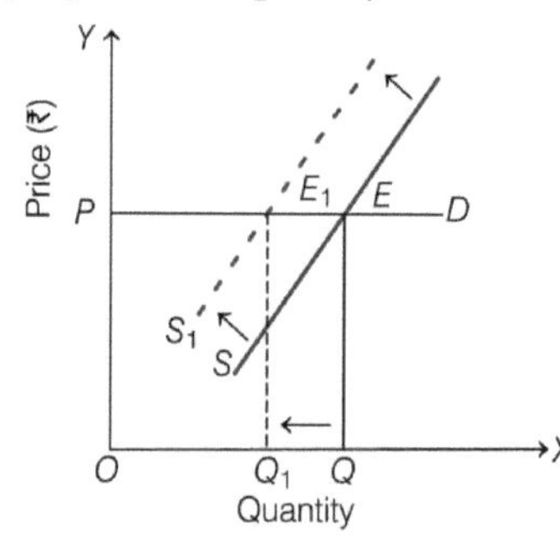

Demand is infinite at existing price. So, decrease in supply does not cause any change in price.

(ii) **Demand is Perfectly Inelastic** Decrease in supply of commodity causes rise in price and equilibrium quantity remains constant when demand for commodity is inelastic.

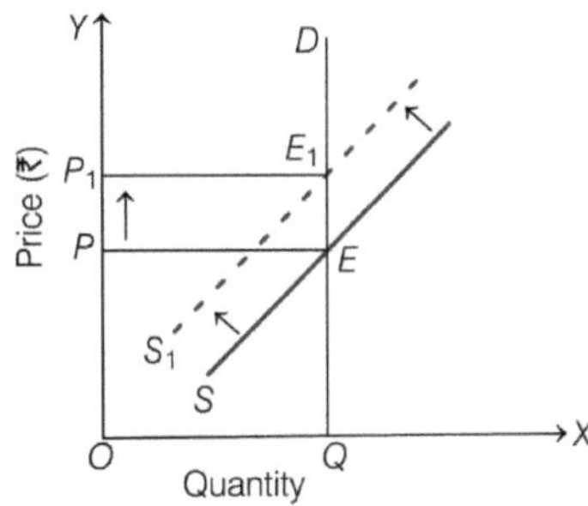

Demand is constant at every price. So, decrease in supply does not cause any change in price.

13. Law of supply derives the relationship between price and quantity supplied. According to this law, quantity supplied of a commodity is directly related to the price of a commodity, provided all other determinants are constant. The quantity supplied increases with increase in price and vice-versa.

Assumptions of the Law of Supply

The various assumptions of the law of supply are given below

(i) There is no change in the price of the factors of production.

(ii) There is no change in the techniques of production.

(iii) There is no change in the goal of the firm.

(iv) There is no change in the price of related goods.

Exceptions to the Law of Supply

The following are the exceptions to the law of supply (any four)

(i) **Agricultural Goods** Law of supply does not apply for agricultural goods, as their supply depends on climatic conditions and not on price.

(ii) **Perishable Goods** Perishable goods like fruits, vegetables, milk and milk products cannot be held for long. Therefore, suppliers are willing to supply these products, even when prices are less, for fear that they would become totally useless.

(iii) **Antique Goods, Rare Articles and Paintings** These goods are highly priced, but still their supply is limited, as supply here is affected by factors other than price. e.g., the supply of Hussain's paintings cannot be increased even if buyers are willing to pay high price for it.

(iv) **Future Expectations regarding Prices** If prices are rising, but sellers anticipate that they would rise further in future, then they would not increase their supply now.

(v) **Lack of Resources** In underdeveloped or backward economies, supply cannot be increased due to lack of resources.

(vi) **Labour Market** In the labour market, it is observed that as the wage rate rises, the workers tend to work for less hours, so as to enjoy more leisure. This causes the supply of workers to decrease at increased wage rate.

Or Law of diminishing marginal product states that with the increase in a variable factor, keeping all other factors constant, the marginal product of the variable factor diminishes after a certain level of production and eventually becomes negative. This law was given by classical economists and related to agriculture.

This law may be explained with the help of an imaginary schedule and diagram

Land (Acre)	**Labour** (Units)	**Total Product** (Quantity)	**Marginal Product** (Quantity)
5	1	50	50
5	2	110	60
5	3	180	70
5	4	260	80
5	5	340	80
5	6	410	70
5	7	470	60
5	8	520	50

Land (Acre)	**Labour** (Units)	**Total Product** (Quantity)	**Marginal Product** (Quantity)
5	9	550	30
5	10	560	10
5	11	560	0
5	12	550	−10
5	13	530	−20

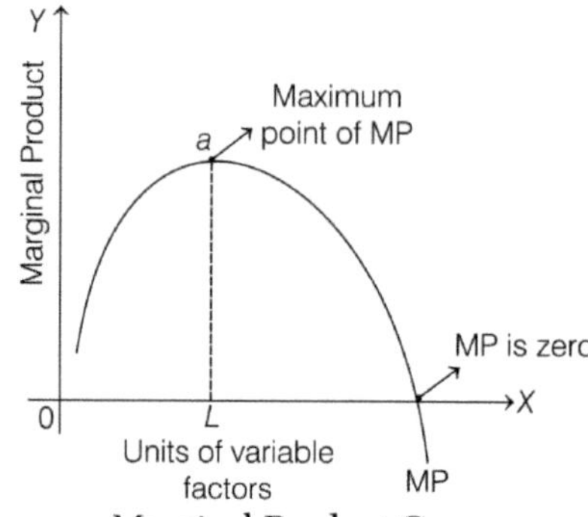

Marginal Product Curve

Note *Law of diminishing marginal product operates in the second stage of law of variable proportion.*

In the above diagram, after point '*a*' on MP curve, marginal product diminishes continuously, showing the law of diminishing marginal product, i.e., with the employment of 6th labour, diminishing returns operates.

14. (i) A firm under perfect competition, is a price taker, not a price maker because of the following three reasons

(a) Large number of buyers and sellers. (b) Homogeneous product. (c) Perfect knowledge.

(ii) A firm under perfect competition earns only normal profits in the long-run. This is because if the firms earn abnormal profits, then this would lead to increase in market supply because of entry of new firms thereby causing the market price to fall upto the level of normal profits.

On the other hand, if the firms earn abnormal losses, then this would force some marginal firms to exit from the market, causing market supply to fall. This will cause the market price to rise upto the level of normal profits.

Or

Equilibrium price refers to the price at which market demand is equal to market supply (i.e., there is no excess demand or excess supply). So, the price with 'excess supply' is not the equilibrium price.

This can be illustrated with the help of the following figure

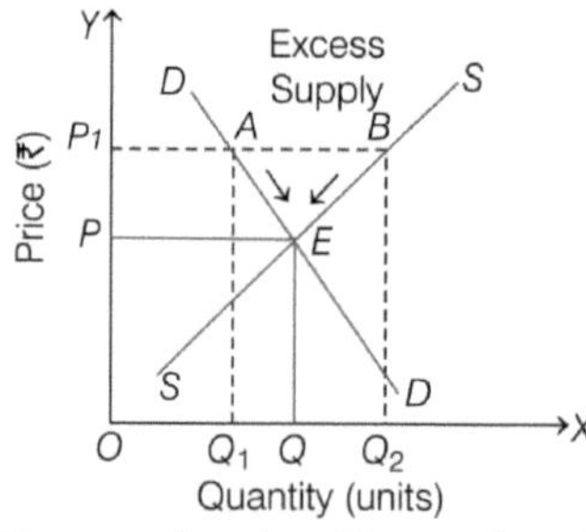

Diagram showing Excess Supply

The given figure depicts, that excess supply is equal to $AB = Q_1 Q_2$. It implies that market supply is greater than market demand.

This puts pressure on price (OP_1) to decline. The producers reduce the quantity supplied at the lower price OP from OQ_2 to OQ. The consumers react by increasing the quantity demanded from OQ_1 (at OP_1 price) to OQ (at OP price). Equilibrium is struck at point '*E*'. Thus, OP and OQ are the equilibrium price and equilibrium quantity respectively with no excess supply.

Practice Paper 2*
(Unsolved)

Instructions

- **Time :** 2 Hours
- **Max. Marks :** 40

1. There are 14 questions in the question paper. All questions are compulsory.
2. Question no. 1–4 and 11 are Short Answer Type Questions. Each question carries 3 mark.
3. Question no. 6–10 are Case Based MCQs. Each question carries 1 mark.
4. Question no. 5 and 12–14 are Long Answer Type Questions. Each question carries 5 marks.
5. There is no overall choice. However, internal choices have been provided in some questions. Students have to attempt only one of the alternatives in such question.

** As exact Blue-print and Pattern for CBSE Term II exams is not released yet. So the pattern of this paper is designed by the author on the basis of trend of past CBSE Papers. Students are advised not to consider the pattern of this paper as official, it is just for practice purpose.*

Section A
Statistics for Economics

Short Answer (SA) **Type Questions** (3 Marks)

1. What are the types of measures of dispersion?

Or Write any three demerits of standard deviation.

2. Draw a scatter diagram and indicate the nature of correlation.

X	5	10	15	20	25	30
Y	2.5	5	7.5	10	12.5	15

3. Explain the meaning of positive correlation and negative correlation alongwith the example and diagram.

4. Calculate coefficient of correlation between the X and Y variables.

X	43	48	56	64	67	70
Y	128	120	138	143	141	152

Or

Calculate standard deviation from the following data using step-deviation method.

Items	10-20	20-30	30-40	40-50	50-60	60-70	70-80
Frequency	4	8	8	16	12	6	4

Long Answer (LA) **Type Question** (5 Marks)

5. The monthly per-capita expenditure incurred by workers of an industrial center for some items are given below. The weights of these items are 75, 10, 5, 6 and 4 respectively. Prepare a weighted index number for cost of living for 2020 with 2010 as base.

Items	Food	Clothing	Fuel and lighting	House rent	Miscellaneous
Price in 2010	100	20	15	30	35
Price in 2020	200	25	20	40	65

Or Mean and standard deviations of two distributions of 100 and 150 items are 50 and 5 and 40 and 6 respectively. Find the combined standard deviation.

Section B
Introductory Microeconomics

Case Based MCQs (1 x 5 = 5 Marks)

Read the following case study carefully and answer the question no. 6 to 10 on the basis of the same.

How quickly will American businesses reopen after COVID-19 lockdowns end? A nationwide survey was conducted of small businesses to measure firms' expectations about their re-opening and future demand. A plurality of firms in our sample expect to reopen within days of the end of legal restrictions, but a sizable minority expect to delay their reopening.

While health-related variables, such as COVID-19 case rates and physical proximity of workers, do explain the prevalence and expected duration of regulated lockdown, these variables have little or no correlation with post-lockdown reopening intentions. Instead, almost one half of closed or partially open businesses said that their reopening would depend on the reopening of related businesses, including customers and suppliers.

Owners expect demand to be one-third lower than before the crisis through autumn. Firms with more pessimistic expectations about demand predict a later reopening. Using an instrumental variables strategy, we estimate the relationship between demand expectations and reopening. These estimates suggest that post-lockdown delays in reopening can be explained by low levels of expected demand.

Source Harvard Business School Working Knowledge Baker Library

6. How has the Covid-19 lockdown impacted the equilibrium price for the commodities other than necessity in the American market?

(a) Increase (b) Decrease (c) No change (d) Either (a) or (b)

7. Assertion (A) Delay in reopening shops lead to decrease in supply of essentials during the covid-19 lockdown.

Reason (R) Lockdowns also led to decrease in demand along with supply of commodities.

Alternatives

(a) Both Assertion (A) and Reason (R) are true and Reason (R) is the correct explanation of Assertion (A)
(b) Both Assertion (A) and Reason (R) are true, but Reason (R) is not the correct explanation of Assertion (A)
(c) Assertion (A) is false, but Reason (R) is true
(d) Both Assertion (A) and Reason (R) are false

8. Statement I Owner's expected demand to be one-third lower than the before pandemic situation, this led to a downward movement along demand curve.

Statement II Expectation about future fall in demand leads to fall in price of the commodities.

Alternatives

(a) Statement I is correct and Statement II is incorrect
(b) Statement II is correct and Statement I is incorrect
(c) Both the statements are correct
(d) Both the statements are incorrect

9. Expected lower demand post lockdown will lead to ……… in equilibrium price.

(a) rise   (b) fall   (c) No change   (d) Can't be predicted

10. Which of the following policy instruments government should use during an abnormal situation like covid-19 to keep the prices of essential goods at a comfortable position?

(a) Price floor   (b) Price ceiling   (c) Taxes   (d) All of these

Short Answer (SA) Type Question (3 Marks)

11. Show that the average fixed cost curve is a rectangular hyperbola.

Or A firm's fixed cost is ₹ 2,000. Compute Total Variable Cost (TVC), Average Variable Cost (AVC), Total Cost (TC) and Average Cost (AC) with the help of the following table.

Output (Units)	1	2	3	4	5	6	7
Marginal Cost (MC) (₹)	2,000	1,500	1,200	1,500	2,000	2,700	3,500

Long Answer (LA) Type Questions (5 Marks)

12. State whether the following statements are true or false. Give reasons.

(i) When there are diminishing returns to a factor, marginal product and total product both diminishes.

(ii) When Marginal Revenue (MR) is positive and constant, Average Revenue (AR) and Total Revenue (TR) both will increase at constant rate.

(iii) As output is increased, the difference between Average Total Cost (ATC) and Average Variable Cost (AVC) falls and ultimately becomes zero.

13. Suppose, free entry and exit are allowed in a freely competitive market and there are identical firms in the market. Following are the demand and supply functions of such a market

Market demand function $(q_d) = 800 - P$

The supply function of a single firm $(q_s) = 10 + P$ for $P \geq 20$; and $= 0$ for $P < 20$

Find out the equilibrium price, quantity and number of firms.

Or Suppose a freely competitive market has identical firms and free entry and exit are also allowed. Market demand function and the supply function of a single firm are given below

Market Demand Function $(q_d) = 590 - P$

Market Supply Function $(q_s) = 8 + 5P$ for $P \geq 10$ and $= 0$ for $P < 10$

(i) What is the significance of $P = 10$?

(ii) At what price will the market be in equilibrium? State the reason.

(iii) Calculate the equilibrium quantity.

(iv) How many firms are required in the market?

14. Explain the relationships between total revenue and marginal revenue curves under the following situation

(a) When price falls with rise in output

(b) When price remains constant for all levels of output

Or Explain any five determinants of elasticity of supply using suitable examples.

Answers

4. $r = 0.897$ *Or* $\sigma = 15.97$

5. CPI $= 185$ (approx) *Or* Combined SD $= 7.45$

6. (a)   **7.** (c)   **8.** (b)   **9.** (a)   **10.** (b)

13. Equilibrium Price $= ₹ 20$; Equilibrium Quantity $= 780$ units; Total Number of Firms $= 26$

Or (ii) Equilibrium Price $= ₹ 10$ (iii) Equilibrium Quantity $= 580$ units

(iv) Number of Firms $= 10$

Practice Paper 3*
(Unsolved)

Instructions

- **Time :** 2 Hours
- **Max. Marks :** 40

1. There are 14 questions in the question paper. All questions are compulsory.
2. Question no. 1-4 and 11 are Short Answer Type Questions. Each question carries 3 mark.
3. Question no. 6-10 are Case Based MCQs. Each question carries 1 mark.
4. Question no. 5 and 12-14 are Long Answer Type Questions. Each question carries 5 marks.
5. There is no overall choice. However, internal choices have been provided in some questions. Students have to attempt only one of the alternatives in such question.

*** As exact Blue-print and Pattern for CBSE Term II exams is not released yet. So the pattern of this paper is designed by the author on the basis of trend of past CBSE Papers. Students are advised not to consider the pattern of this paper as official, it is just for practice purpose.**

Section A
Statistics for Economics

Short Answer (SA) **Type Questions** (3 Marks)

1. Which method is considered as the best method of constructing index numbers and why?

Or

Which measure of dispersion is considered as best and why?

2. If $r = 0.866$, $\Sigma xy = 60$, $\overline{X} = 12$, $\overline{Y} = 8$, $\Sigma y^2 = 48$, find the value of Σx^2?

3. Compute the coefficient of correlation

	X Series	Y Series
Number of items (N)	3	3
Arithmetic Mean	300	150
Squares of Deviations from Mean	18	98

Summation of product of deviations of X and Y series from their respective arithmetic mean $= 40$. Also, interpret the correlation.

Or

From the data given below, find N.

$$r = 0.5, \ \Sigma xy = 140, \text{ Standard Deviation of } Y(\sigma_y) = 4, \ \Sigma x^2 = 49.$$

where, x and y are deviation from arithmetic mean.

4. If the Coefficient of Variation (CV) of X series is 20% and that of Y series is 35% and their means are 72 and 85 respectively, find their standard deviations.

Long Answer (LA) Type Question (5 Marks)

5. Calculate standard deviation from the following data.

Marks	Below 20	Below 40	Below 60	Below 80	Below 100
Number of Students	8	20	50	70	80

Or

Average daily wage of 50 workers of a factory was ₹ 1,200 with a standard deviation of ₹ 40. Each worker is given a raise of ₹ 200. What is the new average daily wage and standard deviation? Have the wages become more or less uniform?

Section B
Introductory Microeconomics

Case Based MCQs (1 x 5 = 5 Marks)

Read the following case study carefully and answer the question no. 6 to 10 on the basis of the same.

Farmers in our country are mostly small and marginal. They produce for self-consumption and hardly have any surplus crop to sell in market. These farmers produce with the help of their family members.

Also due to limited land holding at times, there are more labour working compared with what is actually required, this leads to disguised unemployment.

Use of primitive tools and techniques further reduces the ability of these families to increase production.

6. Assertion (A) Introduction of Green Revolution techniques in agriculture led to failure of law of variable proportion.

Reason (R) Law of variable proportion is a universal law and applicable in every case.

Alternatives
(a) Both Assertion (A) and Reason (R) are true and Reason (R) is the correct explanation of Assertion (A)
(b) Both Assertion (A) and Reason (R) are true, but Reason (R) is not the correct explanation of Assertion (A)
(c) Assertion (A) is false, but Reason (R) is true
(d) Both Assertion (A) and Reason (R) are false

7. Choose the correct option from the options given below
(a) Labour is variable factor of production
(b) Fixity of factors leads to diminishing returns
(c) Land is the only fixed factor of production in agriculture
(d) All of the above

8. In the above situation, productivity was low due to ....
(a) fixity of land
(b) use of primitive tools and techniques
(c) excessive use of variable factor
(d) All of these

9. In case of land, the 'law of returns to factor' is applicable in ....
(a) short-run
(b) medium-run
(c) long-run
(d) Both (a) and (b)

10. In case of disguised unemployment, marginal product of labour is equal to
(a) zero
(b) positive
(c) negative
(d) Either (a) or (c)

Short Answer (SA) **Type Question** (3 Marks)

11. Explain the law of diminishing returns to factors using suitable diagram.

Or

Rapid technological progress leads to postponement of law of returns to factors. Do you agree with this statement? Give suitable reason in support of your answer.

Long Answer (LA) **Type Questions** (5 Marks)

12. Explain the determination of price and quantity in a free market keeping in mind the case of perfectly competitive market. Use suitable schedule and diagram.

13. Answer the following questions
   (i) Complete the following table

Output (Units)	Total Cost (TC) (₹)	Total Variable Cost (TVC) (₹)	Marginal Cost (MC) (₹)
0	12	...	...
1	18	...	...
2	21	...	...

   (ii) Calculate total product and marginal product of a firm, if its average product is as under

Labour	1	2	3	4	5	6
Average Product	10	12	14	12	10	8

Or

State whether the following statements are true or false. Give reasons for your answer.
   (i) When Marginal Revenue (MR) is constant and not equal to zero, then Total Revenue (TR) will be increasing.
   (ii) As soon as Marginal Cost (MC) starts falling, Average Variable Cost (AVC) also starts falling.
   (iii) Marginal Product (MP) starts diminishing from the point of inflexion.

14. A market for garments is in equilibrium. Using suitable example, explain the situation where both demand and supply of garments changed without any impact on the equilibrium quantity.

Or

Explain the following parts
   (i) Implications of large number of buyers and sellers under perfect competition.
   (ii) Difference between floor price and ceiling price.

Answers

2. 100

3. $r = 0.95$ *Or* N = 100

4. Standard Deviation = 14.4 and 29.75

5. Standard Deviation = 22.605 *Or* Old CV = 3.33, New CV = 2.86

6. (c)   **7.** (d)   **8.** (d)   **9.** (a)   **10.** (a)

13. (i)   TVC = 0, 6, 9, MC = –, 6, 3
   (ii) TP = 10, 24, 42, 48, 50, 48;
        MP = 10, 14, 18, 6, 2, –2

Printed by Libri Plureos GmbH in Hamburg,
Germany